THE MAKING OF MEDIEVAL ANTIFRATERNALISM

The Making of Medieval Antifraternalism

Polemic, Violence, Deviance, and Remembrance

G. GELTNER

UNIVERSITY PRESS

OXFORD
UNIVERSITY PRESS

Great Clarendon Street, Oxford, OX2 6DP,
United Kingdom

Oxford University Press is a department of the University of Oxford.
It furthers the University's objective of excellence in research, scholarship,
and education by publishing worldwide. Oxford is a registered trade mark of
Oxford University Press in the UK and in certain other countries

© G. Geltner 2012

The moral rights of the author have been asserted

First Edition published in 2012

All rights reserved. No part of this publication may be reproduced, stored in
a retrieval system, or transmitted, in any form or by any means, without the
prior permission in writing of Oxford University Press, or as expressly permitted
by law, by licence or under terms agreed with the appropriate reprographics
rights organization. Enquiries concerning reproduction outside the scope of the
above should be sent to the Rights Department, Oxford University Press, at the
address above

You must not circulate this work in any other form
and you must impose this same condition on any acquirer

British Library Cataloguing in Publication Data
Data available

Library of Congress Cataloguing in Publication Data
Library of Congress Control Number: 2012930329

ISBN 978–0–19–963945–8

Printed in Great Britain
on acid-free paper by
MPG Books Group, Bodmin and King's Lynn

1 3 5 7 9 10 8 6 4 2

Links to third party websites are provided by Oxford in good faith and
for information only. Oxford disclaims any responsibility for the materials
contained in any third party website referenced in this work.

Q.T.

Prions Dieu que les Jacobins
Puissent manger les Augustines,
Et les Carmes soient pendus
Des cordes des Frères Menus.

[We pray to God that the Jacobins
May eat the Augustinians,
And that the Carmelites may be hanged
From the cords of the Friars Minor.]

                        Jean Molinet (d. 1507), *Graces sans vilenie*

Acknowledgments

Completing this book was a long but hardly lonely task, aided as it was by the encouragement and insights of many, including Oren Ahoobim, Tzafrir Barzilay, Ingrid Bleynat, Jan Burgers, Michele Campopiano, Mary Carruthers, Cesare Cenci, Sam Cohn, Michael Cusato, Trevor Dean, Sharon Farmer, John Fleming, Michelle Garceau, Erica Gilles, James Given, Enrique Gomezllata, Isabelle Heullant-Donat, Katherine Jansen, William Chester Jordan, Andrew Jotischky, Kathryn Kerby-Fulton, Jelle Koopmans, Carol Lansing, Shelly Makleff, Maureen Miller, Christopher Ocker, Marina Rustow, Jens Röhrkasten, Lesley Smith, Richard Schenk, Jeff Schwegman, Nitzan Shoshan, Augustine Thompson, and Chris Wickham. In an act of true generosity, Anne Lester, Stephen Mossman, Neslihan Şenocak, and Amanda Wilkins read a draft of the entire typescript and improved it greatly. I am immensely grateful to all of them, though whatever shortcomings remain are fully my own doing.

In its various incarnations this project has been discussed in seminars, workshops, and conferences in Amsterdam, Berkeley, Leeds, Leeuwarden, London, New Haven, New York, Oxford, Princeton, Santa Barbara, and St Bonaventure, New York. I wish to thank the organizers and participants of these events for their invitation, comments, and kind hospitality. Some materials in this volume have appeared beforehand in different form. "Faux Semblants: Antifraternalism Reconsidered in Jean de Meun and Chaucer," *Studies in Philology*, 101 (2004), 357–80; *William of Saint-Amour's "De periculis novissimorum temporum": An Introduction, Edition, and Translation* (Leuven, etc.: Peeters, 2008); and "A False Start to Medieval Antifraternalism? William of St. Amour's *De periculis novissimorum temporum*," in Michael F. Cusato and G. Geltner (eds), *Defenders and Critics of Franciscan Life* (Leiden: Brill, 2009), 127–43, have been reworked into Chapter 1. The kernel of Chapter 2 has been published as "Friars as Victims: Scale, Scope, and the Idiom of Violence," *Journal of Medieval History*, 36 (2010), 126–41. And the basis for Chapter 3 was laid in "Brethren Behaving Badly: A Deviant Approach to Medieval Antifraternalism," *Speculum*, 85 (2010), 47–64. I wish to thank the editors, reviewers, journals, and publishers, as well as to acknowledge their generosity in allowing me to reproduce segments of these texts. At Oxford University Press, Christopher Wheeler and Stephanie Ireland, along with several anonymous reviewers, have been consistently helpful in improving the typescript and bringing it to print.

A final and very special thanks to the staffs at numerous Italian libraries, museums, and especially archives, who enabled this project over the years; to the

University Library in Amsterdam, the Bodleian Library in Oxford, and Firestone Library in Princeton for handling many odd requests; and to the New York Public Library and Columbia University Library for allowing me to complete the work in the peace and comfort of their reading rooms.

xxx Amsterdam
New Amsterdam
August 2011

Contents

List of Figures and Tables	xii
Abbreviations	xiii

Prologue: Anecdotes and their Value	1
Introduction	4
Part One: Words and Deeds: The World against the Friars	
1. Polemic: False Apostles, False Seemings, False Starts	15
2. Violence: Friars under Fire	45
Part Two: Deeds and Words: The Friars against Themselves	
3. Deviance: Brethren Behaving Badly	81
4. Remembrance: Antifraternalism and Mendicant Identity	103
General Conclusion: Antifraternalism, Anticlericalism, and Urban Discontent	130
Epilogue: A New World Twist	138
Appendix I. Aggression against Mendicant Friars and Convents until 1400	140
Appendix II. Major Offenses and Punishments among Dominican Friars until 1400	154

Bibliography	159
Index of Names and Subjects	183
Index of Places	187

List of Figures and Tables

FIGURES

2.1 Urs Graf, *Two Prostitutes Assaulting a Monk* (1521)	46
3.1 Cover of James Salgado's *The Fryer* (1680)	83
3.2 Cover of James Salgado's *The Slaughter House* (1683)	84
4.1 St Angelus of Jerusalem (*c*.1470)	128

TABLES

2.1 Aggression against friars before 1400, by region	50
2.2 Aggression against friars before 1400, by period	52
3.1 Chronological distribution of major infractions among Dominicans, 1251–1400	91
3.2 Regional distribution of major infractions among Dominicans until 1400	92

Abbreviations

ARCHIVES

AAPi	Archivio Arcivescovile di Pisa
AGOP	Archivum Generale Ordinis Praedicatorum
ASBo	Archivio di Stato di Bologna
ASCMi	Archivio Storico Civico di Milano
ASDL	Archivio Storico Diocesano di Lucca
ASFi	Archivio di Stato di Firenze
ASLu	Archivio di Stato di Lucca
ASPa	Archivio di Stato di Parma
ASVe	Archivio di Stato di Venezia

JOURNALS

AFH	*Archivum Franciscanum Historicum*
AFP	*Archivum Fratrum Praedicatorum*
EHR	*English Historical Review*
JMH	*Journal of Medieval History*
ZfK	*Zeitschrift für Kirchengeschichte*

SERIES AND SOURCES IN PRINT

XXIV Gen.	*Chronica XXIV Generalium Ordinis Minorum*, Analecta Franciscana, 3, (Claras Aquas [Quaracchi]: Typographia Collegii S. Bonaventurae, 1897)
BF	Giovanni Giacinto Sbaraglia (ed.), *Bullarium Franciscanum Romanorum Pontificum*, rev. Conrad Eubel, 4 vols (Rome: Typis Sacræ Congregationis de Propaganda Fide, 1898–1904)
CdF	Cahiers de Fanjeaux
Chronica	Benedictus Maria Reichert (ed.), *Chronica et chronicorum excerpta historiam Ordinis Praedicatorum illustrantia*, MOFPH 7, fasc. I (Rome: Typographia Polyglotta S. C. de Propaganda Fide, 1904)
CUP	H. Denifle and É. Chatelain (eds), *Chartularium Universitatis Parisiensis*, 4 vols (Paris: Delalain, 1889–97)

Abbreviations

De fundatione   Bernard Gui, *De fundatione et prioribus conventuum provinciarum Tolosanae et Provinciae Ordinis Praedicatorum*, ed. P. A. Armagier, MOFPH 24 (Santa Sabina [Rome]: Institutum Historicum Fratrum Praedicatorum, 1961)

De periculis   G. Geltner (ed. and trans.), *William of St. Amour's* De periculis novissimorum temporum: *A Critical Edition, Translation, and Commentary*, Dallas Medieval Texts and Translations, 8 (Leuven, etc.: Peeters, 2008)

Eccleston   A. G. Little (ed.), *Fratris Thomae, vulgo dicti de Eccleston Tractatus De Adventu fratrum Minorum in Angliam* (Manchester: Manchester University Press, 1951)

Glassberger   *Chronica fratris Nicolai Glassberger* (Claras Aquas [Quaracchi]: Typographia Collegii S. Bonaventurae, 1887)

Lanercost   Joseph Stevenson (ed.), *Chronicon de Lanercost, M.CC.I.–M.CCC.XLVI.*, Bannatyne Club Publications, 65 (Edinburgh: Impressum Edinburgi, 1839)

MCH   Adrianus Staring (ed.), *Medieval Carmelite Heritage*, Textus et Studia Carmelitana, 16 (Rome: Institutum Carmelitanum, 1989)

MGH SS   Monumenta Germaniae Historica, Scriptorum

MOFPH   Monumenta Ordinis Fratrum Praedicatorum Historica

Praenarb.   Cesare Cenci (ed.), "De Fratrum Minorum Constitutionibus Praenarbonensibus," *AFH*, 83 (1990), 50–95

Registrum   Thomas Kaeppeli (ed.), *Registrum litterarum Fr. Raymundi de Vineis Capuani, Magistri Ordinis, 1380–1399*, MOFPH 19 (Santa Sabina [Rome]: Institutum Historicum Fratrum Praedicatorum, 1937)

Rolls Series   Rerum Britannicorum Medii Aevi Scriptores

Salimbene   Salimbene de Adam, *Cronica*, ed. Giuseppe Scalia, 2 vols, Corpus Christianorum Continuatio Mediaevalis, 125 and 125A (Turnhout: Brepols, 1998–9) [continuous pagination]

SBF   Cesare Cenci (ed.), *Supplementum ad Bullarium Franciscanum*, 2 vols (Claras Aquas [Quaracchi]: Typographia Collegii S. Bonaventurae, 2002–3)

TSHC   Textus et Studia Historica Carmelitana

Vitae Fratrum   Gerard of Frachet, *Vitae Fratrum Ordinis Praedicatorum*, ed. Benedictus Maria Reichert (Stuttgart: Joseph Roth, 1897)

Westminster   L. C. Hector and Barbara F. Harvey (eds and trans.), *The Westminster Chronicle, 1381–1394* (Oxford: Clarendon Press, 1982)

MODERN STUDIES

Ames   Christine Caldwell Ames, *Righteous Persecution: Inquisition, Dominicans, and Christianity in the Middle Ages* (Philadelphia: University of Pennsylvania Press, 2009)

Andrews   Frances Andrews, *The Other Friars: Carmelite, Augustinian, Sack and Pied Friars in the Middle Ages* (London: Boydell, 2006)

Cotter	Francis J. Cotter, *The Friars Minor in Ireland from their Arrival to 1400*, ed. Roberta A. McKelvie (St Bonaventure, NY: The Franciscan Institute, 1994)
Dupré-Thes.	Eugenio Dupré-Theseider, "L'eresia a Bologna nei tempi di Dante," in *Mondo cittadino e movimenti ereticali nel medio evo (saggi)* (Bologna: Pátron, 1978), 261–315
Lansing	Carol Lansing, *Power and Purity: Cathar Heresy in Medieval Italy* (New York: Oxford University Press, 1998)

Prologue
Anecdotes and their Value

The *New Oxford Book of Literary Anecdotes* opens with a tale featuring Geoffrey Chaucer beating up a Franciscan friar on Fleet Street—a deed lacking any immediate context or explanation, and which cost the perpetrator the sum of two shillings. Undeterred by the fine, so the story goes, the father of modern English set out to have the final say:

> And it seemed his hand ever itched to be revenged, and have his pennyworth's out of them, so tickling religious orders with his tales, and yet so pinching them with his truths, that friars, in reading his books, know not how to dispose their faces between crying and laughing.[1]

Curled into a fist or clenching a quill, Chaucer's hand secured his place within a tradition long considered a staple of Englishness—anticlericalism, here merely replaced with its subgenre, antifraternalism, or opposition to mendicant friars.[2]

Two arguments seem to converge on the editor's use of this anecdote. First and rather circular, if the author of *The Canterbury Tales* and *The Parlement of Fowls* is to epitomize the cultural DNA of the English people, his writings must surely include wit and a healthy dose of antiestablishmentarianism. Secondly and more germane, the abuse of friars, especially when viewed as a metonym for attitudes toward the papal church, gestures at the persistence of a critical stance against Rome well before the Protestant Reformation. Anecdotes used in such a manner promote a teleological approach to English history, also known as "manifest destiny," by reframing the events of the early Tudor era within a continuous narrative of religious and political progress. In other words, the tale demonstrates that England had always been "less medieval" than elsewhere, in part thanks to valiant men such as Chaucer.[3] For whoever had both the gall and the skill to lead a people away from

---

[1] *New Oxford Book of Literary Anecdotes*, ed. John Gross (Oxford: Oxford University Press, 2006), 3, citing Thomas Fuller, *The Church History of Britain* (London: John Williams, 1655), book IV, no. 49 (AD 1399).

[2] Penn R. Szittya, *The Antifraternal Tradition in Medieval Literature* (Princeton: Princeton University Press, 1986), 246, for instance, describes the *Summoner's Tale* as another one of Chaucer's "tales of a church weighed down by hypocrisy and corruption." For a taxonomy of anticlericalism, see José Sánchez, *Anticlericalism: A Brief History* (Notre Dame, IN, and London: University of Notre Dame Press, 1972), 8–11.

[3] See A.G. Dickens, "The Shape of Anticlericalism and the English Reformation," in *Late Monasticism and the Reformation* (London and Rio Grande: Hambledon Press, 1994), 152–3, where the author argues: "English anticlericalism, however defined, underwent a long and massive expansion from the later fourteenth century.... Langland, Wycliffe and Chaucer not only raised the criticism of

Latin (and French) and onto a new linguistic and literary—and by implication national and religious—path, had to do so—violently, if needed—against all that held his country back.[4]

Like many anecdotes, the one relating Chaucer's scuffle with a friar is as telling by its transmission as in its content. The paper trail stretching behind the tale, which is quoted from Thomas Fuller's *The Church History of Britain* (1655), leads us only as far back as Thomas Speght's *The Works of our Antient and Learned English Poet Geffrey Chaucer* (1598).[5] In this influential biography, Speght sought to render Chaucer a more palatable subject to the tastes of audiences in Reformation England. Accordingly, the section dedicated to the poet's education describes how he had rubbed elbows with critical thinkers at Oxford and Cambridge, where he became an accomplished scholar himself, and where his religiosity was deeply shaped by John Wyclif (1324–84), another contemporary whom later reformers would celebrate for his anticlericalism and antifraternalism.[6]

After establishing Chaucer's scholarly acumen, Speght reports—or rather speculates on—the poet's legal training:

It seemeth that Chaucer was of the *Inner Temple* [one of the four Inns of Court in London], for not many years since [the present, a certain] Master *Buckley* did see a Record in the same House where *Geffrey Chaucer* was fined two Shillings for beating a *Franciscan* Friar in *Fleet Street*.

There is no earlier or for that matter firmer evidence for this incident than Master Buckley's alleged testimony.[7] It seemeth that Speght's enthusiasm pushed 1598 hearsay about Chaucer's antifraternal bravado, dating back more than 200 years, into the status of literary anecdote in 1665 and into the present. And its veneer of historical veracity—anecdote, after all, means something unpublished—ensured

---

churchmen to new and striking forms: they eventually transmitted their attitudes to the early Tudor age, when printing swiftly magnified the impact of all three." Dickens's article is a broadside against Christopher Haigh's revisionist article, "Anticlericalism in the English Reformation," *History*, 68 (1983), 391–407, which argues that anticlericalism is a consequence rather than a cause of the English Reformation. Somewhat more useful as a corrective to this thesis is David Loades, "Anticlericalism in the Church of England before 1558: An 'Eating Canker'?," in Nigel Aston and Matthew Cragoe (eds), *Anticlericalism in Britain, c.1500–1914* (Stroud: Sutton, 2000), 1–17.

[4] The Newbolt Report (1921) on English instruction in England and Wales famously asserted that "by the end of the fourteenth century the English language had definitely asserted itself against the results of the Norman Conquest and later French influences"; and that "through the works of Geoffrey Chaucer it became the literary language of the country" (pp. 20 and 28, respectively). Cited here from Brian Doyle, *English and Englishness* (London and New York: Routledge, 1989), 51, 52. The attempt to see Chaucer as the culmination of an early English literary tradition, rather than its beginning, is in Alexander Weiss, *Chaucer's Native Heritage* (New York and Berne: Peter Lang, 1985).

[5] *The Works of our Antient and Learned English Poet Geffrey Chaucer* (London, 1598). On Speght, see s.v. "Speght, Thomas (d. 1621)," *Oxford Dictionary of National Biography*, online edn, Jan. 2008 <www.oxforddnb.com/view/article/26098> (last accessed Feb. 19, 2010).

[6] See *Two Short Treatises, against the Orders of the Begging Friars, compiled by that Famous Doctour of the Church, and Preacher of Gods Word John Wickliffe* (Oxford: Iosph Barnes, 1608).

[7] The comprehensive Martin M. Crow and Clair C. Olson (eds), *Chaucer Life-Records* (Oxford: Oxford University Press, 1966), does not contain any corroborating text other than Speght's.

the tale survived centuries of scrutiny, only to resurface in the twenty-first century as a defining, indeed seminal, moment in English literary and cultural history.

The study of medieval antifraternalism has much more to draw upon than anecdotes. Yet the latter's degree of accuracy or exaggeration, as well as their survival and selective use by later readers, is no less important to understanding pre-modern attitudes toward the friars and toward religious authority in general. The fortunes of the Chaucer anecdote illuminate the changing stakes in perpetuating perceptions of medieval friars' (and by implication the church's) moral laxity, and the righteous responses it provoked from different members of society at different times. The absence of any explanation for Chaucer's act in any of the early modern accounts suggests that, in the religious and political climate of early Reformation England, audiences would justify the violent outburst or were at least implicitly encouraged to do so. For some authors writing as interested parties during and after the religious revolutions of the sixteenth century, men like Chaucer (and Wyclif, and eventually Henry VIII, as well as their parallels across northern and central Europe) championed progress by standing up to a corrupt church and its mendicant vanguard: the bright sparks produced by their efforts illuminate an otherwise dark age, and would soon ignite a great cleansing fire.

Digging deeper, carefully and systematically, into the available evidence concerning medieval antifraternalism, however, reveals a complex and no less telling story: one that does not begin with Chaucer or even with William of St Amour, the so-called Hammer of the Friars, nor lead to the Protestant Reformation, nor end with Nationhood. For the resentment of friars, in England and elsewhere across Latin Christendom, had diverse origins, was shaped by multiple factors, and manifested itself in numerous ways. Nor, on the other hand, does such an investigation exonerate friars from fostering antagonizing practices, since they were capable of them, both by their own accounts and certainly according to the observations of others. But there is another sense in which the brethren were authors of an antifraternal tradition. For beyond unwittingly incurring wrath on account of their misbehavior, they also consciously promoted the memory of their persecution and victimhood, whatever its grounds and however minor its scale.

Introduction

Early in his famous chronicle, the Franciscan friar Salimbene de Adam (1221–c.1290) paused to bemoan his brethren's "many assailants, detractors, enemies, and persecutors, who gladly lay *a blot on the elect* [Eccl. 11.33]."[1] Part of a vibrant if no longer nascent movement, Salimbene made ample room in his writings for recording the hardships of mendicant life, including the ridicule and physical danger to which the brethren were exposed, and which in turn helped brand them as the church's new vanguard. Yet such laments eventually returned to haunt the friars. For, by suggesting the prevalence of hostility aimed at their coreligionists, Salimbene and other mendicant apologists helped cast a lingering doubt over their original appeal and value, a doubt that neatly played into the hands of contemporary and later critics, both of the friars and of the church at large. In this way recorded opposition to mendicants offered proof of the brethren's (and by implication the church's) decadence even during the papacy's alleged golden age.[2]

Driven by curiosity about this core paradox, the present book revisits a major development in medieval Europe—the rise of the mendicant orders—from a number of fresh perspectives. By significantly broadening the traditional documentary basis, geographical scope, and chronology of earlier investigations, and by engaging a number of key debates in medieval social, religious, and urban history, it demonstrates that negative responses to the new orders of friars were scarcely an organized, let alone unified phenomenon: motivations and contexts for dogged treatises, dirty words, and downright violence were highly diverse, even contradictory, running the gamut from calling for the orders' abolition to their internal reform, and from pinpointed assaults to random fighting. Further, it shows that among the forces shaping a medieval antifraternal tradition was not only the brethren's own misconduct but also the orders' self-interest in casting their history in lachrymose terms. Yet, despite their original intent, such narratives would later serve anti-papal critics, both during and after the religious revolutions of the sixteenth century, in framing the vanguard of the church as either corrupt or unpopular—a strategy that in turn influenced the brethren's reputation in the eyes of modern scholars.

---

[1] *Salimbene*, 177: "multos [religiosi] habent mordaces et detractores et inimicos et persecutores, qui libenter ponunt *maculam in electis*."
[2] Geoffrey Dipple, *Antifraternalism and Anticlericalism in the German Reformation: Johann Eberlin von Günzburg and the Campaign against the Friars* (Aldershot: Scolar Press, 1996), 1–17.

Borne out of the revived ideal of apostolic poverty, the medieval mendicant orders—Augustinians, Carmelites, Dominicans, Franciscans, and several other groups—spread across Europe apace, beginning in the early thirteenth century. The friars, as these new monks came to be known, are often seen by modern scholars as fitting the spiritual and socio-psychological needs of Western society like a glove, providing ideal charitable objects in the emergent profit economies of Europe's urban centers, and filling the pastoral gap left by the church's delayed response to urbanization.[3] Yet, alongside their evident success, the brethren also encountered derision, scorn, and even violence, responses duly noted and puzzled over by contemporary and later observers.

Antifraternalism, or opposition to the friars in their early phase (*c*.1220–*c*.1400),[4] is usually understood as a phenomenon driven by competition over material and political resources as well as by envy, a feeling aroused especially among monks and clergymen, members of the church whose income and status the mendicants threatened most.[5] Envy also helps account for antagonism toward friars in another ecclesiastical setting, namely universities, where the new orders' popularity and the perceived opportunism of their recruitment practices undermined the nascent institution's corporate identity and power.[6] The manifest hostility of some churchmen toward mendicants corroborates an observation made by several religious historians in the past—namely, that a characteristic of much medieval anticlericalism was its tendency to concentrate among clerics.

However, and as this study will stress, opposition to the friars' success and conduct exhibits a breadth of scope that pushes antifraternalism beyond the boundaries of medieval church history or the history of church doctrine. Men and women from many walks of life, from poets to prostitutes to peasants, lambasted and occasionally beat religious mendicants, even as the latter's ranks swelled, their treasures grew, and their support by the established church and secular leaders remained stout. Nor, as we shall see, were the brethren's assailants unified under some implicit ideological agenda that somehow foreshadowed the religious revolutions of the early sixteenth century.

How to account for such wide disapproval? Scholarly consensus holds that the early friars sowed the seeds of their own destruction by promoting an ideal that was

---

[3] Jacques Le Goff et al., "Ordres mendiants et urbanisation dans la France médiévale," *Annales: Économies, sociétés, civilisations*, 25 (1970), 924–87; L. Pellegrini, "L'ordine francescano e la società cittadina in epoca bonaventuriana: Un'analisi del 'Determinationes quaestionum super Regulam Fratrum Minorum'," *Laurentianum*, 15 (1974), 154–200; Lester K. Little, *Religious Poverty and the Profit Economy in Medieval Europe* (Ithaca, NY: Cornell University Press, 1978), esp. 97–169.

[4] A period stretching from the orders' diverse foundations to the beginning of their major internal reforms.

[5] Burkhard Mathis, *Die Privilegien des Franziskanerordens bis zum Konzil von Vienne (1311)* (Paderborn: Schöningh, 1928); John R. H. Moorman, *A History of the Franciscan Order from its Origins to the Year 1517* (Oxford: Clarendon Press, 1968), 339–49.

[6] Peter R. McKeon, "The Status of the University of Paris as *Parens Scientiarum*: An Episode in the Development of its Autonomy," *Speculum*, 39 (1964), 651–75; Gordon Leff, *Paris and Oxford Universities in the Thirteenth and Fourteenth Centuries: An Institutional and Intellectual History* (New York: John Wiley and Sons, 1968), 34–47; M.-M. Dufeil, *Guillaume de Saint-Amour et la polémique universitaire parisienne, 1250–1259* (Paris: Picard, 1972).

impossible to sustain over time. On the one hand, and as was common among earlier monastic reform movements, religious mendicancy grew at breakneck speed, leading to undiscerning recruitment practices, lax discipline, and general mismanagement—all of which were reflected to a certain extent by growing internal, clerical, and popular resentment.[7] On the other hand, the prominent role played especially by Franciscans and Dominicans in inquisitorial, missionary, and other diplomatic activities brought them many antagonists, even beyond groups defined as heretical.[8] There is much truth in both views, but even jointly they fall short of explaining the diversity of contexts and motivations for antimendicant hostility in the thirteenth and fourteenth centuries.

To do so, Part One—"Words and Deeds: The World against the Friars"—presents a detailed panorama of medieval antifraternalism broadly redefined as negative responses to the friars, be it their presence, conduct, success, or the rise of organized religious mendicancy. It provides an original and firm basis for understanding antifraternalism in a way that augments a limited doctrinal and literary perspective on the mendicants' early history and then expands that perspective to include the social and political spheres. As such it challenges a traditional and seldom applicable view of the term as limited to a desire to abolish the mendicant orders from the church's hierarchy.

Part One consists of two chapters. The first, "Polemic: False Apostles, False Seemings, False Starts," examines what literary historians have dubbed the medieval antifraternal tradition, a corpus of texts supposedly inspired by the Parisian theologian William of St Amour (d. *c.*1273) and united in its call to do away with the mendicant orders.[9] A comparative reading both of works by St Amour (especially his 1256 *De periculis novissimorum temporum* or *On the Dangers of the Last Times*) and of those of his alleged followers demonstrates, however, that few adhered to William's reactionary ecclesiology, rendering his *magnum opus* something of a false start to the study of medieval antifraternalism. True, accusations against friars were often blatant and at times sincere, but they generally aimed at the orders' reform, not their termination, which was William's stated goal. Thus antifraternal sentiments, some of which actually predate St Amour's vitriol, resonated with criticisms made by members of the mendicant orders themselves and their staunch supporters.

As for writers of medieval fiction and poetry, a subsequent section illustrates that some modern scholars have dubbed them antifraternal on even weaker grounds

---

[7] C. H. Lawrence, *The Friars: The Impact of the Early Mendicant Movement on Western Society* (Harlow: Longman, 1994), 222–3; Andrews, 64; William A. Hinnebusch, *The History of the Dominican Order*, i (New York: Alba House, 1966), 282–8; R. F. Bennett, *The Early Dominicans: Studies in Thirteenth-Century Dominican History* (Cambridge: Cambridge University Press, 1937), 145–56; Moorman, *History of the Franciscan Order*, 155–204.

[8] Holly J. Grieco, "A Dilemma of Obedience and Authority: The Franciscan Inquisition and Franciscan Inquisitors in Provence, 1235–1340," Ph.D. Dissertation, Princeton University, 2004; Ames, 57–93.

[9] See Penn R. Szittya, *The Antifraternal Tradition in Medieval Literature* (Princeton: Princeton University Press, 1986), 3–122.

than they did their theological counterparts.[10] Adding an original study of two famous works to the interpretations of recent literary historians, I argue that friar-characters fabricated by Jean de Meun, Giovanni Boccaccio, William Langland, Geoffrey Chaucer, and other luminaries who comprise the traditional gallery of medieval antifraternal authors offer much more than a ham-fisted critique of the mendicant orders, let alone advocate their obliteration as a matter of course.[11] And, although some of these authors occasionally made use of William of St Amour's writings, they did so in rather complex and ambiguous ways, which occasionally appeared too mild to some of the friars' more committed antagonists. Indeed, several allegedly antimendicant authors seem to have been great enthusiasts of religious mendicancy, as long as the friars clung to their founders' paths (a view that contrasted sharply with St Amour's complete rejection of organized mendicancy), while others used friars (and monks generally) to explore themes of hypocrisy and its role in society and art, without committing to any rigorous ecclesiological viewpoint. Thus, insofar as there was a literary antifraternal tradition, it belonged to the polyvalent realm of medieval estates satire, not to partisan theological polemics, which in turn mostly sought to rehabilitate the orders, not to eliminate them.

Chapter 2, "Violence: Friars under Fire," continues to expand the definition of medieval antifraternalism by establishing the scale and scope of aggression against the brethren, especially physical assaults on individual mendicants and their convents. By adding materials excavated from various archives, such as secular and ecclesiastical court records, as well as from previously published sources, it offers a fresh perspective on the social dimension of antifraternalism, a field heretofore occupied mainly by literary and ecclesiastical historians, and the focus of the previous chapter. The link between the realms of society and church doctrine emerges from this survey, encompassing numerous sources both in and out of print, and enabling us to approximate the frequency and geographical distribution of attacks against friars in the thirteenth and fourteenth centuries. What this broad range of documents attests is a modest, if consistent, rate of physical aggression: a surprise for those (including medieval mendicants) who assumed or sought to establish the prevalence of their victimization.

---

[10] Joseph Spencer Kennard, *The Friar in Fiction, Sincerity in Art and Other Essays* (New York: Brentano's, 1923); Arnold Williams, "Chaucer and the Friars," *Speculum*, 28 (1953), 499–513; John V. Fleming, "The Antifraternalism of the *Summoner's Tale*," *Journal of English and Germanic Philology*, 65 (1966), 688–700; Szittya, *Antifraternal Tradition*.

[11] Jill Mann, *Chaucer and Medieval Estates Satire* (Cambridge: Cambridge University Press, 1973); Jean Batamy, "L'Image des franciscaines dans les 'revues d'États' du XIIIe au XVIe siècle," in André Vauchez (ed.), *Mouvements franciscains et société française, XIIe–XXe siècles*, Beauchesne Religions, 14 (Paris: Beauchesne, 1984), 61–74; Wendy Scase, *"Piers Plowman" and the New Anticlericalism* (Cambridge: Cambridge University Press, 1989); Lawrence M. Clopper, *"Songs of Rechlesnesse": Langland and the Franciscans* (Ann Arbor, MI: University of Michigan Press, 1997); Carlo Delcorno, "La 'predica' di Tedaldo," *Studi sul Boccaccio*, 27 (1999), 55–80; G. Geltner, "Faux Semblants: Antifraternalism Reconsidered in Jean de Meun and Chaucer," *Studies in Philology*, 101 (2004), 357–80; Geoffrey Dipple, "'Si sind all glichsner': Antifraternalism in Medieval and Renaissance German Literature," in Cusato and Geltner (eds), *Defenders and Critics of Franciscan Life*, 177–92.

As for scope, a careful examination of more than 100 cases reveals a wide range of goals and motivations, even within the seemingly cohesive context of anti-inquisitorial violence. To be sure, friars were variously targeted as aliens, political scapegoats, landlords, and abusers of privileges. But they were also hurt as innocent bystanders in military campaigns and during the numerous factional struggles that engulfed Europe at the time, many of which unfolded in an urban context. The friars' ubiquity, accessibility, and wealth often put them in the line of fire. And yet there were few signs of contemporaries' desire to see the brethren disappear from the urban landscape.

Part Two of the book—"Deeds and Words: The Friars against Themselves"—reverses the pendulum swing by shifting the focus from society's reaction to and impact on mendicants to the brethren's own misconduct and ideology. From passive objects and victims, in these chapters the friars become agents within and authors of a medieval antifraternal tradition. Chapter 3, "Deviance: Brethren Behaving Badly," marshals diverse evidence for religious mendicants' normative violations as they emerge mostly from the orders' internal documents. Rather than taking polemicists and authors of poetry and prose fiction at their word, this chapter carefully gauges the frequency and profile of deviance among the brethren, especially but not exclusively Dominicans, whose documentation of the brethren's disobedience, including sexual and violent misconduct, is superior for much of the period under consideration.

It is crucial to isolate mendicant misconduct, since it often paved the way to certain allegations being launched against them and drove locals into social and legal action. Given the brethren's strong presence in urban centers and episcopal and secular courts, their deviancy was hard to conceal and even harder to dismiss in light of the ideals they stood for: humility, obedience, and (at least individual) poverty. Deviance, in turn, exacerbated pressures created by the friars' growing number of antagonists, both within and outside the church, who were able to manipulate potentially isolated events to their own benefit in the context of local and regional power struggles.

While Chapter 3 suggests that friars unwittingly became ensnared in antifraternal narratives crafted by non-mendicants and later polemicists, Chapter 4 asserts the brethren's more conscious and active role in forging an antifraternal tradition from yet another perspective and in a particularly revisionist fashion. "Remembrance: Antifraternalism and Mendicant Identity" documents the various ways in which friars and their advocates perceived of and represented their own victimhood, thereby helping to turn what appears to be a limited phenomenon into a major cornerstone of mendicants' social memory. And, although different orders followed somewhat different paths, jointly they fused somewhat disparate incidents into a misleadingly cohesive, lachrymose narrative, which enabled them to perpetuate yet another antifraternal tradition under the legitimizing guise of mendicant suffering and martyrdom.

This study illuminates the early phase of the mendicant orders from a number of original perspectives. Yet at the same time it offers several broader correctives to the history of anticlericalism and the study of violence, especially in an urban context.

As regards opposition to figures of religious authority and religious institutions generally, the information gathered and analyzed in this book raises several parallels that may be reasonably drawn between antifraternalism and anticlericalism and the extent to which the former can be seen as a proxy to the latter. On the one hand, compared with the picture drawn by some Reformation historians, late-medieval developments do not point conclusively in the direction of a major reform, and, even when they do, resentment against the friars per se offers a rather ambiguous clue. On the other, and contrary to the assumptions of numerous modern historians, articulated resistance to religious authority, albeit under a universal church, did not begin with Humanism or the Enlightenment, let alone with the French Revolution.[12] Either way, it is quite possible to establish very fruitful parallels between opposition to medieval friars and clergymen from a social perspective—for instance, in terms of the immediate triggers to acts of violence, their goals, and their concentration in cities.

As regards urban violence itself, the numerous cases assembled in this book expose medieval society's capacity to balance, subvert, and rewrite power relations between clergy and (at times religiously zealous) laity through organized and often highly nuanced symbolic action. Inspired by several insights, old and new, concerning the role, grammar, and function of violence,[13] this study furthers the development of an interpretative framework based on violence as communicative action.

---

[12] José Sánchez, *Anticlericalism: A Brief History* (Notre Dame, IN, and London: University of Notre Dame Press, 1972).

[13] Hannah Arendt, *On Violence* (Orlando, FA: Harcourt, 1970); Wolfgang Sofsky, *Saggio sulla violenza*, trans. Barbara Trapani and Luca Lamberti (Turin: Einaudi, 1998); Catherine Lutz, *Homefront: A Military City and the American 20th Century* (Boston: Beacon Press, 2001); Slavoj Žižek, *Violence* (London: Profile, 2008).

PART ONE

WORDS AND DEEDS: THE WORLD AGAINST THE FRIARS

Introduction to Part One

On a cold November evening in 2007, I was standing outside a restaurant in New York City's Upper East Side, waiting for a dinner companion. With numb fingers, I began to peruse a free copy of the *Village Voice*, which I had pulled out of the corner dispenser. Within seconds my medievalist's eye caught the title of that issue's society column, which promised, among other attractions, "gossip hot enough to roast a Friar."[1]

The reference and pun concerned a recent event held at the New York Friars Club, a veteran comedy venue in Midtown, where showbiz's finest come to roast.[2] But there was another, probably unintended pun, harkening back to the traditional connotation of roasting as a physical act rather than a speech act. For the expression "roasting a friar" would strike those familiar with medieval and early modern history as an ironic turning of the tables, given how the activities of some friars, especially in their capacity as papal inquisitors in Languedoc, Lombardy, and later in Iberia and Central America, led to numerous burnings of convicted heretics. Historically, the few mendicants actually set ablaze were for the most part radical or Spiritual Franciscans, themselves convicted of heresy during the papacy of John XXII (1316–34). In my (admittedly esoteric) mind, the headline linked such diverse traditions of resisting and thus re-inscribing forms of authority, be they comedic, religious, or both.

For in words (written, spoken) as well as deeds (performed, looming), medieval friars were commonly placed under fire. That is to say, they were publicly exposed or verbally accused of degeneration or corruption, sometimes to the edifying laughter or the mocking cheer of a critical but often orthodox audience. This was done in sermons and theological treatises, through satirical literature and art, and occasionally even by means of physical violence—words and deeds that constitute distinct strands of a medieval antifraternal tradition.

This critical tradition is the subject of the present volume in general and of the following two chapters in particular. The first concerns negative opinions expressed mainly in writing. It examines a corpus of polemical literature and a related group of satirical prose fiction and poetic works that criticize the mendicant orders, their norms, and their activities. Against a common view that stresses these works' antifraternal unison in following the lead of William of St Amour, the so-called

---

[1] *Village Voice*, Oct. 23, 2007 <www.villagevoice.com/2007-10-23/nyc-life/lance-bass-on-pedophilia> (last accessed Mar. 5, 2011).
[2] See <www.friarsclub.com>(last accessed Mar. 5, 2011).

Hammer of the Friars, I will draw a more complex picture that largely isolates St Amour's ecclesiology as radical and lacking in genuine followers. As for poetry and prose fiction, I will posit that, insofar as it is possible to distill an ecclesiology from such diverse texts, it betrays a desire to see the mendicants restored to their erstwhile (and partly imagined) glory rather than promote their eradication—in contrast with their total rejection by St Amour.

The second chapter moves beyond the world of doctrine and literary satire to that of social and political action. It offers an original survey and analysis of incidents of aggression against friars and mendicant convents from their diverse foundations in the early thirteenth century to the end of the fourteenth, when their internal reforms were mostly underway. The more than 100 cases assembled in this chapter attest, on the one hand, the modest scale of documented antifraternal aggression, and, on the other, the variety of contexts in which such violence was perpetrated. Rather than viewing antifraternal violence as a coordinated mobilization driven by a reactionary ecclesiology, these cases can be better understood first and foremost as defensive exercises against social and political instability, a threat that friars were at times thought to pose. Seen from this perspective, urban dwellers' attempts to check the brethren's power were expressions of community building or at least preservation.

1

Polemic: False Apostles, False Seemings, False Starts

> There are no more than two orders among the Disciples... whence this third order emerged we do not know. And what lacks a reason must be extirpated.
>
> William of St Amour, *On the Dangers of the Last Times* (1256)[1]

The deepest furrow of medieval antifraternalism is the intersecting history of doctrine and literature; which is not to say it is its most-documented or even best-understood aspect. Yet polemical texts and literary satire provide easy access to a wider field, via centuries of fine scholarship by intellectual, ecclesiastical, and literary historians, as well as numerous philologists. The seemingly convenient point of departure is misleading, however, since it involves dealing with the burden of some lingering and influential misconceptions about what has come to be known as the medieval antifraternal tradition.

To begin with, "tradition" is a vague term that nonetheless asserts continuity. It suggests or at least implies that there exists a body of Latin and vernacular texts, spanning the length and breadth of Europe, and bound together by common origins, themes, and an ideology. In the words of Penn Szittya, the main proponent of the term, the antifraternal tradition is "a complex of hostile ideas about the friars," which, "in all levels of medieval society... dominated criticism of the friars from the 1250s to the end of the Middle Ages." Indeed,

despite their diversity in genre and purpose, these antifraternal works offer testimony to a common literary tradition. They share a common language, largely derived from the Bible, and a common—theological, symbolic, and prejudicial—perception of the friars that helped to create and preserve many charges against the fraternal orders that were distorted, outdated, or false.[2]

The present chapter joins a number of recent works by historians of medieval literature such as Jill Mann, Jean Batamy, Nicholas Havely, James Andreas, and

---

[1] *De periculis*, 52: "cum enim non nisi duos ordines inter discipulos esse cognovimus... unde iste tertius ordo processerit ignoramus. Et quod ratione caret extirpare necesse est"; citing Gratian, *Concordia discordantium canonum*, pt I, dist. 68, c. v §1, in Emil Friedberg (ed.), *Corpus iuris canonici*, vol. 1 (Leipzig: B. Tauchnitz, 1879), 255.

[2] Penn R. Szittya, *The Antifraternal Tradition in Medieval Literature* (Princeton: Princeton University Press, 1986), p. ix.

Wendy Scase, who—in more and less direct ways—have challenged the idea of an antifraternal tradition as a gross oversimplification. For, insofar as such a literature shares an ancestor—William of St Amour's 1256 treatise *De periculis novissimorum temporum* (*On the Dangers of the Last Times*) being the usual suspect—it has frequently and substantially diverged from it. For even the severest of the friars' literate critics were usually reactionary clerics, not budding anti-papists, proto-reformers, or early prophets of the nation state, all of which are later constructs that have introduced an anachronistic teleology to the original censure of medieval friars. The focus, in short, has been misplaced. And, as a corrective, the following sections will describe, first the source, then its alleged imitators, and then the distance that sets them apart.

Given the abundance and variety of materials, the discussion of theological antifraternalism in the first and second sections had to be rigidly limited to developing the following theses: (1) William of St Amour's approach to religious mendicancy was one of total rejection; he and those he originally spoke for disapproved of the existence of friars and wished to see them deleted from the hierarchy of the church, arguing that their foundation ran against Catholic doctrine. (2) By contrast, *and insofar as their authors wished to make unequivocal statements on the matter*, most other antifraternal theologians, from Nicolas of Lisieux to Jean d'Anneux to Richard FitzRalph, display a desire to curb and reform a corrupted movement, not throw it into history's dustbin. Any more extreme statements regarding the vast majority of antifraternal thinkers can be derived from the sources' silence alone. Thus the following two sections aim to distinguish between a minimalist (total-contrarian) and a maximalist (critical-reformist) interpretation of medieval antifraternalism among ecclesiastical authors.

The third section extends this distinction into the realm of prose fiction and poetry. Here too it proved impossible to cover the span of all relevant thirteenth- and fourteenth-century works. Nor was it germane to refer at every step to an author's general *œuvre*, his literary circle, or his works' general reception and interpretation. Instead, I mainly chose to focus on two works long hailed as staples of medieval antifraternalism, namely Jean de Meun's *Roman de la Rose* (completed around 1270) and Geoffrey Chaucer's *Summoner's Tale* (late fourteenth century), and employ them in support of a growing, but not unopposed, tendency among literary historians to question the presence of clear-cut doctrinal statements against religious mendicancy in other works of medieval fiction.

The conclusion reiterates that focusing on antifraternalism from an abolitionist or total-contrarian point of view will leave us with a puny phenomenon that had little documented impact before the religious revolutions of the sixteenth century. One alternative this leaves us with is to adopt a broader and more inclusive approach to medieval antifraternalism, encompassing the variety of ways in which authors and theologians (and, as Chapter 2 will explore, urban governments and residents) engaged friars, interpreted their ministry, and understood their social role.

ON THE DANGERS OF THE LAST TIMES

The much-vaunted touchstone of medieval antifraternal literature appeared in early 1256, during an escalating legal struggle between mendicant theologians and their allies, on the one hand, and the Parisian university's secular masters and their supporters, on the other.[3] The events' immediate backdrop was the second cessation of teaching at the university in 1253, following the alleged brutalization of several students by the local night watch. The university suspended its activities to protest what it claimed was gratuitous violence. Yet the measure failed to win the immediate cooperation of the popular mendicant *studia*.

The secular masters construed the friars' cool response as a repeated display of their uncolleagiality in the aftermath of the university's Great Dispersion in 1229, during which the brethren, who kept their schools open, gained a lucrative chair in theology. Resentment during the second strike only intensified when the Dominicans—perhaps confirming what behavioral economists have dubbed "the endowment effect," namely that people are more averse to loss than keen about gain, or are generally biased toward maintaining a *status quo ante*[4]—demanded to secure their now-threatened possession of a second theology chair if they were to act in solidarity. In the ensuing conflagration, the secular masters, headed by William of St Amour, appealed to the papal curia and its delegates to eject the mendicant masters from the corporate university body.

On the face of it, the secular masters were dealing with a recurring instance of the friars' success going to their head, opportunism trumping humility. The antimendicant party—and for once we may somewhat accurately speak of one—was quick to point out that the friars had no place at the university to begin with. To some this rang especially true of the Franciscan Order, whose founder, a self-professed *simplex et idiota*, opposed the brethren's pursuit of formal learning.[5] Even the Dominican Order, which was ideologically committed to the study of theology and canon law, conceived of advanced studies as an act of "bending a bow," a preparatory means to the end of preaching missions.[6] Yet by the middle of the thirteenth century Franciscan and Dominican scholars, soon to be joined by their Carmelite

---

[3] Narrative accounts include H. Rashdall, *The Universities of Europe in the Middle Ages*, ed. F. M. Powicke and A. B. Emden, i (Oxford: Clarendon Press, 1936), 370–97; Gordon Leff, *Paris and Oxford Universities in the Thirteenth and Fourteenth Centuries: An Institutional and Intellectual History* (New York: John Wiley and Sons, 1968), 34–47; and *De periculis*, 1–18 (and *De periculis*, 29–34 for an updated bibliography). The classic monograph of this field remains M.-M. Dufeil, *Guillaume de Saint-Amour et la polémique universitaire parisienne, 1250–1259* (Paris: Picard, 1972).

[4] Daniel Kahneman, Jack L. Knetsch, and Richard H. Thaler, "Anomalies: The Endowment Effect, Loss Aversion, and Status Quo Bias," *Journal of Economic Perspectives*, 5 (1991), 193–206.

[5] The Minorites' pursuit of higher education may not, however, have been as problematic as the masters construed it to be or as is often assumed by modern scholars. See Neslihan Şenocak, *The Rise of Learning in the Franciscan Order* (Ithaca, NY: Cornell University Press, 2012), esp. chs 1–2, which complements and revises Bert Roest, *A History of Franciscan Education (c.1210–1517)* (Leiden: Brill, 2000).

[6] M. Michèle Mulchahey, *"First the Bow is Bent in Study...": Dominican Education before 1350* (Toronto: Pontifical Institute of Mediaeval Studies, 1998).

and Augustinian coreligionists, were playing an ever greater role in urban higher education, including the occupation of chairs at the faculty of theology, the crown jewel of the University of Paris.[7]

The friars' conditional solidarity and the apparent discrepancy between their theory and practice in the realm of letters were not lost on their opponents. Indeed, to the latter they offered a strong indictment of the mendicants' hypocrisy.[8] The accusation was strong enough, yet William of St Amour personally did not stop there. As the struggle continued, he took to the pulpit and the quill, claiming that the friars were false apostles who abused their privileges. He also cast those supporting the brethren—a motley crew including numerous bishops and laymen, as well as the Capetian monarchy and the papacy—as accomplices undermining the divinely ordained hierarchy of the church.[9] How well William's ideas resonated with contemporaries outside the university is unclear, for both success and failure could have led him to step up his rhetoric and to publish, in March or April 1256, his most famous work, *De periculis novissimorum temporum*.

William's *magnum opus*, a medium-length, Latin treatise, consists of a prologue, fourteen chapters, and an epilogue. The prologue proclaims the impending disasters of the last times, decries the current state of ignorance and confusion, and presents the exegetical method employed to identify the dangers and confront them. Chapters 1 and 3 argue for the temporal proximity of the last times, while Chapters 2, 4, and 5 announce and then elaborate on the apocalyptic dangers emanating specifically from certain "false preachers." Chapters 6 through 11 emphasize the clergy's central role in identifying and combating false preachers, Chapters 12 and 13 lay out a plan for the proposed struggle, and Chapter 14 enumerates specific signs or signals to help detect false preachers. The brief epilogue reiterates the urgent need to act and underscores the consequences of apathy for the secular clergy and Christendom at large.

Certainly by medieval standards, *De periculis* was a highly contentious work. It develops a series of arguments exposing what William and his alleged collaborators believed were the unorthodoxy of the mendicant orders, the apocalyptic dangers signaled by their proliferation, and the clergy's potentially decisive role in altering

---

[7] E. Randolph Daniel, *The Franciscan Concept of Mission in the High Middle Ages* (Lexington, KY: University of Kentucky Press, 1975); Roest, *A History of Franciscan Education*. The Carmelites settled in Paris around 1256, followed several years later by the Augustinian Hermits. See Franz-Bernard Lickteig, *The German Carmelites at the Medieval Universities*, TSHC 13 (Rome: Institututm Carmelitanum, 1981), esp. 113–79; David Gutiérrez, *The Augustinians in the Middle Ages*, trans. Arthur J. Ennis (Villanova, PA: Augustinian Historical Institute, 1984), 138–9, 143; and Andrews, 42–4, 105–6. In both cases, however, the educational structures were rudimentary well into the second half of the century, and the brethren's formal involvement with the University of Paris weaker by comparison to the larger orders.

[8] Peter McKeon, "The Status of the University of Paris as *Parens Scientarum*: An Episode in the Development of its Autonomy," *Speculum*, 39 (1964), 651–75; Louis Jacques Bataillon, "Les crises de l'université de Paris d'après les sermons universitaires," in Albert Zimmermann (ed.), *Die Auseinandersetzungen an der Pariser Universität im XIII. Jahrhundert*, Miscellanea Medievalia, 10 (Berlin: Walter de Gruyter, 1976), 155–69.

[9] William's output during those months has been finely edited in *The Opuscula of William of Saint-Amour: The Minor Works of 1255–1256*, ed. Andrew G. Traver (Münster: Aschendorff, 2003).

these circumstances (or, read conversely, their present complicity in them). Thus, this treatise, like many late medieval apocalyptic works, was composed as a rallying cry for the restoration of ecclesiastical order.[10] It warns against the impending disasters associated with the last times and carries the dual message of optimism and activism as remedies for these dangers.[11]

At base, then, *De periculis* seeks to identify the secular clergy's responsibility in containing religious mendicancy and to guide them in this effort. In this respect, the work's apocalypticism is subordinate to its political aims—an entirely unexceptional fact, given the literary tradition of apocalyptic eschatology. The clergy's prerogative is stressed throughout the treatise and is reflected in the sheer number of chapters dedicated entirely or predominantly to this task. In promoting the clergy's partisanship and activism, William endorsed the classic two-pronged method of "carrots and sticks," rewards and punishments that will replenish or befall the clergy according to their actions. Importantly, William rarely describes otherworldly events; at least in the case of punishments, he promises God's immediate reprisal, and this, in fact, is precisely the note on which the treatise ends.

One of the greatest ironies of *De periculis* is that it never explicitly names the friars as the harbingers of the Antichrist. Yet the intruders' identity is never in doubt: they are recently arrived and well-educated preachers who have achieved tremendous political and material success, which they leveraged into gaining the ear of the rich and powerful. They appear to be humble and simple but are in fact arrogant and learned. They are thus hypocrites and preach falsehoods. Their main strategy is to target gullible women, and through them gain access to their husbands' homes, pockets, and consciences. By offering personalized services, especially confession, these dangerous men are able to penetrate the homes of numerous people and sow heresy among them under the guise of a genuine apostolic life. And in doing all this they deliver a mortal blow to the only vehicle of human salvation, the divinely ordained church. "Thus it appears from the above who are penetrators of homes and who are the false; it even appears that through such men the dangers of the last times will threaten or already are threatening the entire church."[12]

De periculis completely recast the nature of the struggle between secular and mendicant masters from one over labor politics to a fully-fledged apocalyptic battle. The allegations were audacious, especially considering the friars' enormous popularity and the strong support they received from lay society and the highest echelons of secular and religious powers. Yet William's move was linked in a curious way to a recent event in the Franciscan Order, which may have persuaded him that it was an opportune moment to strike with such force. For among the "incriminating" evidence at William's disposal was a compilation known as the *Liber introductorius*

---

[10] Bernard McGinn, *Apocalyptic Spirituality* (New York: Paulist Press, 1979), 1–16; Bernard McGinn, "Apocalypticism and Church Reform, 1100–1500," in Bernard McGinn (ed.), *Encyclopedia of Apocalypticism*, ii (New York: Continuum, 1999), 74–109.
[11] James Doyne Dawson, "William of Saint-Amour and the Apostolic Tradition," *Mediaeval Studies*, 40 (1978), 223–38, esp. 234–5.
[12] *De periculis*, 58: "Sic ergo patet ex predictis qui sunt penetrantes domos et qui sunt pseudo; patet etiam quod per tales instabunt vel instant pericula novissimorum temporum universe ecclesie."

in evangelium eternum (*Introduction to the Eternal Gospel*). The work, published in 1254 by the Franciscan Gerard of Borgo San Donnino, then residing in Paris, sought to advance one side in an internal debate regarding the correct way of interpreting the Minorites' *Rule*.[13] Although the *Introductorius* was unauthorized and its relation to the original university quarrels tenuous, it contained several inflammatory observations, which William readily exploited to appeal to his audiences and fortify his party's position.

As its title suggests, the *Introductorius* drew on the writings of Joachim of Fiore, a venerated exegete, visionary, and monastic reformer who died in 1202—that is, before the foundation of any mendicant order.[14] Joachim propounded a theology of history in which three ages unfold: that of the Son, the Father, and the Holy Spirit. In this scheme, the latter age, or *status*, would be the culmination of the Godhead's work in the physical world, ushering in a new and complete spiritual understanding of divine truth: an eternal gospel. Importantly, he also claimed that this approaching era would be exemplified by the lives of "new men" (*novi viri*). Despite Joachim's own elusiveness and ambiguity, his Franciscan followers in particular insisted on a literal interpretation of the terms "eternal gospel" and "new men," identifying the abbot's works as the former and their own order as the latter. The Franciscan compiler of the *Introductorius* also established 1260 as the year in which the new age would commence—that is, six years thence.

The appearance of the *Introductorius* could not have come at a worse time for the Parisian mendicants. And, although the work was condemned, burned, and those involved in its authorship severely punished, the antimendicant party employed it to demonstrate that *all* friars were apocalyptic forerunners of the Antichrist, as they prepared to undo the existing church and its basic Scriptures. As William put it in the eighth chapter of *De periculis*, which enumerates several signs of the Antichrist's approach,

The second sign is that, already in the year of the Lord twelve hundred and fifty-four, that teaching which will be preached in the time of the Antichrist, namely, the aforesaid *Eternal*

---

[13] Paolo Cassi, "Per una revisione: Fra' Gherardo da Borgo S. Donnino," *Aurea Parma*, 19 (1935), 5–13; Rino Ferrari, *Fra Gherardo da Fidenza (il Martin Lutero del 1200)* (Parma: STEP, 1950); and Filippo Rotolo, "San Bonaventura e fra Gerardo da Borgo S. Donnino: Riflessi del Gioachimismo in Sicilia," *O Theologos: Cultura Cristiana di Sicilia*, 2 (1975), 263–97. What remains of the condemned *Introductorius* are fragments whose authenticity is questionable. See E. Benz, "Die Excerptsätze der Pariser Professoren aus dem Evangelium aeternum," *ZfK*, 51 (1932), 415–55.

[14] Morton W. Bloomfield, "Joachim of Flora: A Critical Survey of his Canon, Teaching, Sources, Bibliography, and Influence," *Traditio*, 13 (1957), 249–311; and Morton W. Bloomfield, "Recent Scholarship on Joachim of Fiore and his Influence," in Ann Williams (ed.), *Prophecy and Millenarianism: Essays in Honour of Marjorie Reeves* (Harlow: Longman, 1980), 21–52. Later publications include Delno C. West and Sandra Zimders-Swartz, *Joachim of Fiore: A Study in Spiritual Perception and History* (Bloomington, IN: Indiana University Press, 1983); Bernard McGinn, *The Calabrian Abbott: Joachim of Fiore in the History of Western Thought* (New York and London: Macmillan, 1985); Stephen E. Wessley, *Joachim of Fiore and Monastic Reform* (New York: Peter Lang, 1990); Franco Galiano, *Interpretazione esoterica della storia in Gioacchino da Fiore, frate calabrese*, 2nd edn (Cosenza: Brenner, 2000); Matthias Riedl, *Joachim von Fiore: Denker der vollendeten Menschheit* (Würzburg: Königshausen & Neumann, 2004).

Gospel, was publicly submitted for examination in Paris.... Whence it is certain that it would already be preached unless something prevented it....

The seventh sign is that, with the approaching consummation of the era, certain men, who in the church seem most zealous for the faith and appear to love Christ greatly, will cast off the gospel of Christ and adhere to the *Eternal Gospel*, which entirely overwhelms Christ's faith. Whence the love of many, by which the word of God is guarded, will entirely abate.[15]

The unique eschatological role given the friars by the *Introductorius*, as well as what could have been construed as a gross devaluation of the Bible, fell like ripe fruit into the antimendicant party's lap. William personally lost no chance to decry the treatise, and consciously shaped *De periculis* as a complete reversal of (and some would say a parody on) the arguments advanced in it. How, William would repeatedly ask, could such hypocrites blatantly subvert the order of the church and not be recognized as false apostles and the harbingers of the Antichrist?

He who cannot see that these signs are already present in the church is evidently asleep. Whence let him follow the Apostle's counsel, I Thes. 5[:6], *let us not sleep, but be vigilant. Be vigilant*, therefore, *just men*, I Cor. 15[:34], and through the aforesaid signs, which already appear, you will see that the end of the era is near, and that the sorrow, which will come to pass in the time of the Antichrist, already begins.[16]

The friars' degeneration, however, was mostly a red herring. To William's mind, the orders' very existence posed by far the more serious threat to the ordained hierarchy of the church, not because of their comportment, but because they occupied a place outside it. An argument to this effect is propounded especially in the treatise's second chapter, which also questions the legitimacy of the orders' approval by the papacy. Marshaling evidence from Scripture and the Ordinary Gloss, civil and ecclesiastical law, Boethius' *Consolation of Philosophy* and, crucially, Pseudo-Dionysius's *Ecclesiastical Hierarchy* and *Celestial Hierarchy*, William argues that God instituted two and only two orders, with their respective subdivisions, for the direction of the church. The first or "perfect" order (bishops, presbyters, and deacons) was prefigured in the twelve apostles, while the second and inferior order "of those to be perfected" (monks, laymen, and catechumens) follows the path set by the seventy-two disciples (Luke 10:1).

According to this logic, this division precludes any legitimate third order that the mendicants claim to constitute. In the words of Gratian, cited in *De periculis*: "For, since we recognized that there are no more than two orders among the disciples,

---

[15] *De periculis*, 76, 78: "Secundum signum est quod illa doctrina que predicabitur tempore Antichristi, videlicet, *Evangelium eternum* predictum, Parisius... posituri sunt iam publice ad examinandum anno domini mille CC LIIII. Unde certum est quod iam predicaretur nisi esset aliquid quod eam detineret"; and 82: "Septimum signum est quoniam, appropriquante consummatione seculi, quidam qui videntur in ecclesia maximi zelatores fidei at maxime amare Christum, dimittent evangelium Christi et adherebunt *Evangelio eterno*, quod ex toto absorbet fidem Christi. Unde ex toto refrigescet karitas multorum."

[16] *De periculis*, 82: "Qui hec signa non videt iam esse in ecclesia dormire videtur. Unde acquiescat consolio apostoli, I The. V, *non dormiamus sed vigilemus*. Evigilate ergo *iusti*, I Cor. XV, et per signa predicta, que iam apparent, videbitis consummationem seculi prope esse et dolorem qui erit tempore Antichristi iam incohari."

that is, twelve Apostles and seventy-two Disciples, whence this third order emerged we do not know. And what lacks a reason must be extirpated."[17]

With a conscious pun on *ordo predicatorum*, the Dominicans' formal title, William concludes that there can be only one legitimate order of preachers—that is, bishops; anyone else who claims to be filling this office must be exposed as a false preacher. Given the abundance of the latter, however, he concludes that the Antichrist's arrival must be imminent.[18] On this basis the chapter ends on an even more audacious—and in hindsight consequential—note by rejecting the papacy's support of organized religious mendicancy. Producing further favorable statements from Gratian's *Decretum*, William concludes that, "if the Roman pontiff would seem to reject what the Apostles and Prophets taught (let it be far!), he should be demonstrated not to be giving a judgment, but rather to be in error."[19]

Few would deny that the new mendicant orders fit awkwardly into the traditional ecclesiastical scheme, however anachronistically William construed it. Indeed, two of the smaller orders of friars, the Carmelites and the Augustinian Hermits, responded directly to these legitimate charges by reiterating that their origins stretch back to Antiquity and Late Antiquity, respectively.[20] Yet the Franciscans and Dominicans placed little emphasis on their institutional continuities with the early church, perhaps since their success furnished ample proof to the weakening of a traditional division of ecclesiastical labor. William may have voiced the concerns of those who detected this shift in particularly reactionary terms, but even he was painfully aware that few outside the university saw this as a change for the worse.

The legacy of *De periculis* is riddled with irony. Although it failed both as a rallying cry and a legal *pièce justificative*, it became a highly influential work of exegesis and a point of reference for generations of authors concerned with religious mendicancy, church hierarchy, papal infallibility, and the relations between church and state. On the other hand, where William was far from innovative, as when appropriating a prevalent binary apocalyptic narrative that distinguished between the sons of light and darkness (as did the *Introductorius*), he precipitated his own downfall.

For the friars' supporters, who included Pope Alexander IV (a former cardinal protector of the Franciscan Order) and King Louis IX of France (St Louis), the

---

[17] *De periculis*, 52: "cum enim non nisi duos ordines inter discipulos esse cognovimus, id est XII apostolorum et LXXII discipulorum, unde iste tertius ordo processerit ignoramus. Et quod ratione caret extirpare necesse est"; citing Gratian, *Concordia discordantium canonum*, pt I, dist. 68, c. v §1, in Friedberg (ed.), *Corpus iuris canonici*, i. 255.

[18] On the centrality of preaching to the debates, see M. Peuchmaurd, "Mission canonique et predication," *Recherches de Théologie Ancienne et Médiévale*, 30 (1963), 122–44, 251–76; and Rolf Zerfaß, *Der Streit um die Laienpredigt: Eine pastoralgeschichliche Undersuchung zum Verstandnis des Predigtamtes und zu zeinder Entwicklung im 12. und 13. Jahrhundert* (Freiburg: Herder, 1974), 213–43.

[19] *De periculis*, 54, 58, citing Gratian, *Dec.*, pt II, C. 25, q. i, c. 6 (col. 1008): "sunt qui dicent quod si romanus pontifex quod docuerunt apostoli et prophete detestari—quod absit!—videretur, non sententiam dare sed magis errare convinceretur."

[20] Andrew Jotischky, *The Carmelites and Antiquity: Mendicants and their Pasts in the Middle Ages* (Oxford: Oxford University Press, 2002), 261–330. The orders' need to prove their antiquity was exacerbated by (but did not originate with) the Council of Lyons in 1274. See Andrews, 1–2, 17–21, 90–3.

intimate association with the Antichrist seemed grossly unjustified. Soon after the publication of *De periculis*, and following a string of public sermons pitched in a key similar to it, the Capetian ruler identified William as an obstacle to reconciliation between the disputing parties and dispatched the treatise to be examined at the papal court. There, after six months of deliberation, the work was condemned and ordered to be destroyed. William was soon exiled to his native Burgundian town, technically outside Capetian jurisdiction, and his collaborators were forced to recant or lose their positions. By and large they chose the former option.

While in exile William continued to fight for his cause, sparing the friars of none of his vitriol, and even escalating his rhetoric. In a typical passage penned around 1266, for instance, he claimed that mendicants were worse than the Devil, for, while the latter proposed to turn stones into bread, the former were already turning poor people's bread into the stone of their fine churches.[21] Yet the sum effect of his actions was to dissolve the antimendicant party and to conclude the first—and, *strictu sensu*, only—chapter in the history of medieval antifraternalism.

THEOLOGICAL ANTIFRATERNALISM

In the prologue to *De periculis* and elsewhere William of St Amour identifies the work as a collaborative effort.[22] The claim, alongside the masters' jointly written *Apologia* of 1254 and a special tax levied on the various faculties to support William's presentation of the case at the papal court, confirms that contrarian antifraternalism had some appeal among William's academic colleagues.[23] Subsequent texts, however, suggest that such reactionary radicalism was short-lived. Possibly traumatized by William's downfall and subdued by the threat of exile, erstwhile antimendicant partisans such as Gerard of Abbeville (1225–72), in his *Contra adversarium perfectionis christianae* (1269),[24] and his contemporary Nicolas of Lisieux, in his *Liber de Antichristo*, refrained from invoking the eradication of mendicants in their salvos.[25] Instead, they underscored the friars' fallen

---

[21] "Collectiones Catholicae et canonicae scripturae," in William of St Amour, *Guillielmi de S. Amore Opera Omnia...* (Constance [Paris]: Alitophilos, 1632), 462. See Dufeil, *Guillaume de Saint-Amour*, 328–31; Dufeil, "Guilelmus de Sancto Amore, Opera Omnia (1252–1270)," in Albert Zimmermann (ed.), *Die Auseinandersetzungen an der Pariser Universität im XIII. Jahrhundert*, Miscellanea Medievalis, 10 (Berlin: Walter de Gruyter, 1976), 216; John V. Fleming, "The *Collationes* of William of Saint-Amour against St. Thomas," *Recherches de théologie ancienne et medieval*, 32 (1965), 132–8.

[22] *De periculis*, 38. In his subsequent defense of the tract to the papal commission William asserted that he "and others have gathered the aforesaid texts into a book" (*auctoritates praedictas et per multas collationes ego et alii praedicti in volumen unum sub certis rubricis illas redegimus*). See "Les 'Responsiones' de Guillaume de Saint-Amour," ed. E. Garal, *Archives d'histoire doctrinale et littéraire du moyen age*, 18 (1950–1), 360.

[23] Andrew G. Traver, "Rewriting History? The Parisian Secular Masters' *Apologia* of 1254," *History of Universities*, 15 (1997–9), 9–45. For the tax levy, see *CUP* i. 231 (258–9).

[24] Gerard of Abbevile, "*Contra adversarium perfectionis christianae*," ed. S. Clasen, *AFH*, 31 (1938), 276–329; 32 (1939), 89–200.

[25] Nicolas of Lisieux, "Liber de Antichristi," in Edmond Martène and Ursin Durand (eds), *Veterum scriptorum et monumentorum historicorum...*, ix (Paris: Montalant, 1733), cols 1271–1446. And see Palémon Glorieux, "Une offensive de Nicolas de Lisieux contre saint Thomas d'Aquin," *Bulletin de*

state, challenged specific mendicant privileges (especially confession), and called for the orders' return to the path laid by their founders. In doing so, they certainly built upon William's exegesis. But the extent to which such recourse was in keeping with his reactionary ecclesiology was very limited indeed, especially in its avoidance of implicating the friars' supporters in heresy.

Not that the modified strand of opposition calmed the friars. In the immediate aftermath of the university quarrels they continued to consider the antimendicant threat serious enough to solicit learned responses from two of their greatest luminaries, the Dominican Thomas Aquinas (1225–74) and Bonaventure of Bagnoregio (1221–74), recently appointed Minister General of the Franciscan Order. Nor were these apologies produced offhand. Bonaventure's work in particular, the *Apologia pauperum*, is still regarded as one of the finest defenses of religious mendicancy ever composed.[26] Generally speaking, these literary efforts, backed by decisive political action, sufficed to silence truly contrarian antifraternalism for nearly a century. And even then, despite the lingering shadow of William's polemics, its essential spirit would soon vanish.[27]

Within less than a generation, theologians such as Henry of Ghent (d. 1293) and, later, John of Pouilly (d. *c*.1328), household names in the history of antifraternalism, continued to move away from William's original views on the appropriate fate of religious mendicancy. Much like the original remnants of the Parisian antifraternal party, they too chose to focus their energies on defining evangelical perfection in ways that undermined the popularity (but not the legitimacy) of the mendicant model and fought to curb or eliminate individual privileges awarded the brethren, such as confession, preaching, and burial rights.[28] Even a staunch supporter of John XXII such as Jean d'Anneux, in his *Filios enutrivi* (1328), aimed at curbing the Franciscans' privileges, not abolishing the order, although he did claim they were founded on certain errors.[29] And, as Christopher Ocker's work on Konrad of Megenberg (1309–74) reveals, early Reformation propagandists and later scholars were sometimes too quick to dub certain "proto-reformers" as

---

Littérature Ecclésiastique, 39 (1938), 121–9; Roland Hissette, "Nicolas de Lisieux," *Catholicisme*, 9 (1982), 1254–5; Andrew G. Traver, "The Liber de Antichristo and the Failure of Joachite Expectations," *Florensia*, 14 (2001), 1–12.

[26] *SS. Ecclesiae Doctorum Thomae Aquinatis et Bonaventurae Opuscula adversus Guillelmum a S. Amore*, 2 vols (Rome: G. Salomon, 1773).

[27] A full bibliography is in *De periculis*, 33–4. The textual point of departure for most pro-mendicant writers after Bonaventure and Aquinas was *Manus que contra Omnipotentem tenditur*, probably written by the Franciscan Thomas of York. See Max Bierbaum, *Bettelorden und Weltgeistlichkeit an der Universität Paris: Texte und Unterschungen zum literarischen Armuts- und Exemtionsstreit des 13. Jahrhunderts (1255–1272)*, Franzikanische Studien 2. Beiheft (Münster: Aschendorff, 1920), 36–168; F. Pelster, "Der Traktat 'Manus que contra Omnipotentem tenditur' und sein Verfasser," *AFH*, 15 (1923), 3–22; and Andrew G. Traver, "Thomas of York's Role in the Conflict between Mendicants and Seculars at Paris," *Franciscan Studies*, 57 (1999), 1–24.

[28] Sophronius Clasen, *Der hl. Bonaventura und das Mendikantentum: Ein Beitrag zur Ideengeschichte der Pariser Mandikantenstreites (1252–1272)*, Franziskanische Forschungen, Heft 7 (Werl in Wesfalen: Verlag Franziskus-Drukerei, 1940), 1–12.

[29] The treatise is edited in Susanne Starcke-Neuman, *Johannes von Anneux: Ein Fürstenmahner und Mendikantengegner in der ersten Hälfte des 14. Jahrhunderts* (Mammendorf: Septem Artes, 1996), 213–53.

total antimendicant contrarians.[30] William's radical, indeed heretical, stance thus seems to have withered away rather quickly. At least on the Continent it was replaced by a harm-reduction approach of applying constant pressure to limit the friars' privileges without challenging their very legitimacy.

Two fourteenth-century Englishmen, Archbishop of Armagh Richard FitzRalph (1300–1360) and the theologian John Wyclif (c.1328–84), hold pride of place in the gallery of medieval antifraternalism. Both men, despite years of express admiration of and collegial collaboration with friars, especially at Oxford, eventually turned against the brethren in numerous oral and written broadsides. Yet, as often before, neither seems to have followed William's avowed quest to eradicate the mendicants from the church. FitzRalph says so explicitly in the opening words of his most elaborate and influential attack on the friars, the *Defensio Curatorum*, delivered at the papal curia in Avignon on November 8, 1357, and following a series of public sermons preached in London and possibly elsewhere in England: "At the outset of my sermon I affirm that... the destruction or shattering of the mendicant orders, which were approved by the church, is not my intention... Rather, I will argue that these orders must be returned to the purity of their original foundation."[31]

As this sermon and other writings make amply clear, no love was lost between the archbishop and the friars, especially the Franciscans. He found them to be greedy, hypocritical, and grossly inconsiderate. The brethren certainly disturbed the operation of the church, at least as FitzRalph understood it, and it is just plausible that he wished to see them gone. However, the latter goal is never openly articulated in the extant sources, which mostly emphasize the need to reform the orders. The closest FitzRalph ever came to rejecting the orders' legitimacy is in repeatedly reminding his audiences that the church existed for nearly 1,200 years without them—but that is an argument he employs in order to undermine papal support of religious mendicancy as a legal ground for defending the brethren's privileges, not as a way to challenge their very existence. Thus, despite the numerous charges he brings against the friars, his stated purpose in appealing to his fellow bishops, laymen, and the papacy is to curb or annul the orders' privileges, thereby redirecting them toward the narrow path set by their founders.

---

[30] Christopher Ocker, "*Lacrima ecclesie*: Konrad of Megenberg, the Friars, and the Beguines," in Claudia Märtle, Gisela Drossbach, and Martin Kintzinger (eds), *Konrad von Megenberg (1309–1374) und sein Werk Das Wissen der Zeit* (Munich: C. H. Beck, 2006), 169–200.

[31] *Defensio Curatorum*, in Edward Brown (ed.), *Fasciculus rerum expetendarum & fugiendarum*, 2 vols (London, 1690), ii. 466: "In principio mei sermonis protestor quod... non est intentionis meae destructionem seu quassationem ordinum mendicantium approbatum ab Ecclesia... Sed potius suadebo ipsos ordines deberi reduci ad puritatem suae institutionis primariae." It is possible that the statement was designed to protect the speaker from the abolitionism *implicit* in his earlier *De pauperie Salvatoris*. See Katherine Walsh, *A Fourteenth-Century Scholar and Primate: Richard FitzRalph in Oxford, Avignon and Armagh* (Oxford: Clarendon Press, 1981), 377–406; and T. P. Dolan, "Richard FitzRalph's 'Defensio Curatorum' in Transmission," in Howard B. Clarke and J. R. S. Phillips (eds), *Ireland, England and the Continent in the Middle Ages and Beyond: Essays in Memory of a Turbulent Friar, F. X. Martin, OSA* (Dublin: University College Dublin Press, 2006), 177–94.

John Wyclif's departure from Williamine antifraternalism is even more pronounced, given these men's divergent outlooks on organized religion. While St Amour underscored the incongruence of the mendicant orders with the traditional hierarchy of the church, Wyclif denied the very legitimacy of such a hierarchy—a Roman, rather than Christian, invention—in the first place. In other words, what seemed a disease to William (and to a slightly lesser extent, to FitzRalph) was merely a symptom in Wyclif's eyes. Accordingly, and despite his acknowledged debt to FitzRalph on several matters, including his concept of dominion,[32] Wyclif sought the orders' dispersal under the ban of "private religions," as developed in his *De civili dominio* (1375–76) and later in *De apostasia* (1381). One could argue that the Franciscans in particular came closer than most other ecclesiastical orders to the state of propertylessness advocated by Wyclif.[33] However, their gradual accumulation of wealth blurred the boundaries with traditional monks and the secular clergy, a process accelerated by John XXII's clampdown on the Spirituals, which Wyclif seems to have genuinely lamented. None of this is to deny that Wyclif made more prosaic allegations against the brethren, or that these reflected numerous charges made by St Amour a century earlier.[34] But, whatever resentment Wyclif fostered against the friars per se was subsumed within his broader anticlerical campaign.

From a strict, contrarian perspective, then, only FitzRalph approximated Williamine antifraternalism, which explains why later polemicists, including even some who identified themselves as Wyclif's followers, considered only the archbishop's writings as the genuine English basis of an antimendicant position.[35] It is true, however, that Wyclif's views on the friars were sometimes thought to be rather close to those of FitzRalph—so much so, in fact, that several Lollard sympathizers felt compelled to expurgate from their manuscripts certain passages attributed to Wyclif, but which were deemed too hostile toward the brethren.[36] Thus, despite Wyclif's outspoken position on private religion generally and on the mendicants in particular, at least some of his own followers seem to have maintained a positive appreciation of the brethren's ministry.

Numerous canon lawyers and theologians after St Amour criticized the friars' conduct and especially their privileges. With the possible and mostly implicit exception of FitzRalph, however, none of them denied the orders a place within the church, so long as the church itself was recognized as a divinely ordained institution. This may seem at the very least wise, given William's fate, yet assembling an antifraternal gallery of medieval authors proved irresistible in certain circles

---

[32] Elemér Boreczky, *John Wyclif's Discouse on Dominion in Community*, Studies in the History of Christian Traditions, 139 (Leiden and Boston: Brill, 2008), 87–106.

[33] Stephen E. Lahey, *Philosophy and Politics in the Thought of John Wyclif* (Cambridge: Cambridge University Press, 2003), 143–4.

[34] See, e.g., Wyclif's vernacular sermon *Vae octuplex* and his two treatises against the friars, all in *Select English Works of John Wyclif*, ed. Thomas Arnold, 3 vols (Oxford: Clarendon Press, 1869–71), ii. 379–89, iii. 366–429, respectively.

[35] Wendy Scase, *"Piers Plowman" and the New Anticlericalism* (Cambridge: Cambridge University Press, 1989), 11. And see Fiona Somerset (ed.), *Four Wycliffite Dialogues*, Early English Text Society, os 333 (Oxford: Oxford University Press, 2009), p. xlv.

[36] Anne Hudson, *Lollards and their Books* (London: Hambledon Press, 1985), 208–10.

in light of later developments. From the sixteenth century on, a variety of antifraternal polemics, implicitly abolitionist and often falling into the general rubric of anticlericalism or antipapism, became inscribed within teleological narratives of English, Swiss, Dutch, and German anticlericalisms en route to the Protestant Reformation, Enlightenment, secularism, and the nation state. In fact, we owe the first printed edition of two of William's sermons and the publication of his collected works to just such efforts,[37] while the battle still rages over whether FitzRalph's antifraternalism reflects a typically fraught Irish situation or the arch-conservative English environment in which he was raised.[38]

Such narratives have certainly been compelling. Yet, as the foregone section demonstrates, and as will be emphasized throughout this book, opposition to medieval friars was a far more complex phenomenon than the unfolding of William of St Amour's program, much less a striving of critical visionaries to sow the seeds of modernity. Outside of western Europe, tracing the dissemination of William's ideas (and those of his late-medieval followers) still remains a desideratum. With the exception of Vlastimil Kybal's studies on Matthew of Janov (d. 1393),[39] and despite substantial manuscript evidence, little had been said about coeval theologians' attitudes toward friars in central Europe for nearly a century. Things have begun to change of late with Geoffrey Dipple's work on Johann Eberlin von Günzburg (c.1470–1533),[40] Christopher Ocker's investigations on Konrad of Waldhäusen (1320/5–69) and Jan Milíč of Kroměříž (d. 1374),[41] and most recently Olivier Marin's study of pre-Hussite Prague.[42] While these lacunae gradually fill up, it is safe to say that scholars active in late-medieval Europe's main theological faculties (Oxford, Cambridge, and Paris) fail to provide a durable link between William of St Amour's brand of antifraternalism and the prominent role his polemics played in bolstering the theology, ideology, and historiography of the Protestant Reformation.[43] William's legacy, it seems, lies elsewhere.

---

[37] Ortuin Gratius (ed.), *Fasciculus rerum expetendarum & fugiendarum* (Cologne, 1535), 5–137; *Guillielmi de S. Amore Opera omnia quae reperiri potuerunt*... (Constance [Paris]: Alitophilos, 1632; repr. Hildesheim and New York: G. Olms, 1997). A later edition of Gratius' collection, edited by Edward Brown (*Fasciculus rerum expetendarum & fugiendarum*), included FitzRalph's *Defensio Curatorum*.

[38] See Michael Haren, "Diocesan Dimensions of a Die-Hard Dispute: Richard FitzRalph and the Friars in Evolving Perspective," in Howard B. Clarke and J. R. S. Phillips (eds), *Ireland, England and the Continent in the Middle Ages and Beyond: Essays in Memory of a Turbulent Friar, F. X. Martin, OSA* (Dublin: University College Dublin Press, 2006), 164–76.

[39] *Matthiae de Janov Regulae Veteris et Novi Testamenti*, ed. V. Kybal, 6 vols (Innsbruck: Wagner University, 1908–11).

[40] Geoffrey L. Dipple, *Antifraternalism and Anticlericalism in the German Reformation: Johann Eberlin von Günzburg and the Campaign against the Friars* (Aldershot: Scolar Press, 1996).

[41] Christopher Ocker, "Contempt for Friars and Contempt for Jews in Late Medieval Germany," in Steven J. McMichael and Susan E. Myers (eds), *Friars and Jews in the Middle Ages and the Renaissance*, The Medieval Franciscans, 2 (Leiden: Brill, 2004), 145–6.

[42] Olivier Marin, *L'Archevêque, le maître et le dévot: Genèses du mouvement réformateur pragois (1360–1419)* (Paris: Honoré Champion, 2005).

[43] Geoffrey Dipple, "Anti-Franciscanism in the Early Reformation: The Nature and Sources of Criticism," *Franciscan Studies*, 55 (1998), 53–81.

LITERARY ANTIFRATERNALISM

As swan songs go, *De periculis* remained enormously influential. The treatise repeatedly echoes in thirteenth- and fourteenth-century literature, from the poetry of Rutebeuf and Jean de Meun, to the tales of Giovanni Boccaccio and Franco Sacchetti, to the writings of Geoffrey Chaucer, William Langland, John Gower, and others.[44] Williamine *topoi* circulated in Europe throughout the Renaissance, for instance, with Desiderius Erasmus' *In Praise of Folly* (1509), Niccolò Machiavelli's *Clizia* (1525), and François Rabelais's *Pantagruel* (1532) and *Gargantua* (1534), and during the early modern period, notably in Christopher Marlowe's *Doctor Faustus* (posthumously published in 1604).[45] More or less informed depictions of corrupt friars continue to flourish in our times, from G. G. Coulton's *Friar's Lantern* (1906) to *Blackadder's* Friar Bellows ("Blessed are the meek... for they shall be slaughtered" [1983, set in 1498]).

Such frequent recourse to William's works by authors who openly criticized the mendicant orders helps account for his reputation as the wellspring of antifraternal literature. Yet there appears to be a wide range of approaches to his legacy even within his own lifetime and close circle of supporters, a diversity that emerges from wedding social to literary history. To take one example, the Parisian poet Rutebeuf, William's contemporary and partisan, was originally an avid exponent of religious mendicancy.[46] Soon, however, a change of heart following the drawn-out university quarrels and the power politics that had determined their outcome led him to defend his exiled friend and the secular masters' cause by inveighing against what he believed was a corrupted movement. Yet, in doing so, Rutebeuf scarcely maintained William's categorical objection to the existence of friars.[47] Thus tracing the history and pre-history of Rutebeuf's antimendicant rhymes discloses the contingencies of cultural production, including the influence of social networks and the experience of high politics.

Other writers developed several of William's themes in ways that abandoned the original context of *De periculis* as well as its main thrust. Notable among these are Jean de Meun and Geoffrey Chaucer, whose alleged antifraternal poetry is the main focus of the present section. The friar-characters developed respectively in the

---

[44] John V. Fleming, "The Friars and Medieval English Literature," in David Wallace (ed.), *The Cambridge History of Medieval English Literature* (Cambridge: Cambridge University Press, 1999), 354. For a full bibliography, see *De periculis*, 32–3; and Patricia Anne Odber de Baubeta, *Anticlerical Satire in Medieval Portuguese Literature* (Lewiston, NY: Edwin Mellen Press, 1992); Francisco García-Serrano, *Preachers of the City: The Expansion of the Dominican Order in Castile (1217–1348)* (New Orleans: University Press of the South, 1997), 80–1.

[45] See also the anonymous play "The Powers of the Romanists" in Erika Rummel (ed. and trans.), *Scheming Papists and Lutheran Fools: Five Reformation Satires* (New York: Fordham University Press, 1993), 9–47.

[46] Rutebeuf, "Le Dit des Cordeliers," in *Œuvres complètes de Rutebeuf*, ed. Edmond Faral and Julia Bastin, i (Paris: Picard, 1959), 231–7.

[47] Edward Billings Ham, *Rutebeuf and Louis IX*, University of North Carolina Studies in the Romance Languages and Literatures, 42 (Chapel Hill, NC: University of North Carolina Press, 1962).

Roman de la Rose (False Seeming) and the *Summoner's Tale* (Friar John) are engaged in a much broader social critique than can be found in William's contrarian works. Both poems are, moreover, experiments in the fabrication of Cretan-liar characters, through which their authors sought to comment on the meaning of art and poetry and their complex relation to reality.

False Seeming

The *Roman de la Rose* is an enormously learned Middle French poem composed by Guillaume de Lorris around the middle of the thirteenth century and continued (or, if you will, completed) by Jean de Meun several decades later.[48] It traces the confused pursuit of the Rose by Lover—both commonly interpreted as allegorical figures (or abstractions, or verisimilitudes), albeit without a reigning scholarly consensus over their respective objects and relations. Variously seen as morally condoned or ill-advised, Lover's mission propels him to seek advice from different authorities and assemble a baronial host to assault Jealousy's castle, Rose's place of detention. It is with these warriors that False Seeming attempts to ingratiate himself in time to participate in the final push. But, given the importance of the mission and his well-known penchant for deceit, False Seeming is forced by the God of Love to disclose his true self before the barons.

And so, clad in unspecified monastic garb, False Seeming issues forth what has often been portrayed as the chief antifraternal exhortation of medieval literature, which begins, not surprisingly, with the theme of hypocrisy:

> Je mains avec les orguilleus,
> Les veziez, les artilleus,
> Qui mondaines eneurs couveitent
> E les granz besoignes espleitent,
> E vont traçant les granz pittances
> E pourchaçant les acointances
> Des poissanz omes e les sivent;
> E se font povre, e il se vivent
> Des bons morseaus delicieus
> E beivent les vins precieus;
> E la povreté vous preeschent,
> E les granz richeces peeschent
> Aus saïmes e aus tramaus.
>   (ll. 11037–49)[49]

---

[48] There have been numerous editions and translations of the poem, alongside an immense scholarly literature. Basic bibliographies include Karl August Ott, *Der Rosenroman* (Darmstadt: Wissenschaftliche Buchgesellschaft, 1980); Maxwell Luria, *A Reader's Guide to the Roman de la Rose* (Hamden, CN: Archon Books, 1982); and Heather M. Arden, *The Roman de la Rose: An Annotated Bibliography* (New York: Garland, 1993).

[49] Quotations are from *Le Roman de la Rose par Guillaume de Lorris et Jean de Meun*, ed. Ernest Langlois, iii (Paris: Librairie Ancienne Honoré Champion, 1921).

[I dwell among the proud, | the devious, the cunning, | who covet worldly honors and pursue great enterprises | and seek great rewards, | and strive for the acquaintance | of powerful men and follow them. | And they are poor, and they nourish themselves | with luxurious foods | and drink precious wines. | And they preach poverty to you, | and they gather great wealth | with their nets and trammels.]

The existence of want and sumptuousness and of the preaching of poverty and lavish living is not conveyed through concessive conjunctures. It is simultaneous and as such constitutes a state of affairs that, though perfectly coherent to False Seeming, seems paradoxical if not outright jarring to his audiences: instead of empowering the poor as their champion, he flatters the rich; his compulsory poverty gives way to lavish feasting among the worldly.

These initial verses signal what is to come: a narrative elaborating on a basic theme of action contrasted with declared intent, interior corruption with exterior piety, and verbal expression with intended will. False Seeming argues against himself, in confession form, in an attempt to persuade the God of Love and his entourage to admit him into their company, then on the verge of storming Jealousy's castle. (The confessional itself is also paradoxical: a friar, master of all confessors—a theme that will later become crucial to our understanding of the matter—utters a public confession to, of all allegorical figures, the God of Love.) In any case, the history of his treachery and deceit paradoxically wins him the desired trust of the barons. After marveling at his enduring corruption, they welcome him heartily.

Construing the speech as the author's concerted attack on friars or even on ascetic religion generally, however, offers a limited view. It also runs the risk of fragmenting the poem's thematic integrity.[50] Neither is necessary, and False Seeming's habit provides the first clue to the intended ambiguity. His ultimate choice of a friar's garb can perhaps be viewed as tactical, considering his lay audience acting as confessors. Yet at base it is the paradox of the incorruptible-and-deceptive-in-one that offers the greatest momentum to the character's speech. Indeed, there appear to be no limits to False Seeming's capacity to adapt, cutting across the borders of social class, clerical status, religion, geography, age, gender, and language:

> Or sui chevaliers, or sui moines,
> Or sui prelaz, or sui chanoines,
> Or sui clers, autre eure sui prestres,
> Or sui deciples, or sui maistres,

---

[50] Charles Muscatine, *Chaucer and the French Tradition: A Study in Style and Meaning* (Berkeley and Los Angeles: University of California Press, 1960), 91. And see Alan M. F. Gunn, *The Mirror of Love* (Lubbock, TX: Texas Tech Press, 1952), 158–63, 270–3; D. W. Robertson, Jr, *A Preface to Chaucer* (Princeton: Princeton University Press, 1962), 195–204; John V. Fleming, *The Romance of the Rose: A Study in Allegory and Iconography* (Princeton: Princeton University Press, 1969), 161–71. Susan Stakel, *False Roses: Structures of Duality and Deceit in Jean de Meun's Roman de la Rose* (Stanford: ANMA Libri, 1991), interprets False Seeming's role as linchpin for the theme of truth and falsity in the *Roman*. Pierre-Yves Badel, *Le Roman de la Rose au XIVe siècle* (Geneva: Librairie Droz, 1980), 207–62, concludes that contemporaries did not question the unity of the text on stylistic and thematic grounds.

Or chastelains, or forestiers...

(ll. 11189–93)

[Now I'm a knight, now a monk; | now a prelate, now a canon; | now a cleric, at another time a priest; | now a disciple, now a master; | now a castellan, now a forester...]

Or resui princes, or sui pages,
E sai par cueur trestouz langages,
Autre eure sui veauz e chenuz,
Or resui jennes devenuz;
Or sui Roberz, or sui Robins,
Or cordeliers, or jacobins...

(ll. 11195–200)

[Now I am a prince, now a page—| I know by heart many languages. | At one time I'm old and white, | then I become young again; | now I am Robert, now Robin, | now a Cordelier, now a Jacobin...]

Autre eure vest robe de fame:
Or sui dameisele, or sui dame,
Autre eure sui religieuse,
Or sui rendue, or sui prieuse,
Or sui none, or sui abaesse...

(ll. 11207–11)

[At other times I wear a woman's garb: | now I am a maiden, now a lady; | at another time I'm religious: | now a devotee, now a prioress, | now a nun, now an abbess...]

Through rhythmic repetition these verses reinforce the notion that False Seeming's extraordinary talent of disguise is surpassed only by the diversity of his costumes, from prince to dame, from monk to forester, from prioress to mendicant. Once the final choice of disguise is made, however, the warning that "S'est la celee plus seüre | Souz la plus umble vesteüre" ["it is the safest disguise, under the humblest guise"] (ll. 11013–14) reminds us that those who appear poor and holy are perhaps the most effective scoundrels, while the truly poor and humble are ironically the easiest to fool. Yet selecting a friar's garb hardly detracts from False Seeming's exposure of hypocrisy in the church (ll. 11035–162), society at large (ll. 10976–83, 11177–8), the Capetian court,[51] and, of course, the mendicant orders themselves (ll. 11007–10).

False Seeming's explicit appeal to vast and various segments of society evinces and underscores the fruitfulness of combining a broader social approach to the poem. For this penetrating social critique can hardly be said to target the

---

[51] Popular and baronial resentment of Louis IX's mendicant affiliations, which included a rather skimpy wardrobe, was high. See Lester K. Little, "Saint Louis' Involvement with the Friars," *Church History*, 2 (1964), 125–43; William Chester Jordan, "The Case of Saint Louis," *Viator*, 19 (1988), 209–17.

mendicants exclusively. It is exemplified once again through the depiction of a universal attitude toward the poor, virtually anyone's tender prey:

> Trestuit seur les povres genz cueurent,
> N'est nus qui despoillier nes vueille,
> Tuit s'afublent de leur despueille,
> Trestuit de leur sustance humant,
> Senz eschauder touz vis les plument.
> Li plus forz le plus feible robe.
>
> (ll. 11544–9)

[All men want to trample over the poor, | there is no one who does not wish to despoil them; | everyone covers themselves with their spoil, | trampling over their human substance. | Without scalding everyone plucks them. | The more powerful rob the feeblest.]

"But I," continues False Seeming, "who wear my simple robe, dupe the dupers and the duped, rob the robbers and the robbed" (ll. 11550–2). There is no exclusivity, only a general partaking in the universal disgrace.

Jean de Meun's antifraternal partisanship ultimately rests on the narrator's valorizing allusions to William of St Amour and his struggle against religious mendicancy in Paris. The association of De Meun and St Amour was strong enough in certain circles to have led some scribes to attribute parts of the *Roman* to St Amour, occasionally at the expense of Jean de Meun himself. On the other hand, it is possible that the very attribution was intended to eliminate ambiguity in favor of partisanship, by replacing a poet with an outspoken theologian and an icon of antifraternalism.[52] False Seeming's very name, after all, invokes the memory of Rutebeuf, St Amour's Parisian partisan, who developed his figure of Hypocrisy in the *Du Pharisien*, and gave it the name of Faus Semblant in *De Maistre Guillaume de Saint Amour*.[53] Yet, as we have seen, even Rutebeuf steered clear of William's radical antifraternalism.

Above all else looms one basic fact about False Seeming: he is the living image of the Cretan liar's dilemma, a moving field of deceit. His frankness is compromised by his very name, allowing for the existence of two diametrically opposed narratives at every step. This tension only increases toward the moment in which he invokes the fond memory of William of St Amour, his celebrated historical opponent, and vows to carry his message forward even at the cost of his own life (ll. 11501–8). It is the second time that False Seeming vows to surrender his life for the sake of a nobler

---

[52] Ernst Langlois, *Les manuscrits du Roman de la Rose: Description et classement* (Lille and Paris: Champion, 1910), 11, 25, 83, 127, 190, and 131 respectively. All are fourteenth-century works.

[53] See *Œuvres complètes de Rutebeuf*, ed. Faral and Bastin, i. 251–5, 258–66. By this stage in his career Rutebeuf's resentment toward the friars came to replace his original sympathy. The trope of an external garb concealing inner corruption is already tossed around during the monastic debates of the twelfth century. See Giles Constable, "The Ceremonies and Symbolism of Entering Religious Life and Taking the Monastic Habit, from the Fourth to the Twelfth Century," *Segni e riti nella chiesa altomedievale occidentale* (Spoleto: Centro Italiano di Studi sull'Alto Medioevo, 1987), 822–31. As a personification, Religious Hypocrisy's genealogy can be traced to Prudentius (*Psychomachia*, vv. 557–71), and Jerome (*Letter to Eustochium*, 16 and *passim*).

cause. The first instance was prompted by his desire to satisfy the God of Love's command to hear the truth about hypocrisy (ll. 10999–11002). At his lord's insistence False Seeming swiftly changes his position from explicit opposition to total surrender. With such self-service acting as the dominant guideline, it is impossible and indeed futile to locate False Seeming's genuine loyalties.

In sum, the ambiguity of the character and the narrator prohibits us from identifying a partisan authorial voice on one side or the other of a defined ecclesiological border. The very attempt is inherently misguided if we wish to understand the *Roman* in terms of its allegorical art rather than its alleged historical veracity. False Seeming does not *depict* anyone; he *typifies* hypocrisy. The character is a personification and an allegory, created by Jean de Meun to represent the nature of all liars, not all friars. Jean de Meun crafted a protagonist who turns against himself, in defiance of any particular perspective. And if doubts still linger in the reader's mind, the narrator's insistence in a major satellite of the confession, that "ne fu m'entencion | De paler contre ome vivant | Sainte religion sivant... Mais pour quenoistre... Les desleiaus genz, les maudites, | Que Jesus apele ypocrites" ["it was not my intention | to rebuke a person living | according to holy religion... but to identify... the debased people, the evildoers | whom Jesus calls hypocrites"] (ll. 15252–64), again undermines any categorizing of the attack as promoting a Williamine agenda.

Earlier I suggested that the occasional attribution of parts of the work to William of St Amour might have been an attempt to secure a partisan reading of the speech in lieu of a clear antifraternal statement. Manuscript evidence illustrates further ways in which the *Roman*'s illuminators, editors, and readers detected and responded to the inherent ambiguity of False Seeming's confession. For instance, although False Seeming is named a friar in the text, in over 200 manuscripts surveyed by Meradith McMunn, he appears most frequently wearing a Benedictine habit. As a form of gloss to the confession, such depictions suggest a continuing negotiation of the character's identity, at times drawing him to, at times pushing him away from, a mendicant center of gravity and toward a broader allegory of hypocrisy.[54]

Another prevalent method was resorting to fabrication. A later interpolation containing a vehement and unambiguous attack on mendicant privileges appears in more than 30 percent of the extant thirteenth- and fourteenth-century *Roman* manuscripts.[55] Usually inserted between lines 11222 and 11223, but occasionally affixed to the end of the poem, it has come to be known as "the apocryphal chapter on the friars' privileges" and frequently consists of some 150 lines.[56]

---

[54] Personal Correspondence, Aug. 2010. Prof. McMunn is working on a comprehensive catalogue and study of the illustrated manuscripts of the *Roman de la Rose*.

[55] Sylvia Huot, *The Romance of the Rose and its Medieval Readers: Interpretation, Reception, Manuscript Transmission* (Cambridge: Cambridge University Press, 1993), 236–9. The most complete survey of this passage is in the appendix to G. Geltner, "Faux Semblants: Antifraternalism Reconsidered in Jean de Meun and Chaucer," *Studies in Philology*, 101 (2004), 357–80.

[56] See Langlois, *Manuscrits*, 426–30, which also contains the collated text. Beyond the internal evidence for a different author cited by Langlois, the later dating of the interpolation relies on an

In their various forms, these verses offer a brazen attack on the fraternal orders' rights of confession, secured anew in 1282 through the pope's intervention after long years of struggle with the secular clergy. The text diverges from its contiguous narrative in tone and content. False Seeming, now a straightforward representative of the mendicants, boasts his privileged authority to confess and absolve

> Toutes genz ou que je les truisse.
> Ne sai prelat nul qui ce puisse,
> Fors l'apostoile seulement,
> Qui fist cest establissement
> Tout en la faveur de nostre ordre.
>
> (ll. v–viii[1])[57]

[All men or those who I deceive. | No prelate may have such power, | save only the Apostle, | who established these [privileges] | entirely in favor of our order.]

The direct mention of the ecclesiastical forces at play—the prelate, a mendicant order, and the pope—offers for the first time a clearly polarized political picture.

The text was in all probability added in the aftermath of Pope Martin IV's bull *Ad fructus uberes* (December 13, 1281), which, among other provisions, stripped local parish priests from their exclusive monopoly over hearing confessions. Canon 21 of the Fourth Lateran Council (1215), which obliged every Christian to make at least one annual confession to his or her parish priest, resonates from the interpolated verses "chascuns chascuns an a son prestre | Une foiz" ["each person to his own priest | once"] (ll. x–xi). Yet, thanks to Martin IV, the probable referent of the interpolation's "l'apostoile," the decree could be suspended by the friars: "Car nous avons un priviliege | Qui de pluseurs fais les aliege" [" . . . we have a privilege | which relieves us from many burdens"] (ll. xiii–xiv). The local clergy were desolated by the threatening implications of the privilege, as the token speech given by a parishioner reveals. He is no longer dependent on his priest for his salvation, since

> [. . .] cil a cui je fui confès
> M'a deschargié de tout mon fais;
> Assolu m'a de mes pechiez[.]
>
> (ll. xvii–xix)

[he to whom I have confessed | discharged me from all my deeds, | absolved me from all my sins.]

Consequently, he asserts, "Ne je n'ai pas entencion | De faire autre confession" ["I have no intention | to make another confession"] (ll. xxi–xxii). Prelate and curate have lost their hold on their flocks, which no longer seek double absolution inasmuch as it requires any double confession. The parishioner continues:

---

allusion in ll. xi–xii[1] to Pope Martin IV's bull *Ad fructus uberes* (Dec. 13, 1281). See Palémon Glorieux, "Prélats français contre religieux mendiants," *Revue de l'histoire de l'eglise de France*, 11 (1925), 309–31, 471–95.

[57] Line numbers correspond to Langlois, *Manuscrits*, 426–30.

> Je ne dout prelat ne curé
> Qui de confessier me constraigne
> Autrement que je ne m'en plaigne;
> Car je m'en ai bien a cui plaindre.
> Vous ne me pouez pas constraindre
> Ne faire force ne troubler
> Pour ma confession doubler,
> Ne si n'ai pas affeccion
> D'avoir double assolucion.
>
> (ll. xxviii–xxxvi)

[I fear no prelate or curate, | who will constrain me to confess | beyond my will; | for I have one to whom I can very well complain about this. | You can oblige me no more, | neither force me nor trouble, | to make my confession double; | nor am I inclined | to receive double absolution.]

From the clergy's perspective, the loss of confessional monopoly potentially meant a significant reduction in their ability to monitor the morality of their parish members and posed a serious threat to the social and religious cohesiveness of their communities. It could also translate into a major decrease in income for any parish church, whose role as the basic local religious unit was, in a sense, no longer guaranteed. And, while tithes remained obligatory, individuals seeking burial had more than one option.

The privileges were protected by papal authority and supported by the French monarchy, thus rendering futile any attempt to curb the friars' reinforced powers. The parishioner clarifies this point by assuring his priest:

> Je voir juges imperïaus,
> Rois, prelaz ne oficïaus
> Pour moi ne tendra jugement;
>
> (ll. xlv–xlvii)

[I shall be safe from imperial judges, | kings, prelates and officials, | [for] no judgment will be held for me.]

The tone and message are partisan. As all relevant contemporary institutions are named and aligned, from pope to king, the underscored theme becomes one of power and its abuse, not the broader and much more ambiguous one of hypocrisy. Moreover, False Seeming is no longer the focus of the narrative. After relinquishing his place to the parishioner, he is distanced from the scene even further by the introduction of the ruthless and power-thirsty

> [. . .] frere Leus,[58] qui tout deveure,
> Combien que devant le gent eure.
> Et cil, jurer l'os et plevir,

---

[58] Probably a character borrowed from Rutebeuf's *La Discorde de L'Université et des Jacobins*, in *Œuvres complètes de Rutebeuf*, ed. Faral and Bastin, i. 240.

> Se savroit bien de vous chevir;
> Car si vous savra atraper
> Que ne li pourrez eschaper
> Senz honte et senz diffamement,
> S'il n'a dou vostre largement;
> Qu'il n'est si fous ne si entules
> Qu'il n'ait bien de Rome des bules,
> S'il li plaist, a vous touz semondre,
> Pour vous travaillier et confondre
> Assez plus loin de deus journees.
>
> (ll. lvi^1-lviii^9)

[Friar Wolf, who devours all, | however lucky men were before. | These [men] he dares to judge and swear. | He knows well how to protect himself from you. | For he could trap you | so that you could not escape | without shame and dishonor | if he does not receive from you generously; | for he is not so mad nor such a fool | not to obtain from Rome some bulls | (if it so pleases him) to summon you all | in order to exert and confound you, | in a little more than two days' journey.]

Thus, while the secular clergy's ultimate danger lies within two days' journey from Paris, Friar Wolf is everywhere, posing a threat to each and every individual's dignity and purse. He shames and dishonors; he takes, "devours," "traps," "exerts," and "confounds" all. With its strong overtones of heresy, the presence of this friar is necessary to polemicize an otherwise ambiguous text.

Finally, even False Seeming's confession of partiality toward the rich (ll. lxxxi–xc) does not lead, as we would expect, to furthering his image as a hypocrite, but rather reinforces the theme of his political dominance over the prelates. This time he threatens direct violence on prelates who dare grumble at the "loss" of their confessional privileges, in fact a re-delegation of ecclesiastical duties:

> Teus cos leur dorrai seur les testes
> Que lever i ferai teus boces
> Qu'il en perdront mitre et croces.
>
> (ll. xciv–xcvi)

[For this I shall beat them over the head | and cause them such bruises, | that they will lose their miters and crosses.]

"Thus I deceive them all," he concludes, "so formidable are my privileges" (ll. xcvii–xcviii).

The interpolation offers a direct, partisan harangue about the friars' perceived abuse of power. It stands well apart from the deep ambiguity of the uninterpolated speech. Yet, in preceding it, the interpolation efficiently sets the tone of the entire confession; it seems to bring out of the confession a streamlined antifraternal voice that had no central place in it to begin with. But does the interpolation's presence in dozens of manuscripts, or the occasional attributions of parts of the *Roman* to William of St Amour, indicate an enduring consensus among contemporaries over the speech's original ambivalence? The evidence lends itself to different interpretations: was the speech not antifraternal, or not antifraternal *enough*? What can one make, for instance, of Chantilly, Museum Condeé MS 686, which originally omitted nearly the entire speech, but where later, and on separate occasions, both the speech and the interpolation were added? Can this be said to have been motivated by a contrarian or rather by a reformist critique of religious mendicancy? Whatever the case may be, it is clear that some readers of the *Roman* felt compelled to impose greater coherence on a rather tricky text.

Friar John

Chaucer earned his badge of antifraternal honor by composing the *Summoner's Tale* (*ST*), a retort to the *Friar's Tale*, which immediately precedes it in the cycle of the *Canterbury Tales*.[59] In it the summoner, an ecclesiastical functionary, describes the daily routine of John, a mendicant friar in ardent pursuit of food, cash, and sexual gratification. The choice of narrator was an apt one, designed to harp on a bitter in-house ecclesiastical rivalry, an animosity already gesturing at a broader critique of the church. Yet Chaucer introduces a further note of ambiguity to the summoner's censure of the friars by depicting him as a drunk, lecherous man, who "speke and crie as he were wood," "a gentil harlot and a kynde [. . . who] wolde suffre for a quart of wyn | a good felawe to have his concubyn" (*General Prologue*, ll. 636, 647–50).[60] By doing so, he undermines the coherence of the summoner's criticisms of friars, a technique that Chaucer shared—as we have seen—with Jean de Meun.

Rather than in unequivocal antifraternal partisanship, then, the affinities between the *Canterbury Tales* and the *Roman* can be located in the realm of ambiguity. Both works emphasize the tension between the form and the content of a pilgrimage. For Lover, the *Roman*'s chief protagonist, a journey with a defined emotional, if not spiritual, end unfolds in remarkably different terms, climaxing in a ridiculous penetration, the plucking of the Rose. As for the English pilgrims, their joint travels, as well as their individual verbal wanderings—that is, their *errores*—recapitulate those of Lover and his cohort. While the latter is driven by his cupidity, the pilgrims' stories originate in the merry innkeeper's suggestion of a tale-telling contest. From a spiritual point of view, neither progress is particularly edifying.

To be sure, these affinities cannot be reduced to a simple set of mirror images. An intricate web connects many of the characters of the *Roman* and the *Canterbury Tales* without positing a single complementary image for False Seeming. Rather, through Chaucer's appropriation there emerges a variegated resonance of the character's two distinct voices—the partisan and the ambiguous.

Chaucer knew the *Roman* and, to trust his own comment, translated it into the Middle English *Romaunt*.[61] Fragment C of the work contains False Seeming's

---

[59] John V. Fleming, "The Antifraternalism of the *Summoner's Tale*," *Journal of English and Germanic Philology*, 65 (1966), 688–700.
[60] All citations are from *The Riverside Chaucer*, gen. ed. Larry D. Benson (Oxford: Oxford University Press, 1988).
[61] Introduction to Geoffrey Chaucer, *The Romaunt of the Rose*, ed. Charles Dahlberg (Norman, OK: University of Oklahoma Press, 1999), 3–24.

speech in its entirety, including a unique version of the apocryphal chapter on the friars' privileges.[62] Whether or not Chaucer was aware that the text was interpolated, the translation of the work provided him with an opportunity to iron out some stylistic peculiarities in the French text, and to render them less obvious by withdrawing from a partisan, antifraternal voice.

Departing from its French source, the Middle English translation sets the basic plot of the *Summoner's Tale*. Within the space of six lines in the *Romaunt*, the interpolation's original "Touz li monde" and "Chascuns chascun" (l. viii[13], x) are rendered respectively into "husbonde and wyf" and "man and wyf" (*Romaunt*, ll. 6379, 6383). This variation lends a particularistic quality to the text, so that a specific couple (rather than all mankind) falls prey to the friar's manipulations. The couple tends to the friar's needs after his sermon and is finally urged to confess. At this point in the interpolation False Seeming puts into the parishioner's mouth the argument against double confession to be flung at the priest (ll. 6390–440), and then moves to reclaim his own privileged status over that of the secular clergy.[63]

It is a small leap to see how the basic plot in the *Summoner's Tale* is an exact inversion of the translated interpolation: the retaliation, as it were, of the *Romaunt*'s deceived couple. Following his sermon at the local church, Friar John announces himself at the couple's door: "*Deus hic!*" (l. 1770). It is yet another mission to extort money from the affluent Thomas and food and sexual indulgence from his wife—a plot that, however, boomerangs in the shape of a fart directed at John as a form of alms to be shared (equally!) with his brethren. Even his attempt to solicit a confession (l. 2093) is swiftly rebutted by Thomas, in words that echo the *Romaunt*: "I have be shryven [=confessed] this day at my curat" (l. 2095). The shamed friar leaves with empty ears, hands, and belly, and with the unsettling mathematical problem of dividing Thomas's "gift" (l. 2149). Something of a happy ending, especially considering its century-old antithesis.

Yet the plot-driven inversion does not maintain the straightforward partisanship of the interpolation. Despite John's evident immorality—he is a self-indulging glutton: *tipped staf*, marble tables, and all, whose straying from his order's path is manifest—both Thomas and his wife (as well as the people who sustain him along lines 1744–60) are held equally responsible for the situation. Behind the wife's gullibility lies a strong desire to manipulate Friar John. She repeatedly accepts his sexual advances (ll. 1802–5), and her uncensored exposés offer him a bedside view of her conjugal life (ll. 1826–31). Jointly these reveal a character calculating to promote a highly personal agenda. And, although these attempts result in John's shameless monologue on the celestial whereabouts of her deceased child (ll. 1851–68), they raise serious questions about the nature of the wife's piety.

Sluggish Thomas, laying "bedrede upon a couch lowe" (l. 1769), is hardly a more inspiring figure. And, although it is admittedly his wit that ultimately prevails over

---

[62] vv. 6082–7292 (from a total of 7692). The interpolation comprises vv. 6383–472. See full discussion in Geltner, "Faus Semblants," 372 n. 31.

[63] The *Canterbury Tales*' friar's claims to political superiority already emerge in the *General Prologue*, ll. 218–20.

the friar's, his routine handouts to the brethren do not go unnoticed. Nor does a questionable attitude toward charity that emerges from the instrumentalism of his offerings (l. 1951). Yet, unlike Jean de Meun's barons at the end of False Seeming's speech, Thomas, though arguably driven more by economic considerations than by moral righteousness, thwarts John's plan.

The assaulting baronial host had embraced False Seeming in order to gain his support for their expedition; likewise the *Summoner's Tale*'s couple appears to have been repeatedly reliant upon the friar's services as mediator and supernatural intercessor. Complicity and cooperation were necessary in both narratives to perpetuate corruption, and in both cases the authors delegated responsibility over moral decline among all parties involved.

Chaucer's continuous appropriation of False Seeming goes beyond the translation of the *Roman* and the composition of the *Summoner's Tale*. It has long been noted, for instance, that in the *Pardoner's Prologue* and in the *Wife of Bath's Prologue* he drew on the confessional form and ironic tone of False Seeming's original confession. The instances explored above, however, illustrate Chaucer's acute awareness of False Seeming's ambiguous character and his employment of its distilled form.[64] The other facet of False Seeming's character, its interpolated partisan antifraternalism, is isolated in the brief *Summoner's Prologue*: in his vision the Hell-bound friar breathes a sigh of relief at the sight of a mendicant-free cavern. His accompanying angel soon corrects the picture. As they approach Satan, the angel exclaims:

> "Hold up thy tayl, thou Sathanas!" quod he;
> Shewe forth thyn ers, and lat the frere se
> Where is the nest of freres in this place!'
> And ere that half a furlong wey of space,
> Right so as bees out of a swarmen from a hyve,
> Out of the develed ers ther gone dryve
> Twenty thousand freres on a route,
> And thurghout helle swarmed al aboute,
> And comen again as faste as they may gon,
> And in his ers they crepten everychon.
>
> (ll. 1689–98)

The gruesome depiction of numerous friars directly under Satan's tail in Hell appears to be antifraternalism in its pristine form. Yet the scene still inherits the stamp of Jean de Meun's ambiguity, for, on the one hand, the summoner's antagonist along the pilgrimage is, by the summoner's own reckoning, a "false Frere" (l. 1670) who, in D. W. Robertson's words, is "neither a 'typical friar' nor a 'character' of any kind, but... the abstraction 'Faus Semblant' as he appears in the habit of a friar."[65] On the other hand, the summoner himself, as we have seen, is no

---

[64] It is perhaps in recognition of the Wife of Bath's similarity to Faus Semblant that Friar Huberd (who is a "false friar"!) commends her tale, for she has "touched... | In scole-matere greet difficultee" (*Friar's Prologue*, ll. 1271–2).

[65] Robertson, *Preface to Chaucer*, 249.

less guilty of treachery and greediness. In other words, the two characters and their respective tales have strong affinities in that both typify hypocrisy rather than real men or social categories.[66]

In contrast to the *Summoner's Prologue*'s graphic imagery and brutality, the *Summoner's Tale* offers a nuanced critique, which, very much in the spirit of False Seeming's original speech, points fingers in all social directions through an unflattering portrayal of all the characters involved. As Helen Cooper notes, the Friar's "is the most densely populated of all the portraits" in the *General Prologue*—and aptly so.[67] For, by surrounding Friar Huberd and Friar John with numerous contemporaries, who both desired and enabled the brethren's departure from their founders' path, Chaucer was able to overcome the straightforward partisanship of the *Roman*'s interpolation and in this way avoid the constraints of a narrow political or social affiliation.

In sum, Chaucer grasped and emulated the multivalent nature of False Seeming. Familiar with an amended textual tradition and perhaps aware of the interpolation that it contained, he allocated for each of its contrasting voices—the partisan and the ambiguous—a distinct place in the *Canterbury Tales*. In the *Summoner's Tale* he managed to maintain a wider sense of social critique, despite employing the partisan voice associated with the interpolation, by delegating responsibility, not only to Friar John's illicit motives, but also to the calculated hypocrisy of the people he encounters. In the *Pardoner's Prologue* and the *Wife of Bath's Prologue* he retained the superb form of ambiguous confession that characterizes False Seeming's original speech.

It is not the case then that Chaucer, like Jean de Meun before him, wrote exclusively *against* friars. Both authors chose quintessentially hypocritical characters to broaden, rather than limit, their respective social critiques, while exploring the expressive potential inherent to a well-developed character of a Cretan liar.[68] That this choice, at least in the case of the *Roman*, was at odds with that of certain contemporaries seeking a more straightforward antifraternal rhetoric is borne out by the popularity of False Seeming's interpolated confession. Chaucer, in turn, and like other attentive readers of the *Roman*, saw through the false seeming of a friar's garb.

Authors and readers

Jean de Meun's and Geoffrey Chaucer's complex use of friar-characters challenges an engrained view of the latter as passive mirrors reflecting the mendicants' actual conduct and perception in medieval society,[69] or as vessels of a Williamine

---

[66] Robertson, *Preface to Chaucer*, 266–7, 275.
[67] Helen Cooper, *The Canterbury Tales*, 2nd edn (Oxford: Oxford University Press, 1996), 41.
[68] Giovanni Boccaccio employs a strikingly similar technique in portraying "Friar" Tedaldo. See *Decameron*, III. 7, ed. Vittore Branca, 8th edn (Milan: Arnoldo Mondadori, 2001), 275–93.
[69] Joseph Spencer Kennard, *The Friar in Fiction, Sincerity in Art and Other Essays* (New York: Brentano's, 1923), 6, 25–7, 86; David Knowles, *The Religious Orders in England*, ii (Cambridge: Cambridge University Press, 1961), 114; Gerald Harriss, *Shaping the Nation: England, 1360–1461*

ecclesiological critique.[70] The present revision joins a growing body of scholarship that refrains from shoehorning literary fabrications into neatly defined ideological camps. A generation ago, Jean Batamy and Jill Mann independently underscored the enormous debt of antifraternal literature to the long-standing conventions of estate satire—the former arguing that friars are often undistinguishable from monks or clergymen in generic protests against corruption;[71] the latter asserting that, "far from drawing new inspiration from real life, Chaucer seems to have been most stimulated by the possibility of exploiting a rich literary tradition" in his treatment of monks and friars.[72] James Andreas broadened the debate by approaching some of the pertinent characters as carnivalesque heroes;[73] Nicholas Havely has advanced similarly nuanced views of Fra Cipolla and "Fra" Tedaldo in Giovanni Boccaccio's *Decameron*;[74] and, more recently still, Lawrence Clopper has turned a dominant interpretation of yet another staple of medieval antifraternal literature, *Piers Plowman*, virtually on its head by demonstrating that Langland's sincere concerns about religious mendicancy, especially regarding the Franciscan Order, reflect the friars' departure from their founder's ideals rather than a wish to see the brethren eradicated.[75] Last but not least, Wendy Scase has stressed the polemical discontinuities between the thirteenth and fourteenth centuries, arguing that literary and exegetical genealogies of antifraternal (and anticlerical) tropes do not suffice to explain the unique context in which they were appropriated.[76]

The broader implication of these revisions is that the link between William of St Amour's radical ecclesiology and the antifraternalism in works by several literary luminaries is weaker than is usually assumed. To be sure, other authors and especially readers could and at times did harness intentionally ambiguous voices or representations to the service of a strong and even abolitionist antifraternal stance, as the foregone discussion of False Seeming's interpolated speech, where polyvalence gave way to a clear partisan voice, illustrates. The reception of Chaucer's antifraternal critique is another case in point, as Kathryn Kerby-Fulton's study

---

(Oxford: Clarendon Press, 2006), 332; Michael Robson, *The Franciscans in the Middle Ages* (Woodbridge: Boydell, 2006), 157.

[70] Larry Scanlon, *Narrative, Authority and Power: The Medieval* Exemplum *and the Chaucerian Tradition* (Cambridge: Cambridge University Press, 1994), 164–5, 172.

[71] Jean Batamy, "L'Image des Franciscaines dans les 'revues d'États' du XIIIe au XVIe siècle," in André Vauchez (ed.), *Mouvements franciscains et Société française, XIIe–XXe siècles*, Beauchesne Religions, 14 (Paris: Beauchesne, 1984), 61–74.

[72] Jill Mann, *Chaucer and Medieval Estates Satire* (Cambridge: Cambridge University Press, 1973), 17; adding (p. 39): "As with the Monk, Chaucer seems to have more ends in view than moral criticism of the character he is describing." The view is corroborated by Odber de Baubeta, *Anticlerical Satire*, esp. 1–58. And see Arnold Williams, "Chaucer and the Friars," *Speculum*, 28 (1953), 499–513; Fleming, "The Antifraternalism of the *Summoner's Tale*"; Nicholas Havely, "Chaucer's Friar and Merchant," *Chaucer Review*, 13 (1978–89), 337–45.

[73] James Andreas, "'New Science' from 'Olde Bokes': A Bakhtinian Approach to the *Summoner's Tale*," *Chaucer Review*, 25 (1990), 138–51.

[74] Nicholas Havely, "Chaucer, Boccaccio, and the Friars," in P. Boitani (ed.), *Chaucer and the Italian Trecento* (Cambridge: Cambridge University Press, 1983), 249–68.

[75] Lawrence M. Clopper, *"Songs of Rechelesnesse": Langland and the Franciscans* (Ann Arbor, MI: University of Michigan Press, 1997).

[76] Scase, *"Piers Plowman" and the New Anticlericalism*.

of medieval censorship and counter-censorship shows.[77] Kerby-Fulton draws attention to yet another text, *Insurgent gentes*, which contains a prophecy casting the mendicant orders in similar apocalyptic roles to those they were allocated in *De periculis*. Intentionally misattributed to the abbess and mystic Hildegard of Bingen (1098–1179) and probably issued in 1250s Paris, *Insurgent gentes* circulated in several thirteenth- and fourteenth-century manuscripts, suggesting that William of St Amour's original exegesis continued to draw some staunch clerical support.[78]

It is also worth recalling that William viewed the friars' laxity as a symptom, not a disease. Thus, the overall prevalence of the brethren's reform-minded critics, as discussed in the first section of this chapter, prompted authors with a Williamine bent to stress the theologically sound bond between the mendicants' abuses and the onset of a broader moral degeneration as part of the Devil's master plan. The friars' inhabiting of Satan's rectum in the *Summoner's Prologue* is one illustration of such smear campaigns; *The Devil's Letter*, a satirical praise of sin, in which the brethren are particularly complicit, is another.[79] A fourteenth-century poem *Against the Friars* warns that "Ther shal no saule have rowme in helle, | of frères ther is suche throng."[80] And two further instances of this potentially reactionary trend are a text known as *Jack Upland*, which underscores the friars' union with the Antichrist and dubs them as the church's bastard branch,[81] and James le Palmer's *Omne Bonum*, a fourteenth-century encyclopedic work replete with antifraternal theology and lore.[82]

The literary *Nachleben* of *De periculis*, in sum, conforms to no simple pattern. Rather it seems that the medieval antifraternal tradition comprises a broad spectrum of works and authors, whose inspiration by William of St Amour's core

---

[77] Kathryn Kerby-Fulton, *Books under Suspicion: Censorship and Tolerance of Revelatory Writing in Late Medieval England* (Notre Dame, IN: University of Notre Dame Press, 2006), 125–61.

[78] Kathryn Kerby-Fulton, "Hildegard of Bingen and Anti-Mendicant Propaganda," *Traditio*, 43 (1987), 386–99; Kathryn Kerby-Fulton, Magda Hayton, and Kenna Olsen, "Pseudo-Hildegardian Prophecy and Antimendicant Propaganda in Late Medieval England: An Edition of the Most Popular Insular Text of 'Insurgent gentes'," in Nigel Morgan (ed.), *The Millennium, Social Disorder and the Day of Doom: Prophecy, Revolution, Apocalypse and Judgement in Medieval England and France*, Proceedings from the Harlaxton Symposium XVII, July 2000 (Stamford: Paul Watkins, 2004), 160–94.

[79] W. Wattenbach, "Über erfundene Briefe in Handschriften des Mittelalters, besonders Teufelsbriefe," *Sitzungsberichte der königlich preussischen Akademie der Wissenschaften zu Berlin*, 1(1892), 104–16.

[80] Thomas Wright (ed.), *Political Poems and Songs Relating to English History, Composed during the Period from the Accession of Edw. III to that of Ric. III*, i (London: Longman, 1859), 263–8 (originally from British Library, MS Cotton Cleopatra B. ii. fo. 62ᵛ). The following poem (pp. 268–70), which attacks the abuses of the Friars Minor specifically, lacks an explicit eschatological dimension.

[81] P. L. Heyworth (ed.), *Jack Upland, Friar Daw's Reply, and Upland's Rejoinder* (Oxford: Oxford University Press, 1968), 57–9, 65. Heyworth dates the exchange to 1419, which slightly exceeds our chronology, although Fiona Somerset, *Clerical Discourse and Lay Audience in Late Medieval England*, Cambridge Studies in Medieval Literature, 37 (Cambridge: Cambridge University Press, 1998), 135–78, argues for a late fourteenth-century dating.

[82] Lucy Freeman Sandler, *Omne Bonum: A Fourteenth-Century Encyclopedia of Universal Knowledge*, i (London: Harvey Miller Publishers, 1996), 46–7; Szittya, *The Antifraternal Tradition*, 67–81 and apps A and B; Penn R. Szittya, "Kicking the Habit: The Campaign against the Friars in a Fourteenth-Century Encyclopedia," in Michael F. Cusato and G. Geltner (eds), *Defenders and Critics of Franciscan Life: Essays in Honor of John V. Fleming*, The Medieval Franciscans, 6 (Leiden: Brill, 2009), 159–75.

ideology is, at best, intermittent. As such, the tradition shares much common ground, not only with secular theologians who fought the friars' privileges, but also with numerous home-grown critics, from Joachimite Franciscans and their Spiritual successors, through undisputedly orthodox disciplinarians such as Bonaventure and Humbert of Romans, to those who, like the Carmelite Nicholas Gallicus, became disenchanted with the possibility of combining a life of contemplation and an urban ministry[83]—all of whom decried the friars' fallenness in unambiguous terms and for the stated purpose of their improvement, not elimination.

CONCLUSIONS

The extent to which William of St Amour and *De periculis* shaped a medieval antifraternal tradition fundamentally depends on how strictly we delimit a body of texts, produced and circulated in diverse contexts and aimed at different audiences, in keeping with William's total rejection of organized religious mendicancy. We have seen that his firm denial of the mendicants' orthodoxy, including what must have been a jarring dismissal of Francis's and Dominic's lives as exemplary,[84] left no room for a distinction between mendicant ideals and practices. Nor did William bother to construe the friars' history as one of continuous decline from an original golden age, as did numerous other critics, including many members of the orders themselves throughout the thirteenth and fourteenth centuries. The more common idealist-reformist approach discloses the real chasm between William and many of his alleged successors. To that extent, William and *De periculis* are something of a false start to the study of medieval antifraternalism, at least from the broader perspective of religious and cultural history.

De periculis provides a false start in a second sense as well. Even if we treat it as an inspiring text for those disaffected by the friars generally, objections to the brethren's presence, success, and some of their teachings and practices developed in lockstep with the orders' foundations. Peter Linehan was perhaps exaggerating in maintaining that during "the Parisian debates of these years [i.e., the 1250s] secular hostility to the mendicants expressed sentiments which all Europe shared."[85] Yet, and as the next chapter shows, violent opposition to the friars pre-dates the university quarrels by decades. But both before and after the 1250s there is very little evidence of a widespread desire to see the brethren eradicated. A sincere quest for their abolition, at least by more than a fervent few, would recommence in the

---

[83] On the latter and lesser-known case, see Jotischky, *The Carmelites and Antiquity*, 79–105, which challenges the supposedly profound influence of *De periculis* on Nicholas's *Ignea Sagitta*.

[84] See William's responses to Bonaventure's disputed question *De mendicitate*, cc. 17–18, in *Opuscula*, ed. Traver, 134–5. Doubts over Francis's stigmata straddled both mendicants and the regular clergy and apparently were more strategic than William's vitriol. See André Vauchez, "Les stigmates de saint François et leurs détracteurs dans les derniers siècles du moyen âge," *Mélanges d'archéologie et d'histoire*, 80 (1968), 595–625.

[85] Peter Linehan, "A Tale of Two Cities: Capitular Burgos and Mendicant Burgos in the Thirteenth Century," in David Abulafia et al. (eds), *Church and City, 1000–1500: Essays in Honour of Christopher Brooke* (Cambridge: Cambridge University Press, 1992), 84.

early sixteenth century, nearly 300 years after the singular and short-lived campaign led by William of St Amour.

If, therefore, we seek accurately to understand hostility toward medieval friars, a broader and more flexible prism is required, one that includes social and political action alongside cultural production. It is this perspective that we now turn to develop.

2
Violence: Friars under Fire

> Sometimes words lead to lashes.
>
> Richard FitzRalph, 'Unusquisque' (1350)[1]

In the quiet background of an etching, a rural chapel nestles among some shrubs. In the foreground two women are pummelling a kneeling man, a mendicant friar in full garb. His right hand clutches the edge of a small volume; his spread left props him up slightly from the ground. But he is helpless, doomed. The women are standing over him. One, half-crouching, tears at his tonsure and digs her nails deep into his right shoulder. The other stands directly to the friar's left, steadying his head with her left hand and knee, and prepares to deliver a blow with a massive key ring possibly wrestled out of the man's own hand. The friar's mouth is agape and twisted in pain; his eyes are dim with terror. The women's faces, by contrast, emit restraint, almost coolness; their detachment suggests a routine affair. Only their hair, which swings broadly, betrays a more charged emotion, although not quite anger (see Figure 2.1).[2]

A common response to this Swiss Renaissance image—in seminar rooms, public venues, and private discussions—is to assume the friar's culpability. Many viewers even take vicarious pleasure in the women's (rare, as we shall see) assertion of agency in this context, a view governed by the assumption that the man had either molested them beforehand, or tried to do so, or—worse still—did so without paying. On the other hand, it is also possible that the beating followed the friar's refusal to obtain the ladies' services (or those of one rather than the other's), or his

---

[1] L. L. Hammerich, *The Beginning of the Strife between Richard FitzRalph and the Mendicants with an Edition of his Autobiographical Prayer and his Proposition "Unusquisque"* (Copenhagen: Levin & Munksgaand, 1938), 60: "nonnunquam per verba pervenitur ad verbera." The context for this observation was FitzRalph's analysis of the dangers attendant upon the friars' usurpation of the priests' duties.

[2] See Hans Koegler (ed.), *Beschreibendes Verzeichnis der Basler Handzeichnungen des Urs Graf* (Basel: Banno Schwabe & Co., 1926), no. 100 (p. 64); Emil Major and Erwin Gradmann, *Urs Graf* (Basel: Holbein Verlag, 1942), no. 49. Christian Müller, *Urs Graf: Die Zeichnungen im Kupferstichkabinett Basel*, Beschreibender Katalog der Zeichnungen, Band III. Die Zeichnungen des 15. und 16. Jahrhunderts, Teil 2B (Basel: Schwabe, 2001), no. 105 (pp. 207–8). Catalogues and other studies of Graf's works attest his commitment to depicting traditional themes (biblical and mythological scenes, saints' *vitae*, popes, etc.), alongside contemporary daily life, with a notable predilection to violence. Müller, *Urs Graf*, passim, and John K. Rowlands, Fedja Anzelewsky, and Robert Zijlma (eds), *Hollstein's German Engravings, Etchings and Woodcuts*, xi. *Urs Graf* (Amsterdam: Van Gendt & Co., 1977).

Fig. 2.1. Urs Graf, *Two Prostitutes Assaulting a Monk* (1521)
By kind permission of the Kunstmeseum Basel, Kupferstichkabinett; image by Martin P. Bühler.

attempt to better their ways. And there is still a third option—namely, that he paid in order to be treated that way: a twist, perhaps, on mendicant *humilitas*.

In any case, there are many ways here to unpack what linguistic philosophers would call the brute fact of a physical encounter between three individuals, since anything said about the scene beyond this narrow description relies on multiple social and institutional conventions, without which we could never discuss who is doing what to whom, why, and for what purpose.[3] Assaults on medieval friars are a case in point, as the above image suggests. And, as the present chapter will demonstrate, tracing and analyzing the scope of such incidents reveals a broad and at times bewildering array of contexts and motivations for men to transition from launching violent words against the friars to subjecting them to violent deeds. Exploring such events sheds light not only on the mendicants' early history, but also on the dynamics and various dimensions of medieval urban violence.

But first we must address the issue of scale. As the first section of this chapter stresses, both mendicant and non-mendicant sources confirm that violence against

---

[3] G. E. M. Anscombe, "On Brute Facts," *Analysis*, 18 (1958), 69–72.

friars was more common in the late Middle Ages than modern historians have been wont to observe. The oversight owes partly to the absence of discrete sources documenting such violence in that period; even regional surveys are few and far between, and they mostly focus on anti-inquisitorial aggression.[4] Yet there are several ways to compensate for such documentary lacunae concerning the incidence of violent attacks on friars and their convents before 1400. Emerging from a broad range of sources is a picture of an extreme (and thus by definition limited) dimension of medieval social and religious history that has so far been mainly and unnecessarily limited to students of the papal inquisition and mendicant martyrology.[5]

Yet assaulting friars was both broader and more complex a practice than students of the inquisition have shown. First, and as André Vauchez remarked more than forty years ago, physical violence against Franciscan convents could be elicited by "hostility against the Friars Minor and the innovations that they introduced into the ecclesiastical structure."[6] Next, and as a subsequent section reveals, even within the confines of anti-inquisitorial violence, there are discernible differences between cases, which involved different groups and individuals striving toward diverse ends. Further, although the friars' role in the papal inquisition could create local and regional tensions, aggressive responses to their arrival were seldom concentrated in the hands of heretics or their supporters. Most importantly, antimendicant violence is attested well beyond regions particularly associated with the brethren's inquisitorial activities.

In a classic survey, J. R. Hale divided late-medieval urban violence into four categories: personal (for example, assault), group (revolt), organized illegitimate (brigandage), and organized legitimate (war).[7] As we shall see, violence against friars cut across all of these categories, and involved contemporaries, mainly urban residents, in extreme acts. Yet, rather than viewing such recourse to aggression or its threat as a spontaneous, visceral mob response, this chapter will conclude by exploring such events as gestures carefully articulated in the flexible idiom of violence and as such richly suggestive of contemporary experiences of suffering. For, as recent anthropologists have shown, the relations between these two realms were rather close.[8]

---

[4] Yves Dossat, "Opposition des anciens ordres à l'installation des mendiants," in *Les Mendiants en pays d'Oc au XIIIe siècle*, CdF 8 (Toulouse: Privat, 1973), 263–306; Dupré-Thes., 287–96.

[5] Notably, James B. Given, *Inquisition and Medieval Society: Power, Discipline, and Resistance in Languedoc* (Ithaca, NY: Cornell University Press, 1997), 111–40; Lansing, 151–6; Ames. On mendicant martyrs and their iconography, see Bernard Montagnes, "Les Inquisiteurs martyrs de la France méridionale," *Praedicatores, Inquisitores I* (Rome: Istituto Storico Domenicano, 2004), 513–38; S. Maureen Burke, "The 'Martyrdom of the Franciscans' by Ambrogio Lorenzetti," *Zeitschrift für Kunstgeschichte*, 65 (2002), 460–92; and Ch. 4.

[6] André Vauchez, "Les stigmates de saint François et leurs détracteurs dans les derniers siècles du moyen âge," *Mélanges d'archéologie et d'histoire*, 80 (1968), 608.

[7] J. R. Hale, "Violence in the Late Middle Ages: A Background," in Lauro Martines (ed.), *Violence and Civil Disorder in Italian Cities, 1200–1500* (Berkeley and Los Angeles: University of California Press, 1972), 19–37.

[8] Veena Das et al. (eds), *Violence and Subjectivity* (Berkeley and Los Angeles: University of California Press, 2000).

AGGRESSION AGAINST FRIARS: SCALE

The victimization of medieval friars is a staple of mendicant historiography, hagiography, martyrology, liturgy, and iconography.[9] We would be justifiably skeptical of such nostalgic recollections of the brethren's hardships in an earlier and more heroic golden age, recollections that often advance an internal critique of the orders' perceived laxity. Yet aggression against mendicants is attested well beyond the sweet inversions of early mendicant authors—for instance, in urban and monastic chronicles, and in a variety of documents of practice, from the orders' internal correspondence, to papal and episcopal decrees, to criminal court records. The present chapter is based on a broad selection of such sources (see Appendix I), including a sizable sample of more than a century of tribunal records from a number of major Italian city states. The Italian focus was determined by the fine state of preservation of local records and, no less importantly, their accessibility. Moreover, the highly urbanized region of central and northern Italy was particularly rife with mendicant activity throughout the thirteenth and fourteenth centuries, and it seemed plausible that the friars' unique prominence there would trigger a significant response, as indeed it did.[10]

Since the friars' aggressors could vary in socio-economic status and vocation, and given the potential overlap in jurisdictions between communes and local bishops, the present survey combines both civic and (the much scarcer) episcopal criminal court records: laymen could have been adjudicated by both courts; clerics should have stood trial only in the latter. Even where it was theoretically possible, no attempt has been made to exhaust the records of any specific city for the entire period until 1400 or focus on any particular decade throughout Europe. All told, civic criminal courts were surveyed for the following cities and periods: Milan, 1385, 1387, 1390–2, 1397–1400;[11] Lucca, 1331–43, 1357–67, 1398–1400;[12] Bologna, 1285–94, 1325–34, 1354–67;[13] and Florence, 1375–84.[14] The records of bishops' tribunals were examined for Lucca in 1347, 1350–69, 1371–92, 1394–98, a period

---

[9] *XXIV Gen.*, 13; Lorenzo Di Fonzo (ed.), "L'Anonimo Perugino tra le fonti francescane nel secolo XIII. Rapporti letterari e testo critico," *Miscellanea Francescana*, 72 (1972), 16a–b, 17b–c, 19a–24b, 26a, 44b; Jacobus de Voragine, *The Golden Legend: Readings on the Saints*, trans. William Granger Ryan, 2 vols (Princeton: Princeton University Press, 1993), i. 260–1, 261–2; ii. 229. And see the full discussion in Ch. 4.

[10] Augustine Thompson, *Cities of God: The Religion of the Italian Communes, 1125–1325* (University Park, PA: Pennsylvania State University Press, 2005), 419–56.

[11] ASCMi, Cimeli 146–50, 175. These are the only remaining Milanese criminal-court records prior to the fifteenth century. See Ettore Verga, "Le sentenze criminali dei podestà milanesi 1385–1429," *Archivio Storico Lombardo*, 16 (1901), 96–142.

[12] ASLu, Sentenze e bandi 1–9 (the first available decades), 19–23, 25, 28, 33, 36 (an arbitrary decade after the Black Death), 93–6 (closing years of the century), 535.

[13] ASBo, Curia del podestà, Libri inquisitionum 6–31, 115–39, 179–200, 203–4.

[14] ASFi, Capitano del popolo, 848, 892, 896, 947, 954, 1002bis, 1120, 1197bis, 1198, 1255, 1313, 1371, 1427, 1428, 1496, 1521, 1559.

in which the court also adjudicated numerous secular criminal cases;[15] and for Pisa in 1304–12, 1325–1400.[16] The latter two are the sole surviving series among the major bishoprics of central and northern Italy before the fifteenth century.

Scholars have aptly remarked on the problems attendant upon the use of court records for arguing about the nature or incidence of deviancy.[17] For the pre-modern period, as Trevor Dean asserts, the diversity of courts and the fragmentary nature of their paper trail means that even non-sensationalist criminal historians run the risk of holding a magnifying glass to extreme and at times bizarre cases, producing a distorted image that all but normalizes deviant behavior.[18] Gerald Harriss flagged another handicap in noting that allegations of violence in medieval court records were often quasi-procedural, a sort of prudent rhetorical gesture in bringing forth a legal suit.[19] And then there are, of course, the numerous constraints placed upon the responsible interpretation of such data, including, but not limited to, accounting for the relevant documents' haphazard mode of production and intermittent preservation, which, as Daniel Lord Smail has reminded us, was inextricably tied to the status and wealth of defendants and plaintiffs alike.[20] The yawning gap between the extant court records and the original oral exchanges of court procedure, not to mention the offences themselves, can at times be truly huge.

Furthermore, however savvy late-medieval society was becoming about using document-reliant litigation effectively, there were bound to be discrepancies between the bureaucratic handling of different categories of offences. If in the next chapter I speculate that normative violations among medieval Dominicans were probably more prevalent than the available records show, in the present chapter I argue that the submerged iceberg whose tip we are observing is probably modest by comparison. For, unlike the Dominicans' misbehavior and its close internal monitoring, assaults on friars were generally too public to ignore, and, although some incidents have undoubtedly been lost or hidden, many parties—not least the

---

[15] ASDL, Tribunale criminale 1–44. The Lucchese records are by far the richest of their kind for this period, followed from a distance by the fragmentary collection in Pisa. See G. Geltner, "I registri criminali dell'Archivio Arcivescovile di Lucca: Prospettive di ricerca per la storia sociale del medioevo," in Sergio Pagano and Pierantonio Piatti (eds), *Il patrimonio documentario della Chiesa di Lucca: Prospettive di ricerca* (Florence: Edizioni SISMEL, 2010), 331–40.

[16] AAPi, Atti straordinari 1, 3, 4, 6–9, 11. The series is fragmentary.

[17] See Thomas Kuehn, "Reading Microhistory: The Example of Giovanni and Lusanna," *Journal of Modern History*, 61 (1989), 512–34; Robert D. Storch "The Study of Urban Crime," *Social History*, 4 (1979), 117–22; *Historical Research on Crime and Criminal Justice*, Collected Studies in Criminological Research, 22 (Strasbourg: European Committee on Crime Problems, 1985); Judith Pollmann, "Off the Record: Problems in the Quantification of Calvinist Church Discipline," *Sixteenth Century Journal*, 33 (2002), 423–38.

[18] Trevor Dean, *Crime and Justice in Late Medieval Italy* (Cambridge: Cambridge University Press, 2007), 8–9. Among other extreme examples that Dean invokes to make his point is an early fifteenth-century case of two Calabrian friars whose genitalia were cut off by a mob for refusing to pay a prostitute.

[19] Gerald Harriss, *Shaping the Nation: England 1360–1461* (Oxford: Clarendon Press, 2005), 197.

[20] Daniel Lord Smail, "Aspects of Procedural Documentation in Marseille (14th–15th Centuries)," in Susanne Lepsius and Thomas Wetzstein (eds), *Als die Welt in die Akten kam: Prozeßschriftgut im europäischen Mittelalter* (Frankfurt: Vittorio Klostermann, 2008), 139–69.

Table 2.1. Aggression against friars before 1400, by region

Region	Incidents
Italy	40
British Isles	25
France	20
Spain	7
Germany	7
Central Europe	4
Unknown	3
TOTAL	106

mendicant themselves—were interested in recording such events to protect their status and bolster their identity.

With all that in mind, the picture that the available sources reveal is of sustained if infrequent aggression against friars (see Table 2.1). Between the orders' foundation (or assembly) in the early thirteenth century and the close of the fourteenth, 39 instances have been recorded of physical aggression in Italy, and a total of 106 across Europe.[21]

Given the friars' tendency to focus their activities in cities, it is not surprising that all but few of these incidents occurred in urbanized areas, and that, the more urbanized a region, the more represented (and better documented) it is. Most of the cases recorded for Germany, for instance, were set in the relatively urbanized Rhineland (for example, Worms, Cologne) and nearby Strasbourg; and none of the twenty-five assaults documented for England, Wales, Scotland, and Ireland took place outside cities. Three rare exceptions are the murder of the Dominican inquisitor Peter Martyr on the Como–Milan road, the despoiling of a Polish Dominican returning to his convent from a general chapter in Carcassonne, and the kidnapping and rape of a Poor Clare likewise en route to her convent in Arezzo.[22] That said, the decidedly urban profile of antifraternal violence is less obvious than it first seems.

That the vast majority of assaults happened in or near mendicant convents, themselves located somewhere between the outskirts and the centers of medieval cities, may seem trivial. But the friars' constant wandering *between* cities would have rendered them relatively more vulnerable away from home. And yet the countryside is paradoxically where they rarely ran into serious trouble.[23] How to account for the apparent discrepancy? Friars tended to travel in pairs or small groups and reputedly without valuables. This may have rendered them unlikely

---

[21] These are laid out in App. I.
[22] App. I, nos 21, 76, and 94, respectively. See discussion below.
[23] On contemporaries' perceptions of the highway and the uninhabited world as being particularly dangerous places, see Michael E. Goodich, *Violence and Miracle in the Fourteenth Century* (Chicago and London: University of Chicago Press, 1995), 44–8, 103–15.

targets for robbers: the Polish friar's assailants walked away with a few coins and the recent chapter's *acta*. But travelling friars' poverty scarcely deterred heretics or their supporters (as the case of Peter Martyr might suggest), highwaymen with ulterior motives (as in the Poor Clare's case), political or personal enemies, and the generally desperate or simply clueless. In this sense, the literary *topos* of the friar's protective garb, which appears in numerous contemporary sources, seems to reflect anxieties about its limited deterring power rather than the realities of the brethren's travels.[24] But, if the mendicant habit offered little reassurance, so did the mendicant convent, as the second section of this chapter demonstrates.

Plotted chronologically (see Table 2.2), the distribution of incidents exhibits one low and two high peaks. The former comes, perhaps unsurprisingly, during the quarter-century following the onset of Black Death (1351–75) and can thus be attributed to a combination of society's greater focus on regeneration as against conflict, to the friars' perceived heroism during the initial visitation of the plague, and perhaps more prosaically to the deterioration of central administrations and documentary practices during that time. Increases in violent incidents are evident during the orders' formative period (before 1250), especially in northern Italy and southern France, the focus of vigorous settlement and inquisitorial activity; and a full generation later (1276–1300), by which point friars and their convents were fast en route to becoming familiar sites in Europe's urban landscape. The brethren's swift integration, not only as preachers and confessors, but also as religious and secular administrators, boded well only in certain respects. As we shall see, circumstances surrounding antifraternal violence during the last quarter of the thirteenth century were diverse and exceeded (albeit not for the first time) the scope of antagonism created by the friars' foreignness and their inquisitorial activities.

In other words, and to anticipate a later discussion, antifraternal violence in this period did not issue exclusively from heretics or their supporters but rather involved mainly male burgesses, monks, and clergymen alike, even within regions targeted as heretical hotbeds by the papacy. The same point is moot for the British Isles, where the brethren were never systematically deployed to combat heresy. Rather, there as elsewhere, motivations for aggression appear to have ranged from resistance to the settlement of ethnic and linguistic "others," to political and military conflict, to financial disputes.

One major distinction should be drawn between occasional violence and intentional aggression against friars. Of the 106 cases brought together here, 17 seem to have concerned mendicants only incidentally, as when a friar was robbed or (more commonly) a friary was broken into by a mob in pursuit of a non-mendicant enemy

---

[24] Jeanne Ancelet-Hustace (ed.), "Les 'Vitae Sororum' d'Unterlinden: Édition critique du manuscrit 508 de la Bibliothèque de Colmar," *Archives d'histoire doctrinale et littéraire du moyen age*, 5 (1930), 484, describes Hermann of Havelberg, the Dominican provincial minister, offering protection to traveling merchants. Walter of Madeley, an early English Franciscan, found and kept a pair of sandals against the order's rule. He later dreamt of being confronted by two highway robbers who dismissed his claims of being a Franciscan (and consequently of being untouchable) since he was not barefoot. See *Eccleston*, 35.

Table 2.2. Aggression against friars before 1400, by period

Period	Incidents	Incidents in Italy
Until 1250	20	9
1251–75	13	6
1276–1300	26	10
1301–25	15	3
1326–50	12	1
1351–75	6	5
1376–1400	14	5
TOTAL	106	39

or by an invading army in search of booty or a strategic stronghold. Such occasions were apparently frequent enough to explain why local mendicant chroniclers willingly boasted of how their convent was spared the cruel fate reserved for laymen or even other monasteries in times of political unrest.[25] But the broader point here is that being a friar or a mendicant convent was no guarantee for safety. Indeed, the brethren's visibility, location, and growing wealth made them both obvious targets as well as easy scapegoats, although the two are not to be confused.

The remainder of cases, however, suggests that more often than not the brethren were in fact targeted casualties: there were forty-two organized assaults on individual convents outside a military context, at least ten of which culminated with the expulsion of friars from an existing house, as distinct from their rejection as newcomers; and on forty-five further occasions either individual mendicants or groups were assaulted elsewhere in the city. In twenty-two such events violence brought the death of one or more friars. Twelve of these deadly incidents occurred in what can broadly be called heretical or anti-inquisitorial attacks, which constituted just below 21 percent (22 out of 106) of all documented cases of antifraternal aggression.

Recorded assaults are divided across the various orders as follows: forty-nine cases against Franciscans, forty-six against Dominicans, thirteen against Augustinians, eight against Carmelites, two against Sack Friars, and two against Servites. The figures add up to more than 106 cases, since some incidents involved more than one convent, members of more than one order, or else the extant description makes it impossible to tell which order/s were targeted specifically. The distribution of cases seems grossly to reflect the orders' size and geographical spread, as well as the larger orders' involvement with the papal inquisition and superior documentation for this period.

---

[25] The Minorite *Lanercost*, 246, reports how in 1321 the Scots plundered Lancaster and razed all but the local mendicant and Benedictine convents. The army then continued to Preston, where it spared none but the Franciscans. In 1247–48, following Frederick II's excommunication, the Franciscans alone among Zurich's religious were not expelled from the city, according to one Franciscan author. See *Die Chronik Johanns von Winterthur*, ed. Friedrich Bathgen, with C. Brun, MGH SS rer. Germ., new ser. 3 (Berlin: Weidmann, 1924), 11–12.

With the exception of one Poor Clare and the residents of three Dominican nunneries, individual and group casualties comprised male mendicants alone. The marginality of female mendicants here is noteworthy, for they were by no means scarce, at least among the larger orders. Nor was there a general lack of female victims, cloistered or not, in medieval Europe.[26] As always, part of the explanation for the scarcity of assaults against mendicant sisters has to do with the survival of documents. But it seems that gender, more than the mendicant habit, had its benefits in this respect, if only as an unforeseen outcome of the sisters' stricter cloistering, lower public profile, and reduced involvement with the outside world, as compared with their male coreligionists. The orders' women were mostly barred from begging, preaching, or engaging in educational activities outside the convent, and they were typically poorer than their male counterparts.[27] Renowned figures such as Margaret of Cittá di Castello (1287–1320) or Catherine of Siena (1347–80) were exceptional, not only on account of their unique devotion and charisma (which originally rendered them a threat to be managed within the Dominican order), but also because they were tertiary members rather than avowed nuns.[28] Thus it was the nuns' obscurity that, juxtaposed with their brethren's worldliness, may have offered them greater protection or at least helped reduce antagonism.

A similar disparity between men and women emerges from the profile of the assaults' perpetrators. Notwithstanding the etching analyzed above, and insofar as the friars' assailants can be identified, they are almost exclusively adult urban men. As elsewhere in the medieval (and modern) justice system, women were less likely to be arrested and charged and are thus often underrepresented in criminal statistics.[29] However, women were as likely to participate in mob assaults and in any case, as we shall see below, certainly voiced their opinions of the friars' wrongful inquisitorial practices, their illicit recruitment of young children, and their perceived hypocrisy.

It is necessary to underscore the qualitative gap between the systematic sampling at the basis of the Italian survey and the more sporadic references that furnish data on cases outside that region. Despite my heavy concentration on Italian archival sources, and within the most urbanized region of that country in the late Middle Ages, documented assaults there exhibit a similar scale to that of other, less-urbanized regions of western Europe, such as the British Isles. In other words, Italian incidents do not emerge as an order of magnitude greater than elsewhere, which is a curious and unanticipated outcome of the present survey. Further archival investigations elsewhere may prove that the disparity between variously urbanized regions was even smaller.

---

[26] Samuel K. Cohn, Jr., *Women in the Streets: Essays on Sex and Power in Renaissance Italy* (Baltimore: Johns Hopkins University Press, 1996), 107–10; Trevor Dean, *Crime in Medieval Europe, 1200–1550* (London: Longman, 2001), 73–4, 82–6.

[27] Andrews, 34–6, 132–8.

[28] Daniel Bornstein, "Women and Religion in Late Medieval Italy: History and Historiography," in Daniel Bornstein and Roberto Rusconi (eds), *Women and Religion in Medieval and Renaissance Italy*, trans. Margery J. Schneider (Chicago and London: University of Chicago Press, 1996), 1–27, esp. 2–8.

[29] Barbara Hanawalt, "The Female Felon in Fourteenth-Century England," *Viator*, 5 (1974), 253–68; Cohn, Jr., *Women in the Streets*, 16–38; Trevor Dean, "Theft and Gender in Late Medieval Bologna," *Gender & History*, 20 (2008), 399–415.

On the other hand, the intensive examination of Italian court records augmented hitherto-known incidents by around 39 percent: of the forty cases reported here, eleven were excavated from local archives, and have never before—so far as I am aware—made their way into print. There is no comparable survey for any other region. Yet it would perhaps be reasonable to surmise from the Italian case study that a 40 percent increase beyond the currently known incidents is plausible.[30] Applying this principle outside Italy would raise the number of incidents from sixty-seven (documented) to ninety-four (postulated). If we postulate a conservative incidence of violent assaults in regions not covered by the above survey (Scandinavia and the Lowlands), the number of hypothetical cases increases by a further ten cases. According to this calculation, a plausible estimate of incidents (40 for Italy, 94 for regions surveyed, 10 for regions not surveyed) adds up to 144 assaults, or an average of one violent event every fifteen months or so, from the orders' formation to the year 1400.

AGGRESSION AGAINST FRIARS: SCOPE

At this point it would be wise to avoid the temptation of attributing qualitative meaning to quantitative reappraisal. As an order of magnitude, the incidence rate described above (and fully documented in Appendix I), and even that postulated, is relatively low: around eight assaults per decade anywhere in Europe. Setting antimendicant violence against the broader yet comparable category of anticlerical violence confirms the phenomenon's modest scale. In the well-documented diocese of Lucca, for example, priests were reportedly assaulted at least six separate times during the decade 1355–64; that is, clerics were victimized in one episcopal see at an only slightly lower frequency than were friars across the entire continent.[31] Nor is it necessary to correct these figures for the friars' numeric inferiority as compared with priests, for even in large sees such as Lucca the difference would have been at best negligible, given that the city was home to five mendicant convents. In sum, there seems to be little evidence for any widespread victimization of friars.

But does an apparently limited recourse to violence against mendicants suggest a general satisfaction with their presence and activities? Is it possible to juxtapose the brethren's generally positive social reception with the brands of antifraternalism previously imputed from clerical and literary sources, from William of St Amour to Richard FitzRalph and from Rutebeuf to Rabelais? Were, in fine, those laying "a blot on the elect" merely a vocal few exploited by coeval and later propagandists and

---

[30] Given, *Inquisition and Medieval Society*, 113–15, augmented the number of hitherto-known anti-inquisitorial assaults in Languedoc between 1233–1320 by 63 percent, from twenty-seven to forty-four, by recourse to unpublished sources.

[31] ASDL, Tribunale criminale 8, fos 29^{r-v}, 65^{r-v}, 67^{r-v}, 137^{r-v} (1355); 11, fo. 24^r (1357?); 18, fo. 136^r (after May 1363). Other instances of clerical victimization are documented in Myriam Soria, "Les violences anti-épiscopales dans la province de Narbonee (fin XIIe–début XIIIe sècle): Des manifestations anticléricales?"; and Patrick Henriet, "*In injuriam ordinis clericalis*: Traces d'anticléricalisme en Castille et León (XIIe–XIIIe s.)," both in *L'Anticléricalisme en France méridionale (milieu XIIe–début XIVe siècle)*, CdF 38 (Toulouse: Privat, 2003), 161–79, 289–325, respectively; and see Goodich, *Violence and Miracle*, 38–41.

celebrated by modern literary and religious historians? To answer these questions we now turn to examine antimendicant violence more closely. Mapping the scope of such incidents reveals a surprising diversity of contexts, goals, and motivations.

Strangers in a strange land

Beginning in the early thirteenth century, mendicant friars settled in Languedoc, Lombardy, and elsewhere as part of a concerted papal effort to combat heresy.[32] Occasionally upon arrival they met with pockets of resistance, leading in France and the Balkans to several major acts of violence, and epitomized in Italy by the assassination of Peter of Verona, known to posterity as Peter Martyr (d. 1252; canonized 1253).[33] The prevalence of anti-inquisitorial violence—which is treated separately below—has helped obscure the fact that many instances of aggression against friars in this period were not a direct response to the brethren's activities as inquisitors, but rather an outcome, on the one hand, of their unfamiliarity with their new stomping grounds, and, on the other, of broader social, political, and ethnic tensions prompted by their *modus operandi*. In this sense, friars can usefully be viewed as strangers, unfamiliar outsiders in their allocated regions.[34]

Suspicion did not always and everywhere greet the friars. In Holland and Zeeland, for instance, there is no evidence to suggest that their settlement was anything but peaceful, as it had been in contemporaneous Brittany.[35] And yet, as already noted, mendicant chroniclers stressed repeatedly (and not without taking some pride in their predecessors' heroism) that there were at least many superficial grounds for rejecting the new wandering holy men. Even when the brethren did not appear on the scene as papal inquisitors, they still raised locals' suspicion as foreigners, spies, thieves, beggars, and even heretics, especially where they were newcomers to a region. According to the *Lanercost Chronicle*, upon their arrival to Dover in 1224 the Franciscans were accused of being "spies...and thieves" (*exploratores...et latrones*).[36] The cathedral canons in Pamplona likewise treated the brethren publicly as "heretics, worse than Jews and Saracens, and perpetrators

---

[32] This section deals with violence against friars in and on the shifting borders of western Christendom. For the brethren's victimization beyond those borders, especially in Asia and the Near East, see Ch. 4 and the Epilogue.

[33] Anti-inquisitorial violence is discussed below. On Peter, see, most recently, Donald Prudlo, *The Martyred Inquisitor: The Life and Cult of Peter of Verona (†1252)* (Aldershot: Ashgate, 2008).

[34] The literature on medieval linguistic and ethnic "otherness" has been expanding along with scholarly interest in travel, pilgrimage, frontiers, and urban migration. However, with the exception of Uwe Israel, *Fremde aus dem Norden: Transalpine Zuwanderer im spätmittelalterlichen Italien* (Tübingen: Max Niemeyer, 2005), 81–2, 211–12, little direct attention has been given to friars traversing, challenging, and reaffirming such boundaries within Europe itself.

[35] P. A. Henderikx, *De oudste bedelordekloosters in het graafschap Holland en Zeeland*, Hollandse Studiën, 10 (Dordrecht: Historische Vereniging Holland, 1977), 28; Herve Martin, *Les ordres mendiants en Bretagne (vers 1230–vers 1530)* (Paris: Klincksieck, 1975), 137–9. Hostilities are, however, well documented for Brittany increasingly since the fourteenth century, and in the later fifteenth century citizens and clergymen led several armed assaults explicitly protesting what was perceived as the friars' excessive wealth. See Martin, *Les ordres mendiants*, 139–49, 400–1.

[36] *Lanercost*, 30.

of the gravest crimes" (*haereticos, nequiores Judaeis, Saracenis, et gravioribus irretitos criminibus publice asserebant*).[37] And, according to the Franciscan chronicler Jordan of Giano, when a similar mission landed in Germany, the friars were accosted by the locals and "asked if they were heretics, and if they had come to Germany in order to infect it just as they had perverted Lombardy." Unfortunately, the friars replied with the only word they knew in the local dialect, namely, *Ja*. Whereupon,

> some of them were beaten, others imprisoned, and still others stripped naked, taken to a public place, and made a spectacle for men to mock at. Seeing therefore that they could gain no fruit in Germany, the brethren returned to Italy. From this experience, Germany came to have such a cruel reputation among the brethren, that no one but those inspired by a desire for martyrdom dared to return there.[38]

Note the chronicler's adventurous leap from the events at hand to the use of the term martyrdom. By Giano's own account, the friars were "made a spectacle" of, but not even threatened with murder. The locals' action was geared toward the public humiliation of foreign heretics, not their destruction: the brethren were ultimately taken to "a public place" to be mocked, not hung. And, as in other cases to be discussed below, it is the locals' restraint, not violence, that seeks to underscore local power relations, for it demonstrated their agency and control over the situation. As diverse modern observers of violence such as Hannah Arendt, Félix Guattari, Slavoj Žižek, and others have argued, violence can operate as a barometer for vulnerability rather than strength, whether conducted by a minority faction or launched on behalf of a state.[39] Thus the Germans' "cruel reputation among the brethren" seems to rest on exaggerations rather than observed facts or recorded experience, which may well be the author's broader point.[40]

Ironically, both negative and positive receptions could be detrimental to the friars' initial settlement. Some of those who rushed to embrace a life of voluntary poverty were spurned and alienated by friends and relatives, who in turn directed their rage back at the mendicants. In this sense, Francis and Clare of Assisi set powerful examples for the Franciscan Orders, as did, among others, Diana d'Andalò and Thomas Aquinas among the Dominicans.[41] According to Thomas of

---

[37] *BF* i. 429 (Oct. 15, 1244).

[38] *Chronica Fratris Jordani*, ed. H. Boehmer (Paris: Librairie Fischbacher, 1908), 5 (pp. 5–6): "Unde accidit, ut interrogati, si essent heretici et si ad hoc venissent ut Teutoniam inficerent sicut et Lombardiam prevertissent, et respondissent 'ia', quidam ex ipsis plegati, quidam incarcerati et quidam denudati nudi ad choream sunt ducti et spectaculum ludecre hominibus sunt effecti"; see also 6–7 (pp. 6–7), and the parallel description in *Glassberger*, 11.

[39] Hannah Arendt, *On Violence* (Orlando, FA: Harcourt, 1970); Félix Guattari, *Soft Subversions: Texts and Interviews 1977–1985*, ed. Sylvère Lotringer, trans. Chet Wiener and Emily Wittman (Los Angeles: Semiotex(e), 2009), 62–3, 92–3; Slavoj Žižek, *Violence* (London: Profile, 2008). And see Wolfgang Sofsky, *Saggio sulla violenza*, trans. Barbara Trapani and Luca Lamberti (Turin: Einaudi, 1998).

[40] For an updated bibliography on Jordan of Giano, among many other Franciscan chroniclers, see <http://users.bart.nl/~roestb/franciscan/index.htm> (last accessed May 20, 2010).

[41] More famous in her day, Diana (d. 1236) was the co-founder of St Agnes, the first Dominican nunnery in Bologna, and an intimate friend of Jordan of Saxony. See *Love among the Saints: The Letters of Blessed Jordan of Saxony to Blessed Diana of Andalò*, ed. and trans. Kathleen Pond (London: Bloomsbury, 1958).

Eccleston, when Brother Solomon, the first Englishman to join the newly arrived Franciscans, came to beg his sister for alms, she cursed the hour when she ever saw him.[42] Jordan of Saxony's successful recruitment of a nobleman's son led the angry father and his retinue to seek the Dominican's death.[43] And Salimbene de Adam was originally warned by his father not to "put any faith in these piss-in-tunics," by which he meant the Franciscans. But to no avail; when the young Salimbene at last resolved to join the Minorites along with his brother, their father, Guido, exclaimed: "Accursed son, I give you to a thousand devils, along with your brother, who is here a friar with you, assisting in your deception. I lay my everlasting curse upon your head and bequeath you to the infernal demons."[44] Given that Guido de Adam's words expressed (at least according to Salimbene) a sentiment already shared by the wider community, including the local bishop, it is easy to see how violent responses to recruitment, as a form of disrupting community, were only a small step away.[45]

To repeat, however, it would be injudicious to take friars at their word, especially since scorn was a Christological badge of honor worn by or pinned onto many a mendicant sleeve in the movement's early hagiography.[46] Thankfully, for every Thomas of Eccleston or Salimbene there is independent evidence for the brethren's antagonizing recruitment practices, notably among young children, which led to retaliation by oblates' families or friends. In 1288 Pope Nicholas IV recognized the important role that allegations of illicit recruiting practices in Strasbourg played in the violent strife between local citizens and the Dominicans. In a decree aimed at the resolution of the affair, which escalated into the blockading and eventual ejection of the friars from the city (see below), the pope repeated the prohibition on recruiting anyone under the age of 18 without his or her parents' express permission.[47] In 1326 the admission of a young boy into the Franciscan friary in Bologna, evidently against his parents' will, led to a rescue attempt and a brawl.[48] And on July 13, 1392 a London orphan was enlisted under similarly suspicious and

---

[42] *Eccleston*, 12.
[43] *Vitae Fratrum*, III. 14 (pp. 110–11).
[44] *Salimbene*, 56: "Dixit igitur michi pater meus: 'Fili dilecte, non credas istis pissintunicis'"; "'Comendi te mille demonibus, maledicte fili, et fratrem tuum qui hic tecum est, qui etiam de decepit. Mea maledictio vobiscum sit perpetuo, que vos infernalibus commendet spiritibus'."
[45] *Salimbene*, 62, 97–8; *Vitae Fratrum*, IV. 13.8, 17.3, 22.3 (pp. 186, 201, 211); *Eccleston*, 93–6. And see Livarius Oliger, "De pueris oblatis in Ordinis Minorum (cum textu hucusque inediturm Fr. Iohannis Pecham)," *AFH*, 8 (1915), 389–447; Livarius Oliger, "De pueris oblatis in Ordinis Minorum: Additamentum," *AFH*, 10 (1917), 271–88; John Moorman, *A History of the Franciscan Order from its Origins to the Year 1517* (Oxford: Clarendon Press, 1968), 343–4; and T. P. Dolan, "Richard FitzRalph's 'Defensio Curatorum' in Transmission," in Howard B. Clarke and J. R. S. Phillips (eds), *Ireland, England and the Continent in the Middle Ages and Beyond: Essays in Memory of a Turbulent Friar, F. X. Martin, OSA* (Dublin: University College Dublin Press, 2006), 185–6.
[46] See above, n. 9. See also Ch. 4.
[47] Wilhelm Wiegand and Aloys Schulte (eds), *Urkunden der Stadt Strassburg*, ii (Strasbourg: Karl J. Trübner, 1886), no. 150 (p. 106; July 28, 1288): "ut nullum de civitate predicta infra etatis sue annum octavum decimum constitutum absque parentum suorum consensu in ordine predicto reciperant, et quod ad observationem hujusmodi et quorundam aliorum articulorum similium se per suas patentes litteras obligarent."
[48] App. I, no. 74.

in any case antagonizing circumstances.[49] Thus both literary and archival sources attest one contentious aspect of the friars' routine activities, which could and at times did precipitate violent responses.

There were further grounds for tension. Among the better-documented conflagrations of antimendicant resentment and violence were those prompted by the friars' settlement in centers of higher education such as Paris, Salamanca, Cambridge, and Oxford.[50] Despite a propitious initial reception, friars in each of these cities soon clashed with the resident faculty and the local clergy largely in response to their successful recruitment of students and what was perceived as opportunistic academic tactics, as exemplified by the conduct of some orders during the Paris university strikes in the thirteenth century. These chapters in the friars' early history have won due attention, especially thanks to an outpouring of polemical literature from all parties involved. It is important to note, however, that, even in the context of these heated confrontations between secular and mendicant academics, few among the former called for the eradication of the latter. As argued in the previous chapter, William of St Amour's voice in the 1250s was indeed that of the crier in the desert.[51] Few among his cronies, let alone among his supposed later followers, explicitly sought to abolish religious mendicancy from the hierarchy of the church.

Even in regions where friars were active as inquisitors, at least some hostility seems to have been motivated by their material success, or rather its perceived threat to the steady income of existing monasteries and clerical prebends. Thus in the early thirteenth century the Benedictines of Prouille in Languedoc tried to regain by force the first female convent to come under Dominican rule—an event duly noted by the Dominican inquisitor and historian Bernard Gui (1261/1–1331), who was probably keen to underscore instances of antagonism toward his brethren that were ostensibly unrelated to their inquisitorial duties.[52] Yves Dossat's study of opposition to the friars in southern France lists several similar cases: in 1269 Cluniacs sacked the Carmelite convent at Mézin; in 1272 a prior at Rabastens led a beating and expulsion of the local Franciscans; and in 1291 the Franciscans recently settled at Agen were beaten by a mob gathered by a Cluniac prior, who pillaged their convent and injured three brothers.[53] Much like the rejection of the Franciscans in a northern French town by local Benedictines in 1233,[54] that of the Sack Friars by

---

[49] A. H. Thomas (ed.), *Calendar of Select Pleas and Memoranda of the City of London*, iv (Cambridge: Cambridge University Press, 1932), 182.

[50] M.-M. Dufeil, *Guillaume de Saint-Amour et la polémique universitaire parisienne, 1250–1259* (Paris: Picard, 1972); V. Beltran de Heredia, "El convento de s. Esteban en sus relaciones con la iglesia y la universita," *La Ciencia Tomista*, 84 (1926), 95–116; Gordon Leff, *Paris and Oxford Universities in the Thirteenth and Fourteenth Centuries: An Institutional and Intellectual History* (New York: John Wiley and Sons, 1968), 34–47; A. G. Little, "The Friars v. the University of Cambridge," *EHR*, 50 (1935), 686–96.

[51] *De periculis*, 18–22.

[52] *De fundatione*, 10–11. And see Simon Tugwell, "For Whom Was Prouille Founded," *AFP*, 74 (2004), 5–125; Julie A. Smith, "Prouille, Madrid, Rome: The Evolution of the Earliest Dominican Instituta for Nuns," *JMH*, 35 (2009), 340–52.

[53] Dossat, "Opposition des anciens ordres à l'installation des mendiants," 286–91.

[54] *BF* i. 110–11 (Virgiliacum?).

the citizens of Worms in 1264,[55] and the assault led by a local bishop on the newly arrived Franciscans in Orense in 1289,[56] none of these incidents appears to have been a direct response to the friars' inquisitorial activities.

Mendicant apologists such as Gui were probably interested in offsetting the hostility facing friars in their capacity as inquisitors or, as the next section suggests, in mitigating the frequent charges against friars as abusers of privileges. For our present purposes, however, the degree to which the friars' lachrymose history may or may not be valid matters less (the term itself is discussed in Chapter 4). Rather, it is the fact that the majority of cases encountered so far appear to expose the very quotidian nature of aggression against the friars. It is difficult to discern an ideology of Williamine antifraternalism among Cluniacs eager to maintain their estate, local residents wary of supporting a band of scruffy and incomprehensible monks, or parents struggling to direct their children's destiny.

The abuse of privileges

Despite some resistance, the friars' early success has been aptly described as meteoric. In less than sixty years of activity they established over a thousand convents across Europe—a number that increased more than fourfold by the early sixteenth century[57]—and virtually altered the continent's ecclesiastical map.[58] The mendicants' popularity reflected their broad appeal, especially in urban centers.[59] Yet their swift spread was also aided by a number of papal dispensations to administer certain sacraments and in general recognition of their ministry. It was these universal privileges, alongside others, more local by nature, that brought the friars into rather bitter confrontation with the clergy, traditional monks, and civic authorities, who accused them of hypocritically abusing their unique status. The charge's rhetorical force—as William of St Amour was well aware—derived from the juxtaposition of the brethren's

---

[55] Kaspar Elm, "Ausbreitung, Wiksamgeit und Ende der Provençalischen Sackbrüder (Fratres de Poenitentia Jesu Christi) in Deutschland und den Niederlanden," *Francia*, 1 (1973), 267.

[56] App. I, no. 47. And see María del Mar Graña Cid, "La Iglesia Orensana durante la crisis de la segunda mitad del siglo XIII," *Hispania sacra*, 42/86 (1990), 701–2.

[57] Richard. W. Emery, *The Friars in Medieval France: A Catalogue of French Mendicant Convents, 1200–1550* (New York and London: Columbia University Press, 1962), 1–17. By 1300 there were 280 Franciscan and Dominican foundations across the Rhine. See John B. Freed, *The Friars and German Society in the Thirteenth Century* (Cambridge, MA: Medieval Academy of America, 1977), 22–3. According to David Knowles and R. Neville Hadcock, *Medieval Religious Houses: England and Wales* (London: Longman, 1971), 492, (Table H), by 1350 there were nearly 200 mendicant foundations in England. For parallel data on Scotland and Ireland, see, respectively, Ian B. Cowan and David E. Easson, *Medieval Religious Houses: Scotland*, 2nd edn (London: Longman, 1976), 114–42, 152–5; Aubrey Gwynn and R. Neville Hadcock, *Medieval Religious Houses: Ireland* (London: Longman, 1970), 208–305, 307–26. John R. H. Moorman, *Medieval Franciscan Houses* (St Bonaventure, NY: Franciscan Institute, 1983), p. ix, claims that by the division of the Franciscan order in 1517 there were around 4,500 houses spread from Beijing to Cuba.

[58] Hans-Joachim Schmidt, "Establishing an Alternative Territorial Pattern: The Provinces of the Mendicant Orders," in Michael Robson and Jens Röhrkasten (eds), *Franciscan Organisation in the Mendicant Context: Formal and Informal Structures of the Friars' Lives and Ministry in the Middle Ages*, Vita Regularis, 44 (Berlin: Lit, 2010), 1–18.

[59] Lester K. Little, *Religious Poverty and the Profit Economy in Medieval Europe* (Ithaca, NY: Cornell University Press, 1978).

professed humility and their alleged arrogance. If in the eyes of some the habit did not make the monk, in the eyes of many others the friars' special privileges undid much of their initial appeal.[60]

Some of the violent events described above in connection with the friars' early mission and settlement may overlap with the present category of assaults perpetrated ostensibly in response to the friars' abuse of privileges, but the available records do not always enable a neat distinction between the two. Certainly the friars' relative independence from local bishops and, in the case of academic towns, the university's central institutions won them some staunch enemies. Yet numerous incidents can be more directly linked to the friars' real or perceived abuse of privileges. In 1283 the mayor and council of Strasbourg limited the mendicants' rights of inheritance and conditioned the entry of oblates under the age of 18 by their parents' consent. As happened before in Paris, the local Franciscans decided to comply, however grudgingly, while the Dominicans dragged their feet. In early May 1287 several residents, claiming to be backed by the city's magistrates, decided to take matters into their own hands.[61]

What, if any, occasion directly triggered their action remains unknown, yet contemporary accounts convey a consistent picture of what ensued. In an urgent letter to the civic leaders of Strasbourg, the bishop of Tusculum (Frascati) and papal legate to the region fulminated against the citizens' actions:

You violently invaded the houses of those [Dominican] friars with hatchets and horrible cries, breaking the door of that house and terrifying the besieged brethren with many other injuries; and, what is more dreadful, as it is said, you locked those men completely, lest any of the faithful approach them, and no one was allowed to leave.[62]

In a letter written later that month, Bishop Heinrich von Regensburg, the Dominicans' Protector in Germany, added several details in recounting how the Strasbourg laity

revolted against those poor and unarmed [friars] in an uproar, and with an indiscriminate hand invaded the doors of their homes and workshops with hatchets; then, savagely tearing up [the convent from within], the men struck terror with such a lewd rage of their fury, that all alike thought they [i.e., the friars] would lose their lives. Nor were the men satisfied until they had sealed the broken and open doors with strong wooden beams, so that they could not serve as exits, thereby reducing the friars' house to a prison.[63]

---

[60] A. G. Little, *Studies in English Franciscan History*, The Ford Lectures in 1916 (Manchester: Manchester University Press, 1917), 55–122, provides an honest if sympathetic account of the friars' brief golden age.

[61] The event is well documented in Heinrich Finke (ed.), *Ungedruckte Dominikanerbriefe des 13. Jahrhunderts* (Paderborn: Ferdinand Schöningh, 1891), 36–41. For a recent synthetic treatment, see Sandrine Turck, *Les Dominicaines a Strasbourg entre prêche, prière et mendicité (1224–1429)* (Strasbourg: Société Savante d'Alsace, 2002), 39–45.

[62] Wiegand and Schulte (eds), *Urkunden der Stadt Strassburg*, ii, no. 114 (p. 70; May 14, 1287): "violenter domos ipsorum fratrum cum securibus et horrendis clamoribus invasistis frangendo ipsius domus ostia aliasque fratribus opsis multiplices injurias orrogando et, quod est immanius, ipsos, ut dicitur, undique reclusistis, ne ad ipsos pateat fidelibus accessus et eis omnino prohibeatur egressus."

[63] Wiegand and Schulte (eds), *Urkunden der Stadt Strassburg*, ii, no. 118 (p. 74): "contra ipsos puperes et inermes tumultu et manu hostili temere insurrexerunt ac portas domus sue et officinarum hostia securibus invaserunt, [interna] quoque ferociter lacerantes sic fuoris sui inpudica vehementia

Both authors sought to depict the aggressors as a crazed crowd. Yet the hatchets they wielded were only partly destructive, and mostly *con*structive. It is not the impious threat of death but rather the forced cloistering of the friars that emerges from these texts as the citizens' essential act: the humbling of those who should be professionally humble, the external disciplining of those who ought to inspire Christian perfection by those who ought to be inspired. From this perspective, raw violence or its threat superficially mask an eloquent critique, not untouched by irony, of the brethren's conduct. And it demonstrates by contrary example how the absence of power, and not its presence, can lead to extreme violence.

Such airing of grievances, however articulated, was not an isolated event. Envy, alarm, and measured rage were common responses, especially among the clergy, to the friars' popularity and material success. The cup was brimming with allegations brought forward by those disaffected by the brethren's disproportionate power and privilege.[64] If already in 1220 Jacques de Vitry, bishop of Acre, expressed his frustration at how his clergymen were slipping away and into the ranks of the new dangerous orders,[65] scarcely a generation later, the Archbishop of Pisa Federigo Visconti (*c*.1200–77) felt compelled to remind his flock about the friars' unique role in their spiritual welfare.[66] Visconti, along with Robert Grosseteste, bishop of Lincoln (d. 1253), has often been celebrated as an eloquent and vocal supporter of the friars, an eager witness to their rising star.[67] But, set against the backdrop of growing friction between the brethren and the secular and regular clergy, the defensive tone of such encomiums becomes apparent. For, while Grosseteste could occasionally don a Franciscan habit in loving emulation, many of his colleagues were evidently finding it ever more difficult to show emphatic support for the friars or to rise above the endless litigation with them over burial rights,

---

terruerunt, quod vitam suam perdidisse omnes pariter putaverunt, nec hiis contenti omnes portas fractas et apertis sic tabulis ligneis et fortibus obstruxerunt, quod ipsis egredi non valentibus ita quod domus eorum in carcerem est redacta". Henrich specifies the names of fifteen men and sixteen "magistri et consules" who condoned or participated in the attack.

[64] Palémon Glorieux, "Prélats français contre religieux mendiants: Autour de la bulle 'Ad fructus uberes' (1281–1290)," *Revue de l'histoire de l'Église de France*, 11 (1925), 309–31, 471–95; Jean L. Copeland, "The Relations between the Secular Clergy and the Mendicant Friars in England during the Century after the Issue of the Bull *Super Cathedram* (1300)," MA thesis, University of London, 1937; Luigi Pellegrini, "Mendicanti e parroci: Coesistenza e conflitti di due strutture organizzative della '*cura animarum*'," in *Francescanesimo e vita religiosa dei laici nel '200. Atti dell'VIII Convegno Internazionale (Assisi, 16–18 ottobre 1980)* (Assisi: Universitá degli Studi di Perugia, 1981), 129–67; E. Cal Pardo, "Pleito promovido por los freiles de Santo Domingo y San Francisco de Viveiro contra los curas de las parroquias de Santa María y Santiago de dicha villa... Santiago. Rupeforte, 10.V.1334," *Estudios Mindonienses*, 7 (1991), 124–31; John V. A. Fine, *The Bosnian Church: A New Interpretation* (Boulder, CO: East European Quarterly, 1975), 185–6.

[65] Cited in Malcolm Barber and Keith Bate (eds and trans.), *Letters from the East: Crusaders, Pilgrims and Settlers in the 12th–13th Centuries* (Farnham: Ashgate, 2010), 123.

[66] Alexander Murray, "Archbishop and Mendicants in Thirteenth-Century Pisa," in Kaspar Elm (ed.), *Bettelorden und Wirksamkeit der Bettelorden in den städtischen Gesellschaft* (Berlin: Duncker & Humblot, 1981), 19–75. For Visconti's sermons, see Nicole Bériou (gen. ed.), *Les sermons et la visite pastorale de Federico Visconti, archevêque de Pisa (1253–1277)* (Rome: École française de Rome, 2001).

[67] Michael Robson, "The Greyfriars at Lincoln c.1230–1330: The Establishment of the Friary and the Friars' Ministry and Life in the City and its Environs," in Robson and Röhrkasten (eds), *Franciscan Organisation in the Mendicant Context*, 120.

tithes, preaching zones, and confessional jurisdictions. The sinister scenes of corpses being snatched and smuggled at night from mendicant to collegiate churches and vice versa,[68] the periodic expulsions of friars from numerous cities,[69] and other instances of aggression[70]—all speak volumes of the friars' tenuous links with local communities and their double-edged success.[71]

Military and political targets

Individual friars and mendicant houses were scarred by the numerous violent struggles—local and regional—that erupted across Europe in the thirteenth and fourteenth centuries. Whether during the prolonged disputes between England and Scotland (and later Ireland); in the factional strife between the papal and imperial parties throughout Italy and Germany; or in the so-called Peasants' Revolt converging on London in 1381—the brethren were threatened, beaten, abducted, robbed, expelled, and even killed; their convents seized, sacked, and occasionally razed and burnt.

From a purely tactical perspective, friaries were by and large occasional victims. It was not the mendicants' ideology or affiliation but their convents' wealth, location, and defensive potential that rendered them likely objectives of invading armies and victims of besieged cities.[72] Some recognized the imminent threat and asked to be relocated during such episodes.[73] Others stayed put, deluding themselves, like Erik the Viking, about the protective capacity of their habits. During a concerted English and Welsh attack on Scotland in 1335, for example, a number of sailors from Newcastle plundered Dundee and burned the local Franciscan convent, killing at least one friar in the process. The men's opportunism or developed

---

[68] E. B. FitzMaurice and A. G. Little (eds), *Materials for the History of the Franciscan Province of Ireland, AD 1230–1450* (Manchester: Manchester University Press, 1920), 91, 104–5; Luigina Carratori Scolaro et al. (eds), *Carte dell'Archivio Arcivescovile di Pisa, Fondo Luoghi Vari*, iii (Pisa: Pacini, 1999), nos 4–20 (8–82); Vito Tirelli and Matilde Tirelli Carli (eds), *Le pergamene del convento di S. Francesco in Lucca (secc. XII–XIX)* (Rome: Ministero per I Beni Culturali e Ambientali, 1993), nos 75–81, 83–99, 101, 103–13; Antonia Gransden (ed.), "A Fourteenth-Century Chronicle from Grey Friars at Lynn," *EHR*, 72 (1957), 270–8.

[69] *Glassberger*, 159.

[70] In 1272, the Canons Regular of Burgos were charged with instigating the mysterious disappearance of property titles and then of building materials meant for the city's new Dominican convent. See Peter Linehan, "A Tale of Two Cities: Capitular Burgos and Mendicant Burgos in the Thirteenth Century," in David Abulafia et al. (eds), *Church and City, 1000–1500: Essays in Honour of Christopher Brooke* (Cambridge: Cambridge University Press, 1992), 81–110. See also *Calendar of Patent Rolls*, Edward I, iv (London: HMSO, 1898), 79 (Exeter, 1301).

[71] Nor were the friars oblivious to the mounting claims. See, for instance, the anonymous treatise "Quedam dubia apud iuvenes," now part of a Franciscan miscellany at Milan, Biblioteca Ambrosiana, P25, fos 208^r–214^r.

[72] *Lanercost*, 172, 173–5; FitzMaurice and Little, *Materials*, 95. In 1365 the commune of Vivero in north-western Spain agreed to finance repairs to the local Dominican convent, which was damaged *during* the town's preparations for battle. See AGOP, XIV, Lib. I I I, fos 158^v–161^r (Nov. 1, 1356). For a parallel involving the Franciscans at Lincoln, see Robson, "The Greyfriars at Lincoln," 129. According to Linehan, "A Tale of Two Cities," 82, some Spanish convents fell victim to the unpredictability of rivers.

[73] *SBF* 28 and 170A.

sense of irony, however, is confirmed by the fact that they later sold the convent's confiscated bell to none other than the Dominicans of their native town.[74] On other occasions mendicant convents were altogether spared, either individually or along with other monastic houses, although at times the resident friars were replaced with brethren belonging to the triumphant side. Thus, when Edward III ejected the Scottish Augustinians from Berwick in 1333, he installed English friars in their stead, a policy he implemented again after removing French Augustinians from Calais in 1347.[75]

From a political perspective, the friars' fate in Ireland was markedly different. Lasting ethnic tensions between indigenous Irish and Anglo-Irish Franciscans escalated by the end of the thirteenth century, culminating in the infamous provincial chapter at Cork in 1291, where the brethren are reputed to have turned on one another, leaving sixteen men dead. In the early fourteenth century ethnic rivalry resurfaced as different brethren expressed their loyalties with the invading Scots and the ruling English, and it was this relationship—unique, it seems, to the Franciscans—that explains the invading armies' particular targeting of the friars between 1315 and 1317.[76]

More typical was the manner in which the Irish friars were lambasted for their diplomatic efforts on behalf of warring parties.[77] Across Europe, the mendicants' high public profile—notably as royal and princely almoners, confessors, emissaries, and administrators, as well as papal officials and crusade preachers[78]—meant they were prone to becoming embroiled in political strife. For their alleged involvement in a plot against Edward III, for instance, a number of English Carmelites and Dominicans were incarcerated and exiled by Parliament in 1330.[79] Other friars were not as lucky. In 1381 John of Gaunt's physician, the Franciscan William of Appleton, was killed by insurgents during the Peasants' Revolt for his alleged complicity in his master's failed leadership.[80] Ironically, later that year residents of Cambridge broke into the local Carmelite convent and proceeded to burn some of the friars' manuscripts in the market square, citing the brethren's role in stirring

---

[74] *Lanercost*, 282.
[75] Andrews, 103. According to *Lanercost*, 275, the departing Scottish friars despoiled the incoming English brethren of their books, chalices, and vestments.
[76] Cotter, 33–50; Niav Gallagher, "The Franciscans and the Scottish Wars of Independence: An Irish Perspective," *JMH*, 32 (2006), 3–17.
[77] Cotter, 54–9, 123–30, 157–60; Gallagher, "The Franciscans and the Scottish Wars of Independence."
[78] William Chester Jordan, "The Case of Saint Louis," *Viator*, 19 (1988), 209–17; Xavier De La Salle, *Le service des âmes à la cour: Confesseurs et aumôniers des rois de France au XIIIe au XVe siècle*, Mémoires et Documents de l'École des Chartes, 43 (Paris: École des Chartes, 1995); Rita Ríos, "The Role of the Mendicant Orders in the Political Life of Castile and León in the Later 13th Century," in Ausana Cimdiņa (ed.), *Religion and Political Change in Europe: Past and Present* (Pisa: Edizioni Plus, 2003), 21–32; Christoph T. Maier, *Preaching the Crusades: Mendicant Friars and the Cross in the Thirteenth Century* (Cambridge: Cambridge University Press, 1994).
[79] *Chronicon Galfridi le Baker de Swynebroke*, ed. Edward Maude Thompson (Oxford: Clarendon Press, 1889), 44.
[80] Jean Froissart, *Chroniques*, x, ed. Gaston Raynaud (Paris: Jules Renouard, 1897), 111; *Westminster*, 6.

up the same revolt[81]—a fate that also befell both the Dominicans and the Franciscans at York.[82] At least in some cases it seems the friars were easy scapegoats.

In most documented cases, however, rather than being directly identified with particular factions, it seems that the friars' ubiquity and their convents' accessibility placed them in the line of fire. Thus, again in 1381 London, a mob pursuing some resident Flemings, who were especially targeted during the revolt, invaded and damaged the local Augustinian convent, which the Flemings had entered for safety.[83] The pattern of collateral damage is repeated at different times and places: in 1276 a priest seeking refuge at the Franciscan convent in Nice was assaulted there;[84] in 1299 residents of Ludlow violently broke into the local Augustinian friary and seized another asylum-seeker, John le Berner;[85] in 1345 a Lombard residing in London was likewise followed by an angry mob into the Augustinian convent;[86] and in 1362 a criminal on the run, slipping into the Dominican convent in Pisa under the pretext of illness, precipitated a brutal sacking by the pursuing party.[87] As in military affairs, so in these instances, friars were probably the victims of circumstance, not targeted foes. That said, these cases make it clear that neither the mendicants' habit nor the popularity of their convents rendered them or their occasional protégés particularly safe.[88]

Unlike the unanticipated consequences of friaries' accessibility, the brethren's involvement in high politics and the broad support they received from those in power exposed them more directly to the winds of change. According to the continuator of the *Westminster Chronicle*, in 1384 a Carmelite confessor, who may have been mentally ill, implicated certain members of Richard II's court in a plot against the king. The friar was rushed off for safekeeping, but the carriage was seized and its secret human cargo severely tortured. He died of his severe injuries within days, never disclosing his source of information.[89] The following year, an English Franciscan described by the same chronicler as "a decent man but a manifest traitor to the kingdom" (*decens persona set proditor regni manifestus*) was intercepted carrying letters of credence from John of Vienne to Charles VI of France (1380–1422). He was imprisoned at the Tower of London and tortured until he died.[90] The trend's continuity into the early fifteenth century convinced

---

[81] Andrews, 62–4.
[82] Christian D. Liddy, "Urban Conflict in Late Fourteenth-Century England: The Case of York in 1380–1," *EHR*, 118 (2003), 25, 29.
[83] Jens Röhrkasten, *The Mendicant Houses of Medieval London: 1221–1539*, Vita Regularis, 21 (Münster: Lit, 2004), 290–2.
[84] Michel-Jean-Joseph Brial (ed.), *Majus chronicon lemovicense a Petro Coral et aliis conscriptum*, Recueil des Historiens des Gaules et de la France, 18 (Paris: Imprimerie Impériale, 1822), 788.
[85] William W. Capes (ed.), *The Register of Richard de Swinfield, Bishop of Hereford, AD1283–1317*, Cantilupe Society Publications, 3 (Cambridge: Chadwyck-Healey, 1979), 359.
[86] Röhrkasten, *The Mendicant Houses of Medieval London*, 290–2.
[87] AAPi, Atti straordinari 8, fo. 80^{r-v} (Feb. 14, 1362).
[88] See Dino Compagni, *Cronica*, III.10, ed. Isidoro Del Lungo (Florence: Successori Le Monnier, 1889), 186. On the proximity of mendicant convents to hotbeds of criminality and prostitution, see Ch. 3.
[89] *Westminster*, 66–81.
[90] *Westminster*, 136.

Eamon Duffy to accept that the Minorites' pro-Lancastrian stance under Henry IV (1399–1413) led to "more Franciscan friars [being] executed for preaching against Lancastrian dynastic usurpation than Lollards were burned for heresy."[91]

On the Continent, tensions between the competing claims of popes and emperors were paramount in shaping the friars' political fortunes. Most friars, most of the time, stood squarely on the papacy's side and were accordingly prone to incurring the emperor's wrath: the Franciscans in Reggio, Modena, and Cremona were ejected from their cities in 1249 for supporting Innocent IV against Frederick II;[92] their Parisian brethren were similarly expelled from the Capetian capitol in 1303 for their loyalty to Boniface VIII over Philip IV;[93] and, less than a generation later, Dominicans throughout Germany were ordered to leave their convents after lending support to John XXII against Louis IV of Bavaria.[94] Conversely, a number of high-profile Franciscan dissenters found refuge in that same emperor's court as their brethren were violently repressed by the pope from 1318.[95]

Tensions between local needs and the friars' strong links to the papacy continued to influence the orders' political fortunes and, consequently, their ability to carry out their tasks in diverse (and at times adverse) political climates. At least in the Franciscan case, drafting regulations for rapid evacuation was deemed wise already by the mid-thirteenth century.[96] And things would become only more complicated for them and the friars generally as their new recruits were increasingly drawn from local towns or their surrounding countryside, men and women who could not be reasonably expected to remain wholly aloof from local politics, often a clash between family networks of patronage.[97]

Anti-inquisitorial violence

The search for victimized mendicants yields a particularly rich crop among individuals and groups persecuted for heresy.[98] Of the 106 cases listed in the Appendix,

---

[91] Eamon Duffy, *The Stripping of the Altars: Traditional Religion in England, c1400–c.1580*, 2nd edn (New Haven and London: Yale University Press, 2005), p. xxiii. Duffy's statement is not corroborated by actual numbers, but see the *Continuatio Eulogii*, in Frank Scott Haydon (ed.), *Eulogium historiarum*, iii, Rolls Series, 9 (London: Longman, Brown, Green, Longmans, and Roberts, 1863), 389; and *The Chronicle of Adam Usk, 1377–1421*, ed. C. Given-Wilson (Oxford: Clarendon Press, 1997), 175. And see Caroline Barron, "The Deposition of Richard II," in John Taylor and Wendy Childs (eds), *Politics and Crisis in Fourteenth-Century England* (Gloucester: Alan Sutton, 1990), 132–49.
[92] Salimbene, 481–2.
[93] Michael Robson, *The Franciscans in the Middle Ages* (Woodbridge: Boydell, 2006), 144.
[94] *Chronica*, 22.
[95] See Hans-Joachim Schmidt, "Povertá e politica: I frati degli ordini mendicanti alla corte imperiale nel XIV secolo," in Giorgio Chittolini and Kaspar Elm (eds), *Ordini religiosi e società politica in Italia e Germania nei secoli XIV e XV* (Bologna: Il Mulino, 2001), 373–417.
[96] *Praenarb.*, 86–7 (no. 61; V. 16).
[97] On the brethren's provenance, see Ch. 3, n. 86. On the significance of urban kinship, see Jacques Heers, *Family Clans in the Middle Ages: A Study of Political and Social Structures in Urban Areas*, trans. Barry Herbert (Amsterdam and New York: North-Holland, 1977).
[98] Henry Charles Lea, *A History of the Inquisition in the Middle Ages*, ii (New York: Macmillan, 1906), 12–14, 16, 58–9, 214–18, 293–4.

22 appear to fall directly under this category. The frequency of these events is not simply an overrepresentation resulting from the extant documents, though a higher survival rate of inquisitorial records certainly plays an important role here. Rather, it is a reflection of the extreme feelings and high stakes (no pun intended) underpinning the friars' activities as papal inquisitors and those directing the strategies of resistance employed by religious dissidents. Those questioned, threatened, and tortured by inquisitors in Languedoc, Lombardy, and elsewhere stood to lose their lives, if not their souls. It is easy to understand, therefore, their recourse to violence against the chief agents of their impending demise.

On the other hand, anti-inquisitorial violence runs the risk of being the single most overrated aspect of medieval antifraternalism. It is often unclear if it was the friars, religious mendicancy, or an attempt by the papacy to impose religious doctrines that heretics and their diverse supporters were protesting against. Accordingly, locals may have targeted the friars for what they symbolized, such as papal or royal authoritarianism. Indeed, on several occasions in the early thirteenth century such tensions pitted Dominican inquisitors as papal representatives against local residents and their Franciscan allies, in whose convents they could often find a safe haven.[99] Conversely, among medieval Dominican historians of their order, inquisitorial activities were routinely glossed over and marginalized—so much so that one recent historian has dubbed Dominican inquisitors as "strangers to their own order," men whose excessive power and worldliness provoked "hesitation on the part of some and troubling silences among others."[100] And, although there is room for debate on the extent to which such views are representative of the order's members as a whole,[101] it seems that anti-inquisitorial violence is a tricky indicator of antifraternal sentiment.

To illustrate the diversity as well as ambiguity of violent assaults against friars as inquisitors, let us examine two related cases from northern Italy. According to the anonymous *Chronicon parmese*, on October 13, 1279 a servant by the name of Todescha stood to be burned as a heretic. She was convicted by the local Dominican inquisitor as an accomplice of her mistress, Oliva de Fredulfi, herself a confessed heretic who was likewise awaiting execution. Todescha's demise, then, seemed a foregone conclusion when, to the author's evident dismay,

certain evil men, driven by a diabolical impulse, ran to the lodgings of the Friars Preachers, entered them forcefully and looted the place, striking and injuring many of the brethren, and killing a certain friar by the name of Jacopo de Ferrara, who was an aged man and a virgin (as it was said) and who was blind and a member of the order for over forty years. And these incidents could not be stopped by [any] good men.[102]

---

[99] Given, *Inquisition and Medieval Society*, 131–9.
[100] Laurent Albaret, "Inquisitio heretice pravitatis: L'Inquisition dominicaine dans le midi de la France aux XIIIe et XIVe siècles ou la première inquisition pontificale," in Wolfram Hoyer (ed.), *Praedicatores, Inquisitores. I. The Dominicans and the Medieval Inquisition* (Rome: Istituto Storico Domenicano, 2004), 440. William A. Hinnebusch, *The History of the Dominican Order*, 2 vols (New York: Alba House, 1966–73), is a case in point.
[101] Prudlo, *The Martyred Inquisitor*, 97–102; Ames, 1–23. See also Ch. 4.
[102] Giuliano Bonazzi (ed.), *Chronicon parmese ab anno mcxxxvii usque ad annum mcccxxxviii*, Rerum Italicarum Scriptores, 9, pt ix (Città di Castello: S. Lapi, 1902), 35: "tamquam heretica . . . quidam

As in the description of the Strasbourg incident discussed previously, here too the chronicler strains to emphasize the crowd's savageness. True, unlike their Alsatian contemporaries, the Parmese immediately chased the Dominicans out of the city. But the supposed acme of their brutality, the slaying of a blind, sexually innocent old friar, could have been merely a case, however unfortunate, of collateral damage: as they ransacked the friary, only those who literally blindly rather than heroically stood in their way were hurt. No real obstacle presented itself had they truly wished to slay some of the brethren. No real obstacle, that is, except for their desire to communicate being in control of the situation, of being in power, by exercising and signaling their capacity for violence through its restraint.

The chronicler was also at pains to marginalize the perpetrators' action by demonstrating the city magistrates' commitment to the Dominicans' safety and to prosecuting their assailants. All to no avail, however, for the brethren left Parma, marched to Florence, and there convinced the resident papal legate to place their erstwhile host city under interdict. Curiously, the well-intentioned Parmese, despite profuse apologies, a pledge to finance the friary's reconstruction, and the swift punishment of the original assailants, failed to obviate the decree. More curiously still, it took the legate fully eight years to lift the interdict, finally permitting the Dominicans to return to their convent, which they did, triumphantly, in February 1287.[103]

The legate's implied pigheadedness hardly explains the lag, if indeed the violence was perpetrated by a hotheaded handful protesting the inquisitor's verdict of guilt by association. Was the chronicler misrepresenting the event by narrowing its scope? In other words, could Todescha's dubious conviction have merely triggered rather than galvanized a broader resistance to the inquisitors' presence or perhaps even to that of the friars more generally? Unfortunately, Parma's archives offer us nothing to prove or challenge the anonymous chronicler's version. Of the only other contemporary mentions of the event, one, a local chronicle written by a Franciscan Tertiary, matter-of-factly states that "all the Friars Preachers in Parma left the city and went to Reggio because the Parmese rebelled against them after they had a certain woman burned, who was said to be a heretic";[104] and the other, Salimbene's chronicle, subtly casts doubt on the validity of the

---

mali homines, instintu diabolico instigati, cucurerunt ad domos fratrum Predicatorum et ipsas per forciam intraverunt et expoliaverunt, et multos ex fratribus percuserunt et vulneraverunt, et quemdam nomine fratrem Jacobum de Ferariis interfecerunt, qui erat homo annosus et virgo, ut dicebatur, et qui non videbat et quo steterat in ordine per xl annos et plus; et predicta prohiberi non potuerunt per bonos homines."

[103] *Chronicon parmese*, 53. Despite the Dominicans' absence, at least one citizen remembered them in his will. ASPa, *Conventi*, S. Pietro Martire di Parma, Domenicani [= XXXI], B. 3, 12, attests that one Rolandus de Ardemanis of Parma endowed a *beneficium* associated with the church of Sant'Ambrogio, for which "specialiter elligatur et ponatur unus bonus et justus sacerdos per guardianos fratrum minorum et predicatorum di Parma."

[104] Albertus Milioli, *Liber de temporibus et etatibus*, ed. Oswald Holder-Egger, MGH SS 31 (Hanover, 1903), 554: "Et eodem anno fraters Predicatores omnes qui erant in civitate Parme recesserunt et venerunt Regium, quia Parmenses contra eos insurgerunt occasione cuiusdam mulieris quam dicebatur, quod erat caçara, et conburi eam fecerunt."

inquisitor's verdict.[105] (Neither author enters into any detail regarding the violence perpetrated, a decision that, as Chapter 4 will argue, may have had more to do with the victims' identity than a desire to exonerate the citizens.) A distant ray of light, however, may help illuminate the event's dynamics. It concerns a later incident in Bologna, envisaged, according to at least two participants whose confession was taken by the local inquisitor, as an attempt to expel the local Dominicans "as was done in Parma" (*sicud factum fuit Parme*)[106]—an explicit reference to the aforementioned events.

On May 13, 1299, the crowd gathered at Bologna's Piazza dell'Arengheria to witness the burning of two convicted heretics, Giuliano and Bompietro, and of Rosafiore, already long deceased but recently convicted as a relapsed heretic, became outraged when the Dominican inquisitors refused to allow one of the condemned men to confess his sins and die a reconciled Christian. The uproar nearly turned into a mob assault on the friars, but was eventually quelled; the inquisitors left the scene unharmed and continued to operate in the city. Indeed, within a few weeks their leader, Guido da Vicenza, called on anyone who may have witnessed the scene to volunteer information so that offenders could be brought to justice. The Bolognese came forth in droves to repeat what they said, but mostly what "they heard". Their extant depositions comprise a unique survey of attitudes toward inquisitors, yet they also preserve some of the concerns contemporaries had about the friars' conduct more generally.

For the confessions attest not only the outrage that followed the inquisitors' denial of a Christian death; they also disclose the friars' general unpopularity and reputation for corruption. Niccolò, son of Guido de Bonromeo of San Bartolo, claimed that, while awaiting the burning, he heard it said "that if the said Giuliano and Bompietro had had forty lire for bribing, what happened to them would not have happened."[107] Jacopo, a Dominican friar also present that day, overheard similar utterances. Yet he also testified to hearing the aforementioned Niccolò saying "that the friars were bad people; and he spoke other filthy things about the friars... [such as] that the friars were more worthy of being burned than the

---

[105] Salimbene, himself a *parmeggiano*, but no fan of the city's laymen, notes that the inquisitor "had her burned *as* a heretic" (*sicut caçcaram comburi fecerunt*) (emphasis added). Salimbene, 736–7.

[106] Bologna, Biblioteca dell'Archiginnasio, MS B. 1856 (antica 16*-gg-1-l), fo. 42ᵛ (testimony of Pasquale de Agubio, May 16, 1299). The second verbatim comparison to Parma was noted by Susan Taylor Snyder, "Orthodox Fears: Anti-Inquisitorial Violence and Defining Heresy," in Anne Scott and Cynthia Kosso (eds), *Fear and its Representations in the Middle Ages and Renaissance* (Turnhout: Brepols, 2002), 103. The inquisitorial register has been edited by Lorenzo Paolini and Raniero Orioli, *Acta S. Officii Bononie ab anno 1291 usque ad annum 1310*, 3 vols, Fonti per la Storia d'Italia, 106 (Rome: Istituto Storico Italiano per il Medio Evo, 1982–4). The most recent treatment of the event is Augustine Thompson, "Lay versus Clerical Perceptions of Heresy: Protests against the Inquisition in Bologna, 1299," in Wolfram Hoyer (ed.), *Praedicatores, Inquisitores I. The Dominicans and the Medieval Inquisition* (Rome: Istituto Storico Domenicano, 2004), 701–30. See also Dupré-Thes., 287–96.

[107] Bologna, Biblioteca dell'Archiginnasio, MS B. 1856, fo. 40ʳ (May 14, 1299): "quod si dicti Julianus et Bompetrus habuisset quadraginta lib. bon. pro sturione non contingisset sibi quod contingit."

said Bompietro and Giuliano."[108] Another man claimed to have overheard another person yelling (*in alta voce*) that "the inquisitor did this because the said Bompietro refused to give his sister or allow her [to go] to the inquisitor."[109] Tomasina, another local woman, admitted to having said "that the friars committed a grave sin and that the friars were more worthy of being burned than Bompietro and Giuliano."[110] And Chechola, daughter of Bartolomeo, simply asserted that "the inquisitor is the Devil."[111] Emotions evidently ran high, and the anonymity of the crowd afforded those with an axe to grind or a theory to air a misleadingly safe occasion to do so.

For other witnesses, the burnings were merely a point of departure. In his testimony, Bartholomeo, son of Ivan Barberi of San Vitale, tried to deflect allegations that he spoke against the friars by revealing that, "when two Friars Preachers *passed through his neighborhood*," a certain Francesco, son of Gerandello, said: "You Friars Preachers deserve a real beating."[112] In this way witnesses' memories meandered from the event at hand to their own (and others') personal encounters with the friars in different contexts. Contessa, wife of Giovanni Piero of San Leonardo, likewise confessed "that, when two Friars Preachers *passed through her neighborhood*, she said: 'Do not enter this house, for although it is big, there is nothing in it'"[113]— probably a mocking gesture to the friars' appetite, greed, and perhaps even curiosity, and a common *topos* of the friar as a *penetrans domos* (a penetrator of homes) found in the antifraternal literature surveyed in the previous chapter.

In her study of heresy in Orvieto, Carol Lansing argues that the city's first inquisitors—members of the Dominican Order—were treated like political or even military opponents rather than religious figures of authority.[114] That is, their victimization had more to do with local power struggles than with religious ideology. The Orvietan case is typical at least in the sense that, as in the cases cited above, it illustrates how diverse motivations for assaulting friars could be, even within the seemingly more cohesive category of anti-inquisitorial aggression. Moreover, the precise manner by which these events unfolded, insofar as they are knowable, tells us much about the relative strengths of competing claims: what type of force was

---

[108] Bologna, Biblioteca dell'Archiginnasio, MS B. 1856, fo. 40ʳ (May 14, 1299): "quod fratres erant mali homines et dicebat alia verba turpia de fratribus. Item, quod fratres essent plus digni conbustione quam dicti Bompetrus et Julianus."

[109] Bologna, Biblioteca dell'Archiginnasio, MS B. 1856, fo. 41ʳ (May 14, 1299): "inquisitor facit hec quia dictus Bompetrus noluit ei dare sororem suam nec consentire eam ipsi inquisitori."

[110] Bologna, Biblioteca dell'Archiginnasio, MS B. 1856, fo. 41ʳ: "quod fratres faciebant magnum peccatum et quod fratres erant magis digni conburi quam ipsi Bompetrus et Julianus."

[111] Bologna, Biblioteca dell'Archiginnasio, MS B. 1856, fo. 43ᵛ (May 18, 1299): "inquisitor est diabolus."

[112] Bologna, Biblioteca dell'Archiginnasio, MS B. 1856, fo. 42ʳ (May 16, 1299): "dixit, cum duo fratres predicatores transirent per contratum ipsius testis: 'vos fratres predicatores velletis tales bastonatas'" (emphasis added).

[113] Bologna, Biblioteca dell'Archiginnasio, MS B. 1856, fo. 43ʳ (May 18, 1299): "quod dum duo fratres predicatores transirent per contratam dicte testis ipsa testis dixit: 'nolite respicere in domum, quia domus magna est, tamen parum est in ea'."

[114] Lansing, 57–9. Lansing (pp. 137–50) argues that the relative success of a later wave of inquisition at Orvieto, administered by the Franciscans, as it happens, owed to and was shaped by these friars' social and political integration among the city's political elites.

employed, by whom, exactly against whom, where, to what ends, and before which audience—all of these are questions that help map local power in terms of a particular event.

Internal, sporadic, and opportunistic violence

It was no secret, as the next chapter will also demonstrate, that friars could be their own worst enemies, not only by their sometimes lax discipline, but also by committing unequivocally heinous crimes: Caesarius of Speyer, the first Franciscan Provincial in Germany, was either intentionally assassinated or grossly mishandled by a lay brother in 1239 while incarcerated for his strict views on poverty;[115] in 1297 Thomas, an English Carmelite, killed his coreligionist Henry of Oxford;[116] and in 1356 the guardian of the Franciscan house in Newcastle murdered friar Richard Pestel.[117] Most infamously, the Franciscan provincial chapter gathering at Cork in 1291 resulted in the death of some sixteen brothers.[118] True, such events were few and far between, but alongside the violent repression of the Franciscan Spirituals between 1318 and 1329—the outcome of a spiraling *internal* Franciscan dispute—it seems as though a significant portion of mendicant and pro-mendicant casualties were felled by mendicants.[119]

Other cases simply defy categorization in the absence of further details. Salimbene mentions "many rascals and evil doers" who prepared to pillage the Franciscan convent in Reggio in 1287 as well as a botched attempt to storm the Minorites in Monfalcone that same year.[120] It remains equally unclear why either the Pisans attacked the Minorites or the Neapolitans the Preachers in the early thirteenth century.[121] And one can only impute from Fernando III of Castile's (1199–1252) warning to the contrary that some sort of forced (and perhaps repeated) entries into the Dominican convents in Madrid raised the local brethren's concern.[122]

Criminal court records, which occasionally preserve cases of violence involving friars, can be no less frustrating. No grounds are specified, for instance, in a case brought against a monk by the name of Donabonum who, in 1289, led a mob assault against Adam, a Franciscan friar, while he was leading his brethren in prayer near Bologna.[123] Likewise, no grounds are ever specified when three men

---

[115] Angelo Clareno, *Historia septem tribulationum Ordinis Minorum*, ed. Orietta Rossini (Rome: Istituto Storico Italiano per il Medio Evo, 1999), 136–7.
[116] The National Archives: PRO JUST1/369/M22-OCarm.
[117] F. Donald Logan, *Runaway Religious in Medieval England, c.1240–1540*, Cambridge Studies in Medieval Life and Thought, 4th ser., 32 (Cambridge: Cambridge University Press, 1996), 244.
[118] Cotter, 33–50, questions the reliability of the reports, made by "hostile" Benedictine monks. Gallagher, "The Franciscans and the Scottish Wars of Independence," 7–8, restores their credibility.
[119] David Burr, *The Spiritual Franciscans: From Protest to Persecution in the Century after Saint Francis* (University Park, PA: Pennsylvania State University Press, 2001), 213–59. Among the casualties were twelve Franciscan friars, six priests, sixty-eight men, and sixteen women.
[120] Salimbene, 921, 937.
[121] App. I, nos 5 and 1, respectively.
[122] AGOP, XIV, Lib. I I I, fos 15^v–16^r: "que ninguno non sea osado de les fazer turbo, ni demas, ni entrar en sus casas por fuerza, ni en ninguna de sus casas."
[123] ASBo, Curia del podestà, Libri inquisitionum 16, fasc. 8, fos 32^r–43^r (Jan. 20–9, 1289).

(including a priest) were charged with wounding two Augustinian friars in Lucca in 1361;[124] when Agostino, rector of the church of San Iuso and San Lorenzo de Branchaio in the diocese of Lucca, allegedly assaulted Benedetto, a local Augustinian friar, in 1391;[125] or in the charge brought against Ludovico Cittadini of San Miniato in 1398 for assaulting another Lucchese Augustinian, Benedetto di Castro Fiorentino.[126]

Other records are more suggestive of opportunistic violence targeting friars and mendicant convents for material gain and in some cases sexual gratification: in 1334 three Bolognese men robbed Giovanni, a local Franciscan, of a piece of cloth, a tunic, and 40 soldi in cash;[127] a Polish Dominican traveling back from his order's general chapter in either 1338 or 1342 was attacked and robbed, losing little more than the recent chapter's decrees;[128] and in 1383, a Florentine vagabond named Naso abducted, robbed, and raped Francesca, a Poor Clare en route to her convent in Arezzo.[129] Convents were even more attractive targets: in 1355 the former mayor of Bristol broke into the local Augustinian convent and robbed it;[130] and in a similar vein were the London Carmelite and the Lucca Servite convents burglarized in 1305 and 1359, respectively.[131] In 1363 a Venetian named Antonio was charged with multiple burglaries, including at the city's Carmelite, Dominican, and Franciscan convents.[132] And in 1379 Cecco Pieri di Jacopo, another serial thief as well as a rapist and violent offender, broke into the Franciscan convent in Poggibonsi and threatened one of the brethren: "If you don't give me that money which is deposited here, I'll kill you!" For Cecco, the friar was evidently no enemy but merely an obstacle to cash.[133]

Here as elsewhere diversity of motivations continues to emerge as a defining characteristic of antifraternal violence. Over time, the more friars became woven into urban life and its institutions, the more likely they were to develop relationships—hostile as well as friendly—with local men and women. Yet, as already suggested in the above discussion of military and political violence, friars were equally prone to being victims of circumstance or injured as a situation's collateral damage. The mendicant garb, despite attempting to signal its bearer's poverty and holiness, failed to stop all assailants, who were perhaps aware of laymen's cynical use of religious habits, or the employment of friars as couriers of valuables and sensitive

---

[124] ASDL, Tribunale criminale 18, fos 102^r–103^v (Aug. 11–Nov. 8, 1361). A fragment of the original civic proceedings (dated 5 July) is tucked into the register's cover.
[125] ASDL, Tribunale Criminale 42, fo. 55^r (May 29, 1391).
[126] ASLu, Sentenze e Bandi 94, fo. 15^v (May 5, 1398).
[127] ASBo, Curia del podestà, Libri inquisitionum 137, fasc. 4, fo. 2^r (Mar. 30, 1334).
[128] App. I, no. 80.
[129] ASFi, Capitano del popolo 1521, unnumbered folios (May 25, 1383).
[130] App. I, no. 86.
[131] Thomas (ed.), *Calendar of Select Pleas*, 237; ASDL, Tribunale criminale 14, fo. 42^{r-v} (June 25, 1359).
[132] App. I, no. 91.
[133] ASFi, Capitano del popolo 1197, fos 147^v–148^r and 149^r (June 14, 1379): "Se to no me dai quigli denari, i quali sonno deposti equi, io te ocidero." The same record relates that Cecco robbed the local Augustinian convent as well.

documents.[134] As for mendicant convents, they suffered from a combination of being very accessible and increasingly well endowed.

ANTIFRATERNALISM AND THE IDIOM OF VIOLENCE

Evaluating the scale and exploring the scope of antifraternal aggression offers major correctives to the friars' social history. At the same time, the body of evidence it relies upon also furthers our understanding of medieval urban violence more generally. Conformist or heterodox, male or female, local or foreign—the friars' aggressors were seldom discreet. As the foregone pages make clear, most assaults were open and highly communicative events staged before an attentive and sophisticated audience.[135] This is not to argue that such events were always and everywhere ideologically coherent, or that their "thick description" could offer us a privileged view of medieval society's culture and cosmology.[136] Yet understanding these acts as a form of messaging can reveal much about local power relations and participants' status, goals, and the methods deployed to achieve them in an urban setting.

In his classic ethnography of Greek rural life, John Campbell documented an inverse relation between physical proximity and aggression: the further unrelated families' pastures lay (within the allotted territory of a village), the more likely they were to clash.[137] To urban sociologists, anthropologists, and historians, however, such a nexus seems almost paradoxical. For, contrary to popular notions of urban violence, it is seldom shrouded in a vale of anonymity.[138] Assaults on friars, being largely urban affairs, present no exception. As public, communicative events, aggressive acts against mendicants were often exercises in community building or community safeguarding in response to perceived threats on its stability.[139] Medieval urban dwellers appear to have fostered a sense of community and identity, to

---

[134] Dino Compagni, *Cronica*, III.10, ed. Isidoro Del Lungo (Florence: Successori Le Monnier, 1889), 184, notes that in 1304 many among the Florentine Blacks "clad themselves as friars for fear of their enemies, for they had no other defense."

[135] On the medieval city as a theatre of violence, see Claude Gauvard, *Violence et ordre public au Moyen Âge* (Paris: Picard, 2005); David Nirenberg, *Communities of Violence: Persecution of Minorities in the Middle Ages* (Princeton: Princeton University Press, 1996); Esther Cohen, "'To Die a Criminal for the Public Good': The Execution Ritual in Late Medieval Paris," in D. Nicholas and B. Bachrach (eds), *Law, Custom, and the Social Fabric in Medieval Europe: Essays in Honor of Bryce Lyon* (Kalamazoo, MI: Medieval Institute Publications, 1990), 285–304.

[136] Clifford Geertz, "Thick Description: Toward an Interpretive Theory of Culture," in *The Interpretation of Cultures* (New York: Basic Books, 1973), 3–30. For a recent critique, see Daniel M. Goldstein, *The Spectacular City: Violence and Performance in Urban Bolivia* (Durham, NC, and London: Duke University Press, 2004).

[137] J. K. Campbell, *Honour, Family and Patronage. A Study of Institutions and Moral Values in a Greek Mountain Community* (Oxford: Oxford University Press, 1964).

[138] See Joan McCord (ed.), *Violence and Childhood in the Inner City* (Cambridge: Cambridge University Press, 1997); Catherine Lutz, *Homefront: A Military City and the American 20th Century* (Boston: Beacon Press, 2001); Elisabeth Crouzet-Pavan, "Violence, société et pouvoir à Venise (XIVe–XVIe siècles): Forme et evolution de rituels urbains," *Mélanges de l'École française de Rome: Moyen âge*, 96 (1984), 903–36.

[139] Edward Muir, "The Idea of Community in Renaissance Italy," *Renaissance Quarterly*, 55 (2002), 1–18.

which friars were at times construed as a disruptive force: aliens to a place, be it a town, a university, a linguistic region, or the church at large. It was especially crucial here for antagonists to present them as menacing outsiders, often in the face of strong local connections and patronage networks. The discourse of foreignness or unindigenousness, in other words, was never limited to the brethren's opponents among non-Christians or even heretics.

Thus in 1255 Londoners were outraged to learn that the local Franciscans were protecting a number of Lincoln Jews who were in town to be tried for their alleged involvement in the murder of Little St Hugh. Support for the brethren's kindness melted away as they were rumored to be motivated by the promise of Jewish money. The friars were soon ostracized by local residents to the point of starvation, according to Matthew Paris, the monastic chronicler on duty. Paris, hardly a fan of mendicants, nonetheless drew a telling parallel between what he considered a lamentable affair and the Dominicans' recent imbroglio at Paris, where they and their students refused to participate in the university's declared strike: "And just as Londoners' devotion grew tepid toward the Minorites, so did Parisians' charity chill toward the Friars Preachers, who tried to harm the ancient and approved customs of the University."[140] As when defending Little St Hugh, here too the friars were charged with destroying the boundaries that defined local communities. And in both cases they were punished for it, despite the fact that they had long been active members in their localities. Indeed, the severity of the sanctions in both cases was directly related to local familiarity with the friars.

Characterized by sufficient acquaintance between clashing parties, and based upon a shared symbolic language,[141] such aggression sheds further light on what a growing number of medieval social historians have been engaged in defining as the medieval urban public sphere.[142] However spontaneous it may have been, antifraternal violence was a highly scripted process. Putting the friars "in their place" involved messaging all those engaged in the articulation of urban space and the definition of civic identity. This helps explain why, for instance, only three of the acts I was able to document occurred in the

---

[140] Matthew Paris, *Chronica Majora*, v, ed. Henry Richards Luard, Rolls Series, 57 (London: Longman, 1880), 546: "Et sicut Londoniensium tepui devotio penes Minorum, ita et Parisiensium refriguit caritas versus fratres Praedicatores, qui universitatis antiquas et approbatas consuetudines conati sunt infirmare." Two other annalists cast Dominicans, not Franciscans, as the protagonists in the London affair. See Henry Richards Luard (ed.), *Annales monastici*, i, Rolls Series, 36 (London: Longman, Green, Longman, Roberts, and Green, 1864), 347; and *Lanercost*, 24. On this discrepancy, see Ch. 4.

[141] John K. Brackett, "The Language of Violence in the Late Italian Renaissance: The Example of the Tuscan Romagna," in Donald J. Kagay and L. J. Andrew Villalon (eds), *The Final Argument: The Imprint of Violence on Society in Medieval and Early Modern Europe* (London: Boydell, 1998), 97–105; Charles V. Phythian-Adams, "Rituals of Personal Confrontation in Late Medieval England," *Bulletin of the John Rylands Library*, 73 (1991), 65–90.

[142] Gerd Althoff, *Family, Friends and Followers: Political and Social Bonds in Medieval Europe*, trans. Christopher Carroll (Cambridge and New York: Cambridge University Press, 2004), esp. 65–101, 136–59; Daniel Lord Smail, *The Consumption of Justice: Emotions, Publicity, and Legal Culture in Marseille, 1264–1423* (Ithaca, NY, and London: Cornell University Press, 2003); Carol Symes, *A Common Stage: Theater and Public Life in Medieval Arras* (Ithaca, NY: Cornell University Press, 2007), 126–82.

countryside or along highways, which were less accessible, where fewer witnesses were at hand, and where the environment was less coded in a manner fitting urban social relations. By contrast, the mendicant convent, with its typically open design, the civic square, the market, the courtroom (where even evidence from the countryside was discussed), and the local cathedral were all visible, accessible, and familiar arenas for the display and negotiation of identity. As such they constituted mainstays of the medieval public sphere, where acts of violence—as well as of pacification—were more effectively enlisted into partisan service.

Conversely, and as will be more fully explored in Chapter 4, friars subjected to acts of violence were fully aware of its performative and communicative aspects, on both a political and a spiritual register.[143] Accordingly, they used such incidents to underline specific messages such as their vulnerability as the church's vanguard, their apostolic dedication, their independence of (or dependence on) urban governments and local bishops, their utter subordination to the papacy or its direct representatives, and so forth. In the hands of late-medieval mendicants and their supporters, violence and identity were variously intertwined in a discourse of victimhood.

As already mentioned, numerous students of violence have argued that one salient gesture of aggression is the display of moderation: vis-à-vis its capacity for violence, a group's restraint signaled the degree of power to which it laid claim. While plausible and often apt, the inverse relationship between violence and power is at times rather difficult to pin down so precisely. Furthermore, as James C. Scott has famously shown, sheer violence is scarcely the only weapon in the arsenal of the weak. Passivity in the face of authority and hegemonic social order can be no less effective or at least meaningful as a gesture of individual or collective resistance.[144] One must, then, establish rather than assume whether inaction is a willing expression of restraint or a manifestation of fear; and whether unleashing an assault reflects a lack, ignorance, or eventual exhaustion of alternatives.

CONCLUSIONS

Assaults on medieval friars were evocative but ultimately uncommon events, whose unity across space and time is further challenged by the diversity of their circumstances. Even if the overall effect of recounting these incidents is to underscore the brethren's suffering, little if any antimendicant sentiment binds them together. By itself, the total-contrarian rhetoric of William of St Amour apparently failed to resonate either broadly or down the centuries. Grievances against the brethren were no less real for that matter, but they had more to do with real or perceived threats to social order than with any coherent ecclesiology.

---

[143] Ames, 57–93.
[144] James C. Scott, *Weapons of the Weak: Everyday Forms of Peasant Resistance* (New Haven and London: Yale University Press, 1985), 28–37.

Examining antimendicant aggression in detail likewise exposes the fallacy of collapsing antifraternalism into anticlericalism. Just as most antifraternal literature was composed for and by clerics, so a significant portion of the surveyed cases was instigated or led by monks and secular clergymen. In other words, assaults on friars were commonly an ecclesiastical inhouse affair, notwithstanding the major role played by individual laymen and their contingents.

Last, beyond informing mendicant history per se, the brethren's victimization attests contemporaries' critical stance toward putative figures of religious authority, a stance that could and at times was articulated in the idiom of violence. Interrogating the extant sources allows us to qualify allegations of sheer brutality, which they sometimes sought to convey, or its lack, which they occasionally tried to elide. Carefully reading narratives of such violence allows us to focus on how aggression operated as a messaging system in the public sphere, and on how urban dwellers used it to describe, shape, or upset local power relations.

PART TWO

DEEDS AND WORDS: THE FRIARS AGAINST THEMSELVES

Introduction to Part Two

Heated polemics, biting satire, and physical aggression were a modest but painful aspect of the friars' early history. The assaults' circumstances, goals, and motivations varied widely across space and time, and their perpetrators, as explicated in Part One, included laypeople, clergymen, and even the brethren themselves, variously prompted by a desire to reform their orders, driven to action by intramendicant rivalry, or eager to maintain local networks of support. While the latter occasions imply at least some measure of agency among the friars, they only indirectly generated resentment toward religious mendicancy. However, the brethren contributed to the development of an antifraternal tradition in two rather more straightforward ways.

The first was through their misbehavior. The friars' mischief is recounted in numerous contemporary tales, and as such it continues to be taken as firm evidence of their dubious morals and lax discipline. This book opened by making a case for carefully distinguishing between social realities and the fabrications of authors such as Jean de Meun, Boccaccio, and Chaucer. In the first of the following chapters, however, we reverse this perspective by returning to the brethren's misbehavior as documented by their orders' administrative accounts. These disclose an ongoing struggle of local and regional priors against their underlings' deviancy, not only for the sake of the latter's spiritual salvation, but also, and one suspects at times especially, out of fear of public scandal and even reprisal.

But if some friars authored this aspect of an antifraternal tradition unwittingly, Chapter 4 explores a second and more conscious effort to bolster it—namely, the framing of the brethren's suffering as a pillar of mendicant identity and of the orders' lachrymose history. Here we are no longer concerned with the rhetoric of fallenness and reform, but rather with the friars' active remembrance of their victimhood in a mode designed to underscore the orders' eschatological role as the church's vanguard and by extension their unique status and privileges. This chapter will show how mendicant writers and their supporters shaped their past for their own corporate benefit, thereby completing our survey of the development of medieval antifraternalism. The friars' performed deeds (Chapter 3) as well as their written words (Chapter 4) complement the picture painted in Part One, not only through relying on different sources but also by demonstrating the shifting agency of antifraternal resentment from assailant to victim and back.

3

Deviance: Brethren Behaving Badly

> I was trying to grasp why the splendor of our Order has been somewhat obscured.
>
> Bonaventure, *First Encyclical Letter* (1257)[1]

Harsh as they could be, words and deeds directed against the friars leave us unapprised of the brethren's actual misconduct and what role, if any, it might have played in obscuring the early splendor of their orders. As we have seen in Chapter 1, mendicant deviancy was usually construed by their critics in terms of a failure to imitate Christ and the Apostles or—somewhat closer to home—as a departure from the admittedly narrow paths set by the orders' founders. When antifraternal resentment occasionally took a violent turn, as explored in Chapter 2, allegations assumed a seemingly more concrete form, from shady recruitment practices of children to treason and espionage. Yet most extant sources—chronicles, letters, court records—seldom reveal much about the pre-history of such assaults. Thus the rhetoric of spiritual or moral fallenness, on the one hand, and the opacity of the sources regarding antifraternal violence, on the other, prevent us from assessing the friars' behavior and in turn impede a well-rounded reconstruction of antifraternal resentment from a social perspective. To do so we must ponder, along with the Franciscan Minister General Bonaventure, what, on earth, went wrong.

A NORMATIVE APPROACH TO ANTIFRATERNALISM

The present chapter explores whether or not there is room for understanding opposition to the friars also as a reformist response to the brethren's deviance from a broad normative point of view: a perspective distinct, on the one hand, from that of monastic perfection, and, on the other, from a reactionary ecclesiology espoused by William of St Amour. It asks to what extent resentment of friars grew out of a genuine concern about the brethren's actual or perceived misbehavior on a human, rather than angelic, plane. To date, the question of the friars' deviancy has not been addressed in any comparative way beyond local studies and based on

---

[1] Bonaventurae of Bagnoregio, *Opera omnia*, viii (Claras Aquas [Quaracchi]: Typographia Collegii S. Bonaventurae, 1898), 469: "Sane perquirenti mihi causas, cur splendor nostri Ordinis quodam modo obfuscatur."

documents of practice covering the orders' first centuries of activity.[2] When it came to assessing mendicant unruliness, diverse modern scholars have been wont to take medieval poets and polemicists—including disgruntled members of the orders themselves—at their word. For instance, the prolific literary and theater historian Joseph Spencer Kennard (1859–1944), in several studies of friars in pre-modern texts, concludes that the friar's image as deceitful and immoral "represent[s] the typical friar as found in real life during those centuries."[3] The English Benedictine and doyen of monastic history David Knowles (1896–1974) asserts that "it is hard to escape the conviction" that Langland, Wyclif, and Chaucer "are in their different ways witnesses to a corruption among the mendicants...which was only too real."[4] And Gerald Harriss (b. 1925), an eminent parliamentary and administrative historian, remarks that the friars' "proselytizing and poverty made them butts for anticlerical satire and denunciations, exemplified in Langland and Chaucer and in the vitriolic attacks of Wyclif and the Lollards."[5]

While many medieval authors no doubt participated in shaping an antifraternal tradition, such statements by modern specialists and generalists alike run dangerously close to placing literary satire, doctrinal polemics, and the discourse of spiritual reform on a par with each other, and—no less disturbing—as straightforward historical sources that communicate an unmitigated social reality. One could expect as much from later religious propagandists such as James Salgado (fl. 1666–84; see Figures 3.1 and 3.2), a former Spanish priest who came out vehemently against the Catholic Church and the papal inquisition. His series of "histories" culled "out of several Authors of sundry Nations, who were Roman Catholicks themselves," relied strongly on the tales of Boccaccio and others.[6]

---

[2] A partial exception is R. F. Bennett, *The Early Dominicans: Studies in Thirteenth-Century Dominican History* (Cambridge: Cambridge University Press, 1937), 145–56. Local and regional studies include Peter Linehan, *The Ladies of Zamora* (Manchester: Manchester University Press, 1997), 41–76; Jens Röhrkasten, *The Mendicant Houses of Medieval London, 1221–1539*, Vita Regularis, 21 (Münster: Lit, 2004), 167–74; Sylvain Piron, "Un couvent sous influence: Santa Croce autour de 1300," in Nicole Bériou and Jacques Chiffoleau (eds), *Économie et religion: L'Expérience des ordres mendiants (XIIIe–XVe siècle)* (Lyons: Presses universitaires de Lyon 2009), 331–55; and Michael Vargas, "Weak Obedience, Undisciplined Friars, and Failed Reforms in the Medieval Order of Preachers," *Viator*, 42 (2011), 283–307. A parallel study for the Cistercian Order is A. Dimier, "Violence, rixes et homicides chez les Cisterciens," *Revue des sciences religieuses*, 46 (1972), 38–57.

[3] Joseph Spencer Kennard, "Some Friars in English Fiction," in *The Friar in Fiction, Sincerity in Art and Other Essays* (New York: Brentano's, 1923), 6. In Germany antimendicant writers conveyed a picture of "virulence and truth...but the great body of friary was gangrened to the core and no physician could avail, no medicine work a cure" ("The Friar in German Fiction," in *The Friar in Fiction*, 25–7). Friars who reached Dante's *Paradiso* did so on personal merits, rather than because of any mendicant affiliation. See "The Friars of Dante, Boccaccio and Machiavelli," in *The Friar in Fiction*, 86. And see, to a similar effect, Peter S. Taitt, *Incubus and Ideal: Ecclesiastical Figures in Chaucer and Langland*, Salzburg Studies in English Literature, 44 (Salzburg: Institut für Englische Sprache und Literatur, 1975), 20.

[4] David Knowles, *The Religious Orders in England*, ii (Cambridge: Cambridge University Press, 1961), 114.

[5] Gerald Harriss, *Shaping the Nation: England, 1360–1461* (Oxford: Clarendon Press, 2006), 332.

[6] James Salgado, *The Fryer, or An Historical Treatise*, 2 vols. in 1 (London, 1680), preface. The Boccaccian tales are mainly appropriated in the second, "comic" volume.

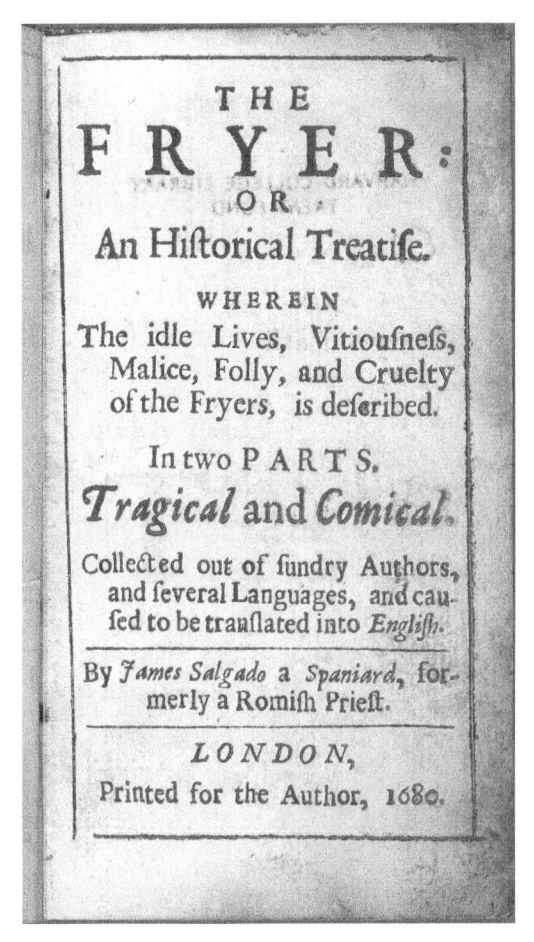

Fig. 3.1. Cover of James Salgado's *The Fryer* (1680) Typ 605.80, Houghton Library, Harvard University.

But different yardsticks should apply when it comes to a critical evaluation of the friars' behavior and its broad perception by contemporaries, all the more so when many alternative sources are available to that end. Indeed, numerous records afford a nuanced view of mendicant discipline both in and out of the convent: internal administrative correspondence, the *acta* of the orders' general and provincial chapters, and external documents of practice such as wills, ordinances, letters, and court protocols. Building on such records, the present chapter offers a fresh view of mendicant misbehavior. As such, however, it does not provide an explanation for the friars' deviance, real or perceived, or commit to the accuracy of internal documents describing disobedience. Nor does it suggest a cause-and-effect relationship between mendicant deviancy and allegations made against the brethren by their critics. Rather, as part of a multifocal study of medieval antifraternalism, it seeks to identify yet another strand of this tradition in which the friars took an active if unwitting role.

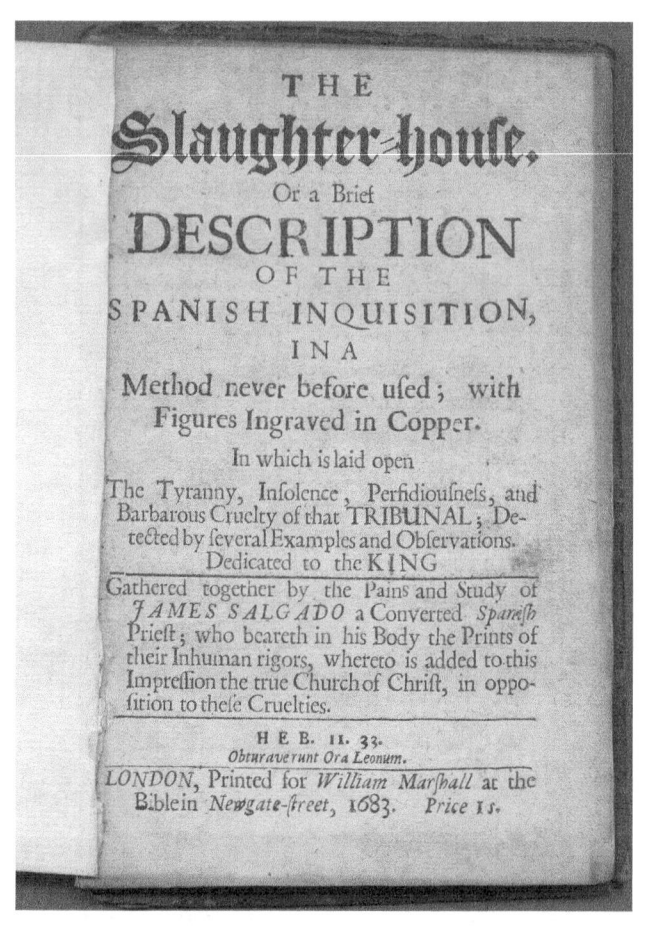

Fig. 3.2. Cover of James Salgado's *The Slaughter House* (1683) Courtesy of Columbia University Libraries.

Spotlighting mendicants' deviance is not an indictment of the orders themselves.[7] Friars' misconduct, as the Dominican scholar Thomas Masetti acknowledged long ago, is part and parcel of their history, although, unlike modern sociologists, he attributed delinquency to innate human corruption, not to social maintenance.[8] But

---

[7] Even if it contrasts with the idealized accounts of Galvano Fiamma, *Cronica Ordinis Praedicatorum ab anno 1170 usque ad 1333*, ed. Benedikt Maria Reichert, MOFPH 2 (Rome: In Domo Generalitia, 1897), 39–51; and Pietro Lippini, *La vita quotidiana di un convento medievale: Gli ambienti, le regole, l'orario e le mansioni dei frati domenicani del trecesimo secolo*, Collana Attendite ad Petram, 5 (Bologna: Studio Domenicano, 1990), 351–9.

[8] Thomas Masetti (ed.), *Monumenta et antiquitates veteris disciplinae Ordinis Praedicatorum ab anno 1216 ad 1348*, i (Rome: Camera Apostolica, 1864), 162: "Nec putare debemus temporibus de quibus disserimus, improbos defuisse, qui propriae immemores conditionis intra vel extra Claustra Praelatis haud modicas inferebant molestias; id nos inficiari nec volumus, nec possumus, quin etiam pluribus in

whatever its "origins," *official* deviance is simpler to define and identify among medieval friars (and monks) than it would be among most other contemporaries. After all, if there is any pre-modern candidate for the title of a "total" institution, it would be the monastery, for it, like the modern prison, military academy, or mental asylum, is "a place of residence and work where a large number of like-situated individuals, cut off from the wider society for an appreciable period of time, together lead an enclosed, formally administered round of life."[9]

True, friars were not as spatially confined as most medieval monks; in fact, they were often accused of being *gyrovagi*, or wanderers, famously detested by St Benedict.[10] But they did lead common, theoretically egalitarian, and highly regulated lives according to a written rule that was enforced by their superiors. Moreover, however ambiguous as a term, obedience was central to the friars' spirituality, and punishments meted out for undermining it were common and potentially harsh.[11] Whatever the peculiarities of mendicant life, normative borders were as explicit and well demarcated among medieval friars as within any monastic order, presenting the social historian and the historical sociologist with a useful site for studying the construction of deviancy.

In other words, there is a relatively clear divide between friars' licit and illicit conducts, at least from the point of view of the orders' normative texts and administrative records. And yet there has been no attempt to examine the frequency and character of mendicant indiscipline across Europe and prior to their internal reforms at the end of the fourteenth century. As a corrective, the first section of this chapter marshals data on mendicants' major infractions, especially among Dominicans. (Their major violations are listed in chronological order in Appendix II.) The relative gravity of an infraction has been determined on the basis of the act's description in the sources (usually some form of violence, sexual misconduct, or gross insubordination) and in view of the reprimand that ensued. By and large, major offenses were those punishable by incarceration, relocation, or banishment, rather than by lighter penances such as fasts, masses, or flagellations.

The focus on the followers of Dominic is due to the fact that, for the period under discussion, the order's pertinent documentation is superior to that of any

---

locis ingenue confessi sumus. Sed quoadusque homines erimus corruptae naturae miserias ferre cogimur, quas reprimere quidem ac coercere, extinguere vero non possumus."

[9] Erving Goffman, *Asylums: Essays on the Social Situation of Mental Patients and Other Inmates* (Garden City, NY: Anchor Books, 1961), p. xiii—commonly regarded as the seminal definition of the term "total institution." And see Michel Foucault, *Surveiller et punir: Naissance de la prison* (Paris: Gallimard, 1975); and Samuel E. Wallace (ed.), *Total Institutions* (Chicago: Transaction Books, 1971).

[10] Ramona Sickert, "*Extra obedientiam evagari . . . :* Zur zeitgenössischen Deutung der Mobilität von Franziskanern und Dominikanern im 13. Jahrhundert," in Sébastien Barret and Gert Melville (eds), *Oboedientia: Zu Formen und Grenzen von Macht und Unterordnung im mittelalterlichen Religiosentum*, Vita Regularis, 27 (Münster: Lit, 2005), 159–80; and Ramona Sickert, *Wenn Klosterbrüder zu Jahrmarktsbrüdern werden: Studien zur Wahrnehmung der Franziskaner und Dominikaner im 13. Jahrhundert*, Vita Regularis, 28 (Berlin: Lit, 2006), 191–9.

[11] Barret and Melville (eds), *Oboedientia,* is a recent re-examination of the term in the monastic context, exposing the variety of its meanings and, indeed, historical constructions. And see Thomas Füser, *Mönche im Konflikt: Zum Spannungsfeld von Norm, Devianz und Sanktion bei den Cisterziensern und Cluniazensern (12. bis frühes 14. Jahrhundert)*, Vita Regularis, 9 (Münster: Lit, 2000).

other major order, including the Franciscans, both in quantity and in precision.[12] As the acclaimed Franciscanist A. G. Little once admitted: "If you want to know what happened, the Dominicans will be the safest guides: if you want to know how it struck a contemporary... consult the Franciscans."[13] To avoid perhaps pleasing Little too much by marshaling evidence exclusively drawn from Dominican records, all subsequent sections report similar infractions among Augustinian, Carmelite, Servite, and Franciscan monks and nuns, although these are illustrative, not comprehensive.

Maintaining a distinction between reality and perception is crucial, for the available information cannot be evaluated in statistical terms alone. Deviant friars in any city or region were, by definition, few and far between. Yet, as the chapter's second section demonstrates, mendicants' high public profile amplified what otherwise might have been glossed over as isolated events and exposed the brethren, as they were well aware, to allegations of scandalous behavior. Most importantly, the friars' general disrepute, whether truthful or exaggerated, spread through different channels and could be manipulated to different ends: tensions between the church and urban regimes, the envy of clergymen and monks, local property disputes—all played a role. But, whatever the catalyst of infamy, it is deviancy itself, in conjunction with a reactionary ecclesiology, constant calls for reform, and the brethren's high public profile, which supplies a more satisfying context for the early development of antifraternal sentiments.[14]

DOMINICAN DEVIANCE: A CASE STUDY

In his nearly twenty years of service as master general of the Dominican order, Raymond of Capua (1330–99) dealt directly with numerous infractions perpetrated by his underlings. On what must have been a particularly demoralizing day, March 18, 1387, he addressed several disturbing incidents discovered among the Italian brethren. First, he asked Antonio, prior of Urbino, to look into allegations made against a certain fra Marino "regarding a crime committed by him in the city of Camerino" (*super crimine commisso per eum in civitate Camerinensi*). Should Marino confess his misdeed, which remains typically obscure, he is to be

---

[12] Franz Ehrle (ed.), "Die ältesten Redactionen der Generalconstitutionen des Franziskanerordens," *Archiv für Literatur- und Kirchengeschichte des Mittelalters*, 6 (1892), 1–138. A unique exception is Luzern, Zentralbibliothek, MS BB.129.4°, a Franciscan formulary excerpted in Clément Schmitt, "Documents sur la province franciscaine de Strasbourg aux XIV–XVe siècles d'après un formulaire de Lucerne," *AFH*, 59 (1966), 209–300, esp. 216–17 and no. 15 (235), which attest several major violations among local Minorites.

[13] A. G. Little, "Chronicles of the Mendicant Friars," in *Franciscan Papers, Lists, and Documents*, Publications of the University of Manchester, 284; Publications of the University of Manchester, Historical Series, 81 (Manchester: Manchester University Press, 1943), 41.

[14] A similar emphasis on deviant behavior over a religious world view is laid, albeit in a different polemical context, by Israel Jacob Yuval, *Two Nations in your Womb: Perceptions of Jews and Christians in Late Antiquity and the Middle Ages,* trans. Barbara Harshav and Jonathan Chipman (Berkeley and Los Angeles: University of California Press, 2006), 135–204.

incarcerated for six months at the order's prison in Faenza. Next, Raymond instructed Caterina, the prioress of St Archangel in Fermo, to imprison Sister Vagnola, "on account of the many crimes committed by her" (*propter crimina plurima per ipsam commissa*), specifying that, while incarcerated, she is to fast three days a week on bread and water. An accomplice of Vagnola's, Brother Venanzio of Camerino, was likewise to be imprisoned by the prior of Rimini "on account of the crime committed [by him] with the said Sister Vagnola" (*propter crimen commissum cum sorore Vagnola supradicta*). The day's labor was not complete, however, until Raymond dispatched yet another letter, this time to Ugo of Ravenna, prior of the Ancona convent, ordering him to incarcerate Brother Ugolino of Pesaro and examine him "regarding intolerable excesses repeatedly committed by him in the convents of Pesaro, Recanati, and others, and especially concerning what he did on a public way to the prior of Faenza" (*de intolerabilibus excessibus multoties per ipsum commissis in conventu Pesauriensi et Racanatensi et aliis, et maxime super quae fecit in strata publica priori Fanensi*).[15]

Raymond's extant correspondence suggests that, although March 18, 1387 may have been an unusually taxing day, the offenses themselves were typical both among and beyond the order's Italian convents and throughout its rank and file: the prior of Rimini was charged in 1389 with physically assaulting two of the brethren and destroying the convent's vineyards; Guillaume, a lay brother, was expelled from the convent at Bruges in 1390 for what appears to be theft; large-scale disobedience and *scandala* were detected at the Viterbo convent in 1390; in early 1398 Sister Ursula of Sechdorf (Eschdorf?) left her convent along with nine other sisters, all of whom refused to return until their joint sentence of excommunication had been lifted; later that year, Brother Ivo of Gladbach impregnated an unnamed sister at the convent of St Gertrude of Cologne while serving as her confessor; and so it goes on.[16] On average, the Dominican master general intervened in two or more major incidents a year, from internal uprisings to sexual promiscuity to theft and violence.

With one exception to be discussed below, Raymond's register is the only extant Dominican (and, so far as I am aware, mendicant) collection of quotidian correspondence prior to 1400, the cut-off date of the present study. Even assuming that the surviving dossier is complete, however, it probably relates a fraction of the friars' major violations in that period. What underlies this assumption is that the Dominican constitutions delegated disciplinary responsibilities down the order's hierarchy, from the master general, through the provincial *diffinitores* and priors, to the priors and subpriors of individual houses. In theory, then, few cases should have required Raymond's direct intervention, and little else by way of more local correspondence survives.[17] Further, even within the context of a general chapter, most disciplinary

---

[15] *Registrum*, "Provincia Lombardiae inferioris," 30–3 (10).

[16] *Registrum*, "Provincia Lombardiae inferioris," 147 (23); "Provincia Franciae," 9 (2); "Provincia Romana," 367–9 (99); "Provincia Teutoniae," 249–50 (150), and 279 (154).

[17] Humbert of Romans, "Instructiones de officiis ordinis" 1.4, in *Opera de vita regulari*, ed. Joachim Joseph Berthier, ii (Rome: Typis A. Befani, 1889), 184–5.

actions were discussed and concluded by tribunals appointed for that purpose, and without the master general's ruling.[18] From the standpoint of deviancy, therefore, Raymond's writings reveal the tip of an iceberg, notwithstanding his particular commitment to the order's moral reform.

One rung lower on the order's administrative ladder, the annual general assemblies generated a more detailed picture of the brethren's infractions, but it, too, is far from complete. Although a nearly unbroken record of such *acta* or redacted protocols survives from 1220 onward, their texts seldom describe violations in detail, preferring instead the use of opaque terms such as *scandalum, crimen, excessus,* and *irreverentia*.[19] Moreover, and as already mentioned, most infractions were handled by special tribunals or committees, a precis of whose decisions was brought before the general assembly and approved en bloc. In their current recorded form they provide little specific information about the offenses perpetrated.[20] Nor are these committees' specific procedures anywhere clarified.[21] Judging by the great variety of offenses that *were* discussed at the general chapters, from minor disobediences to grave crimes, there seem to have been no rigid criteria for differentiating between incidents that found their way into the official minutes and those omitted from them.

Nonetheless, the proceedings' *iniunctiones penitenciarum* or clauses *de penitenciis*, which appear almost continuously from 1240 onward, add precious information on misbehavior and its repercussions among early Dominicans. Virtually all such sections deal with minor disobediences, such as failing to reach the chapter on time or doing so uninvited, acting insolently to a superior, preaching outside a convent's allocated area, accepting illicit gifts, and pawning the convent's possessions without permission. The prescribed punishments themselves are usually a combination of traditional penances, such as fasts, prayers, masses, and flagellations. Occasionally, however, the offense is deemed graver and the judges' (or the assembly's) response is harsher, ranging from the cancellation of certain privileges, a status, or an office, to a fixed-term banishment or permanent relocation, to temporary or perpetual incarceration. Following an ancient monastic tradition, the ultimate penalty for serious and repeat infractions was expulsion from the order.[22]

---

[18] G. R. Galbraith, *The Constitution of the Dominican Order, 1216 to 1360*, Publications of the University of Manchester, Historical Series, 44 (Manchester: Manchester University Press, 1925), 83–4; William A. Hinnebusch, *The History of the Dominican Order*, i (New York: Alba House, 1966), 169–250.

[19] In an attempt to overcome similar vagueness, the Franciscan constitutions glossed an early thirteenth-century injunction against imprisoning brethren "for anything but a great and evident excess" (*nisi pro enormi et manifesto excessu*) as either a sexual offense, heresy, major theft, or repeated misdeeds. See *Praenarb.*, 77 (no. 34 and VII. 3).

[20] Hinnebusch, *History*, i. 182. On the general chapters' sequence, see Simon Tugwell, "The Evolution of Dominican Structures of Government, II: The First Dominican Provinces," *AFP*, 70 (2000), 100–9.

[21] Simon Tugwell, "The Evolution of Dominican Structures of Government, III: The Early Development of the Second Distinction of the Constitutions," *AFP*, 71 (2001), 110; C. Douais (ed.), *Acta capitulorum provincialium Ordinis Fratrum Praedicatorum . . . (1239–1302)*, 2 vols (Toulouse: Privat, 1894–5), i, pp. xliii–xliv.

[22] Humbert of Romans, "Instructiones de officiis ordinis" 2.6, in *Opera de vita regulari*, ii. 198.

Whether or not the punishments were ever meted out is hard to tell. Yet a survey of penitential clauses promulgated by the general chapters for the period 1240–1400 reveals dozens of severe violations, involving scores of friars throughout the order's provinces (see Appendix II). In 1267, for instance, the priors of Stralsund and Greifswald, near the German Baltic shore, were removed from their offices "on account of the scandals perpetrated by them and by their brethren in the city of Greifswald" (*propter scandala facta ab ipsis et fratribus eorum in civitate Gripsvaldensi*) in the course of a dispute over begging rights. In addition, they were both given a string of penances, though only the prior of Greifswald was to leave his convent, never to return unless by a special dispensation. Johannes of Bremen, a third friar implicated in the affair, suffered long penances and was permanently removed "from his convent and land" (*et removemus eum de conventu et terra sua*).[23] In 1301 more than twenty Rhineland friars were involved in a series of unspecified *scandala*, for which many of them were relocated, stripped of their sometimes high offices, deprived of their privileges of preaching and confession, and barred from re-election to any office for different durations.[24] In 1321 two friars from the convent of Strasbourg "beat their provincial prior, threw him to the ground, seized and violently incarcerated him; and they wished to kill him, and injured both his *socius* and his servant." The assailants were sentenced to perpetual incarceration on bread and water.[25] Simon, the prior of Rouen, was removed from his office and exiled in 1342 for his negligence, "on account of which... disorders and quarrels abounded in that convent, in both spiritual and material affairs."[26] At the same meeting, another French friar, Guillaume Calatot, was convicted of forging letters of his provincial prior. He was sent "*misericorditer*" to prison and lost all his privileges.[27] As with the evidence drawn from Raymond of Capua's register, a list limited to major infractions alone would fill many more pages, despite the paucity of information contained in the sources.

Further evidence of the friars' disciplinary infractions emerges from a unique manuscript documenting the order's administrative practices. It is a register containing some 150 letters, mostly written by the German provincial Hermann von Minden (1286–90). The dossier's discovery in a Berlin manuscript more than a century ago was instrumental for the study of a specific event in the history of the Dominicans in Alsace—namely, the strife between the brethren and the city of Strasbourg from the mid to the late 1280s—an incident that culminated with the

---

[23] Benedikt Maria Reichert (ed.), *Acta capitulorum generalium Ordinis Praedicatorum*, 9 vols, MOFPH 3, 4, and 8–14 (Rome: Typographia Polyglotta S.C. De Propaganda Fide, 1898–1904), i. 139–40.

[24] Reichert (ed.), *Acta*, i. 307–9.

[25] Reichert (ed.), *Acta*, ii. 135: "priorem provincialem verberaverunt, ad terram prostraverunt, ceperunt et violenter in carcerali custodia detinuerunt; ac interficere voluerunt et socium eius et famulum vulneraverunt." According to Dimier, "Violence, rixes et homicides chez les Cisterciens," the White Monks displayed a strong tendency to assault their own priors and visitators.

[26] Reichert (ed.), *Acta*, ii. 281–2: "quia propter indiscriminacionem ipsius in regimine multe turbaciones et disceptaciones in spiritualibus et temporalibus in dicto conventu contigerunt et graviores futuras verisimiliter formidamus."

[27] Reichert (ed.), *Acta*, ii. 281–2.

friars' temporary ejection from the city, an ensuing interdict, and the gradual spread of tensions to adjacent towns.[28] For our present purposes, however, the collection illuminates the order's routine disciplinary activities at the provincial level.[29]

Hermann addressed a number of major infractions, some of which were closely linked to the regional tensions. In early 1289, for instance, he instructed the prior of Colmar to punish two of the brethren, Erbonus and Humbertus, for illicitly entering the convent of St Agnes in Strasbourg, probably in order to administer confession to the nuns during the interdict. He also scolded the local abbess for accepting or perhaps even inviting the friars in the first place and then expressed his dismay at a similar incident involving the local Franciscans, who avoided the magistrates' wrath, and the Dominican nuns, who remained *in situ*. Later that year the provincial dispatched a friar to one of the local convents for an unstated offense, ordering the local prior to incarcerate him perpetually or expel him from the order unless the culprit was able to secure himself a place in a different order outside the province.[30] All told, Hermann's extant letters mention a dozen major events over a period of four years.[31]

The provincial prior's extant correspondence sheds light on isolated incidents only. Moreover, in this particular period the province's Dominicans had to adjust to the peculiarities of carrying on with their mission while the brethren were mostly exiled and the nuns remaining in the city were besieged by locals, some of whom continued to seek entry into the convent in order to participate in the liturgy. A relatively broader picture emerges from the examination of the provincial chapters' *acta* over a longer period. It is these documents, by far the wealthiest single source on early Dominican discipline, to which we now turn.

Compared with the well-kept protocols of the order's general chapters, the extant records of provincial assemblies from the early thirteenth to the end of the fourteenth century are sparse. Despite the best efforts of Dominican historians, many of these texts have been lost for centuries, others are yet to be unearthed, and not all of those that have been identified are easy to access.[32] Among the known *acta*, moreover, many are fragmentary or otherwise do not (or no longer) contain

---

[28] Heinrich Finke (ed.), *Ungedruckte Dominikanerbriefe des 13. Jahrhunderts* (Paderborn: Schöningh, 1891), 36–41. And see Sandrine Turck, *Les Dominicaines à Strasbourg, entre prêche, prière et mendicité (1224–1420)*, Publications de la Société savante d'Alsace et des regions de l'Est, Collection Recherches et Documents, 68 (Strasbourg: Du Cerf, 2002), 39–45; Andreas Rüther, *Bettelorden in Stadt und Land: Die Straßburger Mendikantenkonvente und das Elsaß im Spätmittelalter*, Berliner historische Studien, 26; Ordenstudien, 11 (Berlin: Duncker & Humblot, 1997).

[29] For a Franciscan parallel, see *Monumenta Germaniae Franciscana*, 2.1: *Die Kustoden Goldberg und Breslau*, 1 Teil: *1240–1517* (Düsseldorf: L. Schwann, 1917), no. 256 (p. 45), in which Werner, the Provincial of Saxony, writes to Rodiger, the Custodian of Goldberg, about misbehavior among the province's brethren (Dec. 24, 1337); and Ludovic Vialler, "Le Role du gardien dans les couvents franciscains," in Michael Robson and Jens Röhrkasten (eds), *Franciscan Organisation in the Mendicant Context: Formal and Informal Structures of the Friars' Lives and Ministry in the Middle Ages*, Vita Regularis, 44 (Berlin: Lit, 2010), 234–5.

[30] Finke (ed.), *Ungedruckte Dominikanerbriefe*, nos 110, 112, 140 (132–3, 153).

[31] Finke (ed.), *Ungedruckte Dominikanerbriefe*, nos 93, 96, 109, 113–14, 124, 141 (pp. 116, 119, 131–2, 134–5, 143, 154–5).

[32] Masetti (ed.), *Monumenta*, i. 29.

Table 3.1. Chronological distribution of major infractions among Dominicans, 1251–1400

Period	Infractions
1251–60	5
1261–70	3
1271–80	7
1281–90	11
1291–1300	3
1301–10	10
1311–20	6
1321–30	6
1331–40	6
1341–50	2
1351–60	8
1361–70	4
1371–80	7
1381–90	14
1391–1400	33
TOTAL	125

penitential clauses. Still, nearly full protocols remain from the Italian and Aragonite provinces, and along with other partial records from central and northern Europe, notably those gathered by Donald Logan for England,[33] they afford a fuller view of the brethren's major infractions (see Table 3.1).

Documents issued by Dominican provincial administrations, augmented by the recorded cases discussed above, report 125 major incidents between 1251 and 1400. Jointly these incidents involved hundreds of friars convicted of rebellion, violence, forgery, desertion, rioting, wrongful imprisonment, heresy, apostasy, debt, gross mismanagement, and sexual depravity.[34] In most cases the punishment

---

[33] F. Donald Logan, *Runaway Religious in Medieval England, c.1240–1540,* Cambridge Studies in Medieval Life and Thought, 4th ser., 32 (Cambridge: Cambridge University Press, 1996), 241–2. Logan's monumental study provides arrest and/or prosecution dates for nearly all the twenty-four friars charged with apostasy between 1251 and 1400. Of the seven cases for which no accurate date is specified, three fall within the period 1301–50, and four between 1351 and 1400. In order to distribute these cases in the table I have arbitrarily added one case to each of the six decades between 1321 and 1390.

[34] None of the following incidents overlaps with those previously mentioned: Fritz Bünger (ed.), "Ein Dominikaner-Provinzialkapitel in Luckau (1400)," *ZfK*, 34 (1913), 85, 86; Heinrich Finke, "Zur Geschichte der deutschen Dominikaner im XIII. und XIV. Jahrhundert," *Römische Quartalschrift für christliche Altertumskunde und für Kirchengeshichte*, 8 (1894), 383; Thomas Kaeppeli (ed.), "Acta capitulorum provinciae Lombardiae (1254–93) et Lombardiae inferioris (1309–1312)," *AFP*, 11 (1941), 156; Thomas Kaeppeli and Antoine Dondaine (eds), *Acta capitulorum provincialium provinciae Romanae (1243–1344)*, MOFPH 20 (Santa Sabina [Rome]: Institutum Historicum Fratrum Praedicatorum, 1941), 14, 39, 124, 140–1, 142, 167, 171, 175, 197, 200, 228–9; Benedikt Maria Reichert (ed.), "Akten der Provinzialkapitel der Dominikanerordensprovinz Teutonia, 1398, 1400, 1401, 1402," *Römische Quartalschrift für christliche Altertumskunde und für Kirchengeschichte*, 11 (1897), 300, 311; Thomas Kaeppeli (ed.), "Ein Fragment der Akten des in Friesach 1315 gefeierten Kapitels der Provinz Teutonia," *AFP*, 48 (1978), 73; and Douais (ed.), *Acta*, i.

Table 3.2. Regional distribution of major infractions among Dominicans until 1400

Region	Infractions
Italy	38
Germany	38
England	27
France	12
Spain	9
Other	1
TOTAL	125

remains obscure or is delegated to a local prior, convent, or secular official. Yet in thirty-five cases the offenders were ordered to be relocated to another convent; in twenty-seven cases they were incarcerated, sometimes for life;[35] and at least eleven cases were resolved by permanently expelling the offenders from the order. The many hundreds of friars convicted of minor disobediences not covered by the present survey suffered lighter punishments, usually a combination of fasts, flogging, and prayers.

There are limitations to using the provincial and general *acta*, of course. Their laconic nature, undoubtedly an aid to officialdom, frustrates any hope of understanding the circumstances of individual events and pushes attempts to reconstruct motivations for violations beyond the realm of responsible speculation. Moreover, given the haphazard survival of relevant records, the offenses' apparent distribution across time is often misleading. For instance, the seven cases documented for the decade 1271–80 involved at least triple that number of offenders, and at least thirty friars were complicit in the ten cases reported for 1301–10. Arguing meaningfully for any distribution across space (see Table 3.2) is equally problematic since a single occasion—for instance, a rebellion among the German brethren in 1301—could have involved numerous men spread among different convents.

100, 147, 203, 280, 290, 427; and Zaragoza, Biblioteca Universitaria, MS 185 [=a sixteenth-century copy of the medieval Aragonese chapter *acta*], 107–8 (1321), 233 (1352), 247–8 (1353), 288–90 (1357), 304 (1358), 376–7 (1369), 397 (1371), 448 (1377), 590 (1395). The latter manuscript, which I have consulted and therefore cite, has a partial parallel in Barcelona, Biblioteca Universitaria, MS 241. Both have been the basis of an edition of the fourteenth-century *acta* by Adolfo Robles Sierra and, later, Vito T. Gómez García, in *Escritos del Vedat*, 20–7 (1990–7) and 31–5 (2001–5). This is not a complete list of published *acta* of provincial chapters in the examined period and region but only of those that document major violations, as discussed above.

[35] Prisons became required facilities in every Dominican convent (or province) at least from 1238. See Reichert (ed.), *Acta*, i. 10. Detailed instructions on how to construct and run a prison were promulgated by the Ferrara provincial chapter in 1279. See Kaeppeli (ed.), "Acta capitulorum provinciae Lombardiae," 156. In 1277 Ieronimo of Ascoli, the Franciscan minister general, similarly instructed "quod carceres fortes et multiplices habeantur" throughout the order's provinces, according to *Glassberger*, 89. The Franciscan general chapter meeting in Padua that year promulgated a similar resolution. See A. G. Little (ed.), "Decrees of the General Chapters of the Franciscan Order, 1260–1282," *EHR*, 13 (1898), 707.

As a rule, however, where the surviving documentation is better, the number of infractions is higher. Thus, toward the end of the fourteenth century, the internal reform spearheaded by Raymond of Capua, which mainly focused on Italy and Germany, generated more reports of infractions. And the same is valid for England, where numerous royal writs for arresting apostate friars are extant, and for northern Spain, where many provincial *acta* have been preserved. But whether a similarly powerful magnifying glass placed over any other region, at any other period, would have exposed a similar picture is currently impossible to know. In sum, beyond attesting the ubiquity of major violations, the available records do not allow us to generalize about particular periods or regions, for instance, regarding the influence of the order's recruitment practices after the onset of the plague cycle in 1347, differences in landowning patterns among various cities, and a region's degree of urbanization.

BEYOND THE DOMINICAN CASE

The composite image emerging from the Dominican records can be improved if we extend our search to include other sources and orders. Mendicant authors, often engaged in creating narratives of decay, routinely allude to friars involved in activities that were dubious, unorthodox, criminal, and even traitorous;[36] and comparable instances can be gleaned or inferred from non-mendicant chronicles, urban statutes, sermons, papal letters, saints' lives, and canonization processes. No systematic survey has been attempted here, but canvassing published sources has yielded numerous instances of apostasy, theft, destruction of property, sexual misconduct, and embezzlement, as well as violent rivalries and deadly internal disputes, most infamously at the Franciscan provincial chapter of Cork, in 1291, where the Irish and Anglo-Irish Minorites allegedly turned on one another, leaving sixteen of their brethren dead.[37]

---

[36] Philipp Jaffé (ed.), *Annales colmarienses maiores*, MGH SS 17 (Hanover, 1861), 203, 222, 224; Salimbene, 111, 117, 473, 932–3; *XXIV Gen.*, 87–8, 469; Andrea Maiarelli (ed.), *La cronaca di S. Domenico di Perugia*, 59, Quaderni del Centro per il Collegamento degli Studi Medievali e Umanistici nell'Umbria, 36 (Spoleto: Centro Italiano di Studi sull'Alto Medioevo, 1995), 50–1; Jordan of Saxony, *Liber Vitasfratrum*, II, ed. Rudolf Arbesmann and Winfrid Hümpfner (New York: Cosmopolitan Science & Art Service, 1943).

[37] John Clyn, *Annalium Hiberniae Chronicon ad annum MCCCXLIX*, ed. R. Butler (Dublin: Irish Archaeological Society, 1849), 17 (which post-dates the event to 1325). See Cotter, 33–40, 69. Other instances are documented in Gerard Cagnoli (ed.), "La leggenda del B. Gerardo Cagnoli, O.Min. (1267–1342) di Frà Bartolomeo Albizi. O.Min. († 1351)," *Miscellanea Francescana*, 57 (1951), 442–5; Christopher Tyerman, *God's War: A New History of The Crusades* (London: Penguin Books, 2007), 778 n. 27; *SBF* 9, 27, 40, 140, 142, 159, 175, 178, 180, 182, 199, 205; and App. I, nos 13, 46, 50, 82; Auguste Coulon and Suzanne Clemencet (eds), *Lettres secrètes et curiales du pape Jean XXII (1316–1334) relatives à la France*, iv (Paris: Fontemoing, 1972), no. 17,248 (p. 264); Andrea Sabatini (ed.), *Atti dei capitoli provinciali di Toscana dei carmelitani, 1375–1491*, Archivum Historicum Carmelitanum, 4 (Rome: Institutum Carmelitanum, 1975), 23, 32, 35, 36, 61; and Balbino Velasco Bayon, *Historia del carmeli español*, i, TSHC 17 (Rome: Institutum Carmelitanum, 1990), 151–4.

Other, less accessible documents of practice such as unpublished court records throw further light on the scale and scope of mendicant deviance. Since the brethren were theoretically autonomous or else answered directly to the pope, their prosecution by local bishops or secular magistrates was sporadic at best. Yet such cases do occasionally emerge: in 1326 Bartolo, a Bolognese Franciscan, was fined 500 lire and later incarcerated at the municipal prison for admitting a boy into the order against his parents' wish (the incident was later followed by a rescue attempt and a brawl);[38] Thomas, the subprior of the Dominican convent in Pisa, was convicted in 1362 of harboring a relative at the cloister while the latter was being pursued as a criminal;[39] in 1369 the Pisan Dominicans Jacopo dela Seta and Jacopo di Petri were defrocked and clapped into prison in the order's convent in Lucca, allegedly for siding with the emperor;[40] and in 1373 Antonio, an Augustinian prior, fled the convent, city, and diocese of Lucca carrying with him "the funds and numerous goods belonging to that monastery" (*cum thesauro et nonnullis bonis ipsius monasteri deprehensus*).[41]

Other kinds of archival sources can also be revealing. In her testament, Jacobella, a Venetian matron, bequeathed six ducats to an Augustinian friar named Benedetto, who had been incarcerated for an unspecified offense.[42] The money could have been used for purchasing his pardon or simply alleviating his conditions of captivity, despite the fact that incarceration in Venice was—untypically for that period—free.[43] Another Augustinian friar, likewise incarcerated indefinitely in Venice, made his documentary debut several years later, when his escape, along with that of a certain nobleman, prompted the local magistrates to organize a search party.[44] However sporadically they resurface, such cases move us closer to a broader and better-grounded reconstruction of medieval mendicants' social history.[45]

On the basis of this survey, there is no reason *not* to take satirists and polemicists at their (face-level) word or to dismiss the self-criticism of mendicant reformers as a rhetoric of fallenness. Official deviance among friars was substantial according to both their own administrative accounts and an array of external sources and regardless of how favorably it might have compared with misconduct by their lay

---

[38] ASBo, Governo, Riformagioni e provvigioni 200, fos 312^v–313^r (Feb. 21, 1326). For similarly antagonizing recruitment practices among the London friars, see A. H. Thomas (ed.), *Calendar of Select Pleas and Memoranda of the City of London*, iv (Cambridge: Cambridge University Press, 1932), 182 (July 13, 1392). The trope of kin being appalled by a member's taking a friar's habit is common in mendicant hagiography. See *Vitae Fratrum*, III. 14; IV. 13.7, 17.3, 22.3 (pp. 110–11, 186, 201, 211); and *Eccleston*, 12, 23.

[39] AAPi, Atti Straordinari 8, fo. 80^{r-v} (Feb. 14, 1362).

[40] ASDL, Tribunale Criminale 23, fo. 24^{r-v} (Apr. 11, 1369).

[41] ASDL, Tribunale Criminale 30, fos 46^r–47^v (Feb. 14, 1373).

[42] ASVe, Cancellaria inferiore, Miscellanea testamenti, Notai diversi B. 22, no. 782 (Oct. 13, 1388).

[43] See G. Geltner, *The Medieval Prison: A Social History* (Princeton: Princeton University Press, 2008), 12–17.

[44] ASVe, Consiglio di dieci, Deliberazioni (miste) 8, fo. 13^r (Sept. 10, 1393).

[45] The murder of a London Carmelite by a fellow friar is attested in The National Archives: PRO JUST1/369/M22-OCarm. (1297).

or clerical contemporaries.[46] But what role, if any, did such behavior play in the development of resentment against friars? To begin answering this key question, we now move to examining how contemporary observers learned about and construed the friars' deviance.

SECRETS, SCANDALS, AND THE PUBLIC SPHERE

The Dominican constitutions emphasized the brethren's strict routine and hierarchy and placed a high premium on obedience. Yet, whether owing to their innate human corruption or to integrated social mechanisms with which societies address the internal tensions and even contradictions upon which they are built, the brethren overstepped their prescribed normative boundaries on a more or less routine basis. That this should be typical of any society, including a community of religious, was originally put forward by social philosopher Émile Durkheim (1858–1917): "Imagine a society of saints, a perfect cloister of exemplary individuals. Crimes, properly so called, will there be unknown; but faults which appear venial to the layman will create there the same scandal that the ordinary offense does in ordinary consciousnesses."[47]

Durkheim sought to demonstrate that crime and deviancy are routine and relative rather than pathological and absolute. Reworked by Alexandre Lacassagne (1843–1924), a founding father of modern criminology, this approach succeeded in popularizing the notion that societies "have the criminals they deserve."[48] Without detracting from the veracity of this maxim, it is doubtful whether what could count for deviancy in a "community of saints" would appear merely "venial to the layman." After all, laymen were invested in imaging groups such as monks as pillars of perfection, and it is thus quite possible that, however unavoidable, minor

---

[46] On late-medieval crime rates, a subject riddled with documentary and interpretative problems, see Claude Gauvard, *Violence et ordre public au moyen âge*, Les Médiévistes Français, 5 (Paris: Picard, 2005); Anthony Musson (ed.), *Boundaries of the Law: Geography, Gender and Jurisdiction in Medieval and Early Modern Europe* (Aldershot: Ashgate, 2005); Karen Jones, *Gender and Petty Crime in Late Medieval England: The Local Courts in Kent, 1460–1560*, Gender in the Middle Ages, 2 (London: Boydell, 2006); Valérie Toureille, *Vol et brigandage au moyen âge* (Paris: Presses universitaires de France, 2006); Trevor Dean, *Crime and Justice in Late Medieval Italy* (Cambridge: Cambridge University Press, 2007); and G. Geltner, "I registri criminali dell'Archivio Arcivescovile di Lucca: Prospettive di ricerca per la storia sociale del medioevo," in Sergio Pagano and Pierantonio Piatti (ed.), *Il patrimonio documentario della chiesa di Lucca: Prospettive di ricerca* (Florence: SISMEL, 2010), 331–40.

[47] Émile Durkheim, *The Rules of Sociological Method*, trans. Sarah A. Solovay and John H. Mueller, 8th edn (New York: Free Press, 1962), 68–9. A fine survey of the pertinent sociological theory is David Downes and Paul Rock, *Understanding Deviance: A Guide to the Sociology of Crime and Rule-Breaking*, 5th edn (Oxford: Oxford University Press, 2007). And see Mary Douglas, *Purity and Danger: An Analysis of Concepts of Pollution and Taboo* (Abingdon: Routledge, 2007 [orig. pub. 1966]), 173–95; Dennis H. Wrong, *The Problem of Order: What Unites and Divides Society* (New York: Free Press, 1994), 202–44.

[48] Alexandre Lacassagne, "Les transformations du droit pénal et les progrès de la médecine légale, de 1810 à 1912," *Archives d'anthropologie criminelle*, 28 (1913), 364: "Les Sociétés ont les criminels qu'elles méritent."

96   *Deeds and Words*

violations among them would resonate not only within the perfect community but also, and perhaps especially loudly, outside it once they became known.

Moreover, there was a direct relation between religious perfection (or an order's reputation thereof) and the brethren's ability to carry out their duties outside the convent. According to an exemplary tale written by the Augustinian Jordan of Saxony (c.1299–c.1380; not to be confused with his Dominican namesake), a certain friar who had a habit of roaming the city without cause was chastised for his practice by his prior, who forbade him from leaving the convent unless he had an urgent need. The friar, however, feigned various excuses—"now pretending to be called by a sick person, now to buy some parchment, now candles, now this, now that" (*nunc pretendendo se vocatum ad infirmum, nunc ire ad emendum pergamenum, nunc candelas, nunc haec, nunc illa*). On one of these dubious excursions he came across a man possessed by a demon, and, seeking to cure him, the friar, invoking John's Gospel and the virtue of holy obedience, ordered the demon to depart. Predictably, the demon responded, from within the possessed man's body, that he sees no reason to obey one who is himself a false observer of that virtue ("Quid tu habes mihi praecipare in virtute sanctae oboedientiae, qui numquam verus oboediens fuisti?").[49] *Pace* Durkheim, then, the tale's import is that violating even a peculiarly monastic virtue such as obedience could be poorly perceived beyond the cloister.

By focusing on major violations and reprimands, the previous sections sought to adjust the parameters from angelic to human ones: violence, fraud, sexual promiscuity, desertion, and rebellion would have struck contemporaries as serious offenses, to judge by secular jurisprudence and penal practices.[50] But whatever the scale—monastic or civic, religious or secular—Dominican and other mendicant administrators were eager to keep allegations, confrontations, and violations confined to their order's concentric circles: convent, province, order.[51] What happened within them was no stranger's business; indeed, it was a *secretum*. And the purpose of defending such *secreta*, as repeatedly stated in the chapters' proceedings, was to avoid scandal.[52]

---

[49] Jordan of Saxony, *Liber Vitasfratrum*, II. 2, ed. Arbesmann and Hümpfner, 83.
[50] See Bernard Schnapper, *Les peines arbitraires du XIIIe au XVIIIe siècle: Doctrines savantes et usages français* (Paris: R. Pichon et R. Durand-Auzias, 1974); Marco Cattini and Marzio A. Romani (eds), *Il potere di giudicare: Giustizia, pena, e controllo sociale negli stati d'Antico regime*, Cheiron, 1 (Brescia: Grafo, 1983); Nicole Gonthier, *La châtiment du crime au moyen âge, XIIe–XVIe siècles* (Rennes: Presses universitaires de Rennes, 1998).
[51] Reichert (ed.), *Acta*, i. 5 (Paris, 1234); Douais (ed.), *Acta*, i. 119 (Limoges, 1266). For a Franciscan parallel, see *Praenarb.*, 71–4 (nos 12–26; VIII. 7–X. 25).
[52] Kaeppeli and Dondaine (eds), *Acta*, 228 (Castello, 1323); G. Stephens (ed.), "Brottstycken av en Dominikaner-Ordens eller Predikare-Brödernas Statut- eller Capitel-Bok infrån XIII. Århundradet, och gällande för 'Provincia Dacia'eller de Nordiska Riken," *Kirkehistoriske Samlinger*, 1 (1849–52), 545–642; 2 (1853–6), 128–9; Berthold Altaner (ed.), "Aus den Akten des Rottweiler Provinzialkapitels der Dominikaner vom Jahre 1396," *ZfK*, 48 (1929), 8–9; *Analecta Sacri Ordinis Fratrum Praedicatorum* (Rome: Ex Curia Generalitia ad S. Sabinam, 1893–), iii. 411–36; iv. 479–93. Jacques Guy Bougerol, *Les manuscrits franciscains de la Bibliothèque de Troyes*, Spicilegium Bonaventurianum, 23 (Grottaferrata: Collegii S. Bonaventurae ad Claras Aquas, 1982), 12–13 (K.55, V.879), mentions a collection of *quaestiones* dealing specifically with friars' *scandala*. And see, to the same effect, the exemplum related in *Eccleston*, 86–7.

It is no accident that the term *scandalum* in Dominican as well as other mendicant documents is closely linked to the brethren's relations with the outside world and the disclosure of the orders' *secreta*.[53] Already in 1239, the general chapter gathered at Paris admonished "lest our brethren go to the houses of secular men or clerics on funeral processions or receive [anything] to provoke evident scandal."[54] And henceforth the term appears frequently in similar contexts: in 1242 the chapter meeting at Bologna warned the priors "lest they allow fugitives or apostates to join other orders or let them wander elsewhere, causing a scandal to our order";[55] a decade later, the brethren were instructed to avoid supplying "prelates or clerics anywhere with grounds for disturbance or scandal, but rather hold them in reverence and respect";[56] and the 1268 chapter assembled at Viterbo insisted that the friars should avoid "issues . . . and grounds from which a scandal might arise."[57]

Nor was the term's use in such contexts unique to the Friars Preachers: in 1335, for instance, an Augustinian provincial chapter condemned recent dressing practices among the brethren as strange, effeminate, and leading to "a scandal in the eyes of secular men" (*scandalum in oculis secularium*);[58] and in 1362 the Carmelite general chapter prescribed incarceration or expulsion for anyone provoking public brawls, noting that they cause "a scandal in the presence of secular men" (*scandalum coram secularibus*).[59] Perhaps most famously, Bonaventure's *First Encyclical Letter to the Friars Minor* (1257), composed upon his becoming Minister General, laments an order compromised by "scandals [in the eyes of] secular men" (*scandala mundadorum*) and brethren "leaving behind them scandals rather than good examples" (*non exempla post se relinquunt vitae, sed scandala potius animarum*) by behaving in

---

[53] On the essentially public nature of scandal in the Middle Ages, see Lindsay Bryan, "Scandle is heaued sunne," *Florilegium*, 14 (1995–6), 71–86; Lindsay Bryan, "*Periculum animarum*: Bishops, Gender, and Scandal," *Florilegium*, 19 (2002), 49–73; and Katherine Gill, "*Scandala*: Controversies Concerning *Clausura* and Women's Religious Communities in Late Medieval Italy," in Scott L. Waugh and Peter D. Diehl (eds), *Christendom and its Discontents: Exclusion, Persecution, and Rebellion, 1000–1500* (Cambridge: Cambridge University Press, 1996), 177–203, esp. 184–7.

[54] Reichert (ed.), *Acta*, i. 11: "ne fratres nostri vadant ad domos secularium vel clericorum pro funeribus, nec recipiant cum scandalo evidenti." Repeated verbatim in the acts of the Bologna chapter of 1240 (Reichert [ed.], *Acta*, i. 15).

[55] Reichert (ed.), *Acta*, i. 24: "Monemus priores ne in scandalum ordinis nostri fugitivos et apostatas nostros in aliis religionibus stare vel alias vagari permittant." Repeated verbatim in Reichert (ed.), *Acta*, i. 29 (Bologna, 1244).

[56] Reichert (ed.), *Acta*, i. 63 (Bologna, 1252): "Caveant fratres ubique ne prelatis vel clericis dent materiam turbacionis vel scandali, sed pocius eos habeant in reverencia et honore." A similar injunction appears in the proceedings of the Franciscan general chapter at Lyons in 1274. See Ehrle, "Die ältesten Redactionen," 43.

[57] Reichert (ed.), *Acta*, i. 143: "questiones . . . et causas de quibus potest oriri scandalum."

[58] E. Esteban (ed.), "Definitiones antiquorum capitulorum provinciae Franciae, O.N.," *Analecta Augustiniana*, 4 (1911–12), 163. See also letters 1 and 2 of William of Cremona, "Litterae Prioris Generalis Fr. Guillelmi de Cremona," *Analecta Augustiniana*, 4 (1911–12), 29–32, 57–65; and letter 7 of Gregory of Rimini, in "Litterae Prioris Generalis Ordinis Fr. Gregorii Ariminensis," *Analecta Augustiniana*, 5 (1913–14), 7.

[59] Gabriel Wessels (ed.), *Acta capitulorum generalium Ordinis B. V. Mariae de Monte Carmelo*, i (Rome: Apud Curiam Generalitiam, 1912), 50; see also pp. 58, 119. For the order's range of medieval prescriptive sources, see Carlo Cicconetti, *La Regola del Carmelo: Origine, Natura, Significato*, TSHC 12 (Rome: Institutum Carmelitanum, 1973).

ways that "give rise to many rumors, suspicions, and scandals" (*ex qua suspiciones, infamationes et scandala plurima oriuntur*).[60] It is in this normative and semantic range that the penitential clauses surveyed above dubbed a brother's deviance as "scandalous."[61] Disobedience was indeed sinful, but public exposure itself caused serious damage, for it rendered obsolete the available systems of evasion, or a community's capacity to ignore trespasses that otherwise would have remained—at worst—open secrets.[62]

But what to do when the infractions themselves are perpetrated in the open, as can be inferred from some of the examples cited in the previous section? To recall, Brother Marino of Urbino was prosecuted for "a crime committed by him *in the city* of Camerino"; Ugolino of Pesaro's prior was instructed to investigate "intolerable excesses . . . especially concerning what he [Ugolino] did *on a public way*";[63] the two Baltic priors were ejected for "scandals perpetrated by them and by their brethren *in the city* of Greifswald";[64] and the records regarding both Bartolo, the Bolognese Franciscan, and Thomas, the Pisan Dominican, likewise situate their offenses in the public view.[65]

There is no shortage of similarly visible incidents: in 1352 three Dominicans left their convent at Panyana without permission and were later discovered consuming chicken and wine in public, provoking a "manifest scandal and disgrace" (*scandalum et opprobrium manifestum*).[66] In 1372 a group of armed friars stormed the cathedral at Arles after being denied the right to preach there. They interrupted the service and insulted the vicar general and the members of the local chapter.[67] And in 1370 the Dominican nuns of St Marx, St Nikolaus in Undis, and St Katharina in Strasbourg abandoned their convents and were promptly excommunicated. In response, and perhaps revealing some of the motivations for their departure, the sisters brought forward allegations of material corruption and sexual depravity among their male counterparts. True, false, or exaggerated, the charges were taken at face value and amplified by local clergymen and civic leaders in order to

---

[60] Bonaventure, *Opera omnia*, viii. 468–9.

[61] The church's omnipresence and claims to authority, on the one hand, and the myriad critiques launched against its members' shortcoming, on the other, rendered it a fulcrum of the pre-modern public sphere—a participatory discourse more aptly described for that period by Mikhail Bakhtin, *Rabelais and his World*, trans. Hélène Iswolsky (Cambridge: Cambridge University Press, 1968), than by Jürgen Habermas, *The Structural Transformation of the Public Sphere: An Inquiry into a Category of Bourgeois Society*, trans. Thomas Burger with Frederick Lawrence (Cambridge, MA: MIT Press, 1989). Eschewing Habermas's chronology, but not his analytical framework, is Carol Symes, "Out in the Open, in Arras: Sightlines, Soundscapes, and the Shaping of a Medieval Public Sphere," in Caroline Goodson, Anne E. Lester, and Carol Symes (eds), *Medieval Cities, Texts and Social Networks, 400–1500: Experiences and Perceptions of Medieval Urban Space* (Aldershot: Ashgate, 2010), 279–302.

[62] On "systems of evasion," see Bronislaw Malinowski, *Crime and Custom in Savage Society* (London: Kegan Paul, 1926), 80–4.

[63] *Registrum*, "Provincia Lombardiae inferioris" 32, 10 (emphases added).

[64] Reichert (ed.), *Acta*, i. 139–40 (emphasis added).

[65] See above, nn. 38 and 39, respectively.

[66] Zaragoza, Biblioteca Universitaria, MS 185 (previously 97), 247–8.

[67] Louis Stouff, "Le couvent des prêcheurs d'Arles, XIIIe–XVe siècle," in *L'Ordre des Prêcheurs et son histoire en France méridionale*, CdF 36 (Toulouse: Privat, 2001), 71–2.

advance their converging agendas—namely limiting the Dominicans' access to urban property.[68]

The latter incident also highlights another major public aspect of mendicant misbehaviour—namely, a friar's (or in this case, a sister's) abandonment of a convent, an act usually understood in coeval terms as a form of apostasy. Francis Cotter discovered several such cases among Irish Franciscans in 1310, 1318, and 1320;[69] and I have been able to locate several others for the diocese of Lucca in the later fourteenth century.[70] Most famously, Donald Logan's magisterial study of apostasy among members of English and Welsh religious houses lists no fewer than ninety-four cases among the four major mendicant orders there prior to 1400. In some instances, wayward brethren were accused of further offenses such as theft, heresy, and illicit marriage.[71]

General awareness of the friars' abuses and misbehavior was understandably a serious concern, especially given their exposure to the world, for, unlike most traditional monks, mendicants usually congregated in urban centers. And, since some of their staple missions—preaching, holding masses, and conducting burials—were highly public affairs, it became all the more difficult to avoid open scrutiny.[72] Moreover, as discussed in Chapter 2, the friars' proliferation meant that their ubiquitous convents became accessible to city-dwellers and visitors alike. Their intentional location, at least initially, near the physical edges of cities, among lepers, vagabonds, and prostitutes, created a proximity that offered a mixed blessing. Mendicants themselves acknowledged the tension: toward the end of the thirteenth century the Sienese Servites urged the local commune to enforce a prostitute-free zone around their convent precisely on such grounds;[73] and it was with similar concerns in mind that the Bolognese Dominicans helped prosecute the proprietors of an adjacent brothel in 1360.[74] The vicinity of prostitutes, however, could prove too tempting. The criminal records of Winchester, for instance, reveal that friars were particularly numerous among local clients.[75] And, according to Ruth Mazo Karras, a "monkwhore" or "friarwhore" could mean the mistress of a member of a religious order, although she (and at times he) might also

---

[68] Michael Tönsing, *Johannes Malkaw aus Preussen (ca.1360–1416): Ein Kleriker im Spannungsfeld von Kanzel, Ketzerprozess und Kirchenspaltung*, Studien zu den Luxemburgern und ihrer Zeit, 10 (Warendorf: Fahlbusch, 2004), 142–3; Rüther, *Bettelorden in Stadt und Land*.

[69] Cotter, 27.

[70] ASDL, Tribunale criminale 34, fos 89ʳ–90ᵛ (Nov. 8, 1382); 39, fos 103ᵛ–104ᵛ (Nov. 23, 1386), and fo. 128ᵛ (Sept. 1, 1387).

[71] Logan, *Runaway Religious in Medieval England*, 241–50; for the range of meanings of apostasy in the Middle Ages, see pp. 9–41.

[72] Jacques Le Goff et al., "Ordres mendiants et urbanisation dans la France médiévale," *Annales: Économies, sociétés, civilisations*, 25 (1970), 924–87; *Les ordres mendiants et la ville en Italie centrale*, extrait de *Mélanges de l'École Française de Rome. Moyen Age, Temps Modernes*, 89.2 (1977), 557–773.

[73] Franco Andrea Dal Pino (ed.), *I Frati Servi di S. Maria, dalle origini all'approvazione (1233 ca.– 1304)*, ii. *Documentazione*, Recueil de Travaux d'Histoire et de Philologie, 4th ser. 50 (Louvain: Bureau du Recueil, Bibliothèque de l'Université, 1972), 225 (p. 359), 288–9 (pp. 416–17).

[74] ASBo, Curia del podestà, Libri inquisitionum 191, Reg. 4, fos 101ʳ–103ᵛ.

[75] Derek Keene, *Survey of Medieval Winchester* (Oxford: Clarendon Press, 1985), 391.

be a sex worker who catered particularly for those groups.[76] As one male sex worker confessed, friars (and priests) simply paid better.[77]

Mendicants drew negative attention to themselves also through other practices that were considered abusive. The previous chapter remarked the more or less constant flow of allegations against the friars' greed, as well as several cases of illicit recruitment, especially of children, which could result in assaults on mendicant convents. The public eye was ever watchful over the friars' conduct, even at the height of their popularity. Thus, for instance, their assistance to plague victims during the Black Death was widely hailed, especially by mendicant authors, as a supreme act of altruism. Yet, in the event's aftermath, the brethren came to be perceived as disproportionately benefiting from the ensuing chaos, which provided them with increased access to property. The Augustinians of Winchester, for example, moved unannounced and without permission from the local (and rather sympathetic) bishop into new dwellings in the city center, leaving their extramural convent, including its graves, unattended.[78] This seems to have been typical enough. As one chronicler put it:

It was believed that this Mammon of iniquity wounded the regular clergy very much, but wounded the mendicants fatally. The superfluous wealth poured their way... in such quantities that they scarcely condescended to accept oblations. Forgetful of their profession and rule, which imposed total poverty and mendicancy, they lusted after things of the world and of the flesh, not of heaven. Superfluous finery was everywhere: in their chambers, at table, in riding—all unauthorized and prompted by the devil.[79]

Nor did it help the brethren that, at least according to one report, by the Vicar of Narbonne, friars or at least men dressed as friars were rumored to have placed noxious aromatic potions in churches, homes, wells, and food supplies, thereby bringing the plague to Languedoc.[80]

Yet, as scholars have often remarked, and as noted in the previous chapter, the brethren's main vulnerability stemmed from their involvement with and the support

---

[76] Ruth Mazo Karras, *Common Women: Prostitution and Sexuality in Medieval England* (New York: Oxford University Press, 1996), 30. She asserts that "priests, monks, and friars were certainly among the [sex workers'] clients" (p. 45).

[77] David Lorenzo Boyd and Ruth Mazo Karras, "'Ut cum muliere': A Male Transvestite Prostitute in Fourteenth Century London," in Louise Fradenburg and Carl Freccero (eds), *Premodern Sexualities* (London: Routledge, 1996), 111–12.

[78] Aubrey Gwynn, *The English Austin Friars in the Time of Wyclif* (Oxford: Oxford University Press, 1940), 77–8.

[79] James Tait (ed.), *Chronica Johannis de Reading et Anonymi Cantuariensis 1346–1367* (Manchester: Manchester University Press, 1914), 109–10: "Creditur ergo Mammona hoc iniquitatis regulares plurimum laesisse, ordinem tamen mendicantium letaliter"; "superfluae divitiae affluebant ut vix sibi oblate dedignabantur admittere. Illico, suae professionis obliti et regulae, quae in omni paupertate ac mendicatione consistent, undique superfluo ornatu in cameris, mensis, equitaturis ex parte diaboli ceterisque inordinatis, terrene carnalique non coelestia appetebant." For similar observations by a German Dominican, see *Liber de rebus memorabilioribus sive chronicon Henrici de Hervordia*, ed. A. Potthast (Gottingen: Dieterich, 1859), 268–9.

[80] Christian Guilleré, "La Pest noire a Gerone (1348)," *Annals de l'Institut d'Estudis Gironins*, 27 (1984), 103–4 and n. 80.

they received in their various capacities from lay rulers.[81] To external as well as internal critics, such familiarity with secular power, epitomized by the abundance of mendicant confessors in royal and princely courts, undermined their dedication to a life of evangelical poverty and humility. The papacy, too, made ample use of the brethren's services as preachers, missionaries, inquisitors, jurists, teachers, envoys, and theologians, and raised many of them to positions of influence and authority.[82] In Ireland alone, for instance, at least twenty-six Franciscans were elevated to the episcopate between 1247 and 1400.[83] Across Europe, Williell R. Thomson documented at least forty-seven (and up to fifty-eight) Franciscan prelates, including nine archbishops, before 1261, thirteen of which positions were immediately or shortly filled by other Minorites.[84] And R. F. Bennett estimated that, within less than a century since the foundation of the Dominican Order, there were some 450 ecclesiastical dignitaries from among their ranks alone, including two popes and a dozen cardinals.[85] Such power and prominence must have been gratifying but also compromising. For success furnished the friars' internal critics and external opposition with solid arguments for accusing the brethren of straying from their founders' path.

CONCLUSIONS

Charting misbehavior among mendicants lays an important, albeit not exclusive, foundation for understanding the friars' disrepute and the role it may have played in forging a medieval antifraternal tradition. Deviance among the brethren may have fed into society's perception of them, if not that of religious mendicancy itself, for it is clear that opposition to the friars was never exclusively couched in ecclesiological terms, but rather more commonly made normative claims as well. That said, too much can be imputed from the apparent correlation between the friars' reported misbehaviour and

---

[81] Notably, but not exclusively, with Louis IX of France (St Louis). See Lester K. Little, "Saint Louis' Involvement with the Friars," *Church History*, 2 (1964), 125–43; William Chester Jordan, *Louis IX and the Challenge of the Crusade: A Study in Rulership* (Princeton: Princeton University Press, 1979), 135–213; Xavier de La Salle, *Le service des âmes à la cour: Confesseurs et aumôniers des rois de France du XIIIe au XVe siècle*, Mémoires et Documents de l'École des chartes, 43 (Paris: École des Chartes, 1995), 99–109, 261–83, 310–15, 318–22. See also P. A. Henderikx, *De oudste bedelordekloosters in het graafschap Holland en Zeeland*, Hollandse Studiën, 10 (Dordrecht: Historische Vereniging Holland, 1977), 121–9; Herve Martin, *Les ordres mendiants en Bretagne (vers 1230–vers 1530)* (Paris: Klincksieck, 1975), 149–58; Francisco García-Serrano, *Preachers of the City: The Expansion of the Dominican Order in Castile (1217–1348)* (New Orleans: University Press of the South, 1997), 90–115; David Gutiérrez, *The Augustinians in the Middle Ages*, trans. Arthur J. Ennis (Villanova, PA: Augustinian Historical Institute, 1984), 48–54; and, more broadly, C. H. Lawrence, *The Friars: The Impact of the Early Mendicant Movement on Western Society* (Harlow: Longman, 1994), 166–201.
[82] For one very active Carmelite, see *The Life of Saint Peter Thomas by Philippe de Mézières*, ed. Joachim Smet, TSHC 2 (Rome: Institutum Carmelitanum, 1954).
[83] Cotter, 137.
[84] Williell R. Thomson, *Friars in the Cathedral: The First Franciscan Bishops, 1226–1261*, Studies and Texts, 33 (Toronto: Pontifical Institute of Mediaeval Studies, 1975), 150–8. All but one were members of the order before being raised to the episcopate.
[85] Bennett, *The Early Dominicans*, 131–2.

their stereotyping by contemporary and later authors, who wrote in different genres to different audiences, and, most importantly, with different goals in mind. In this sense, the present chapter does not seek to draw a direct link between the brethren's internally documented deviancy and their cultural representation, let alone identify a causal mechanism rigging misbehavior to opposition. After all, our ability to chart mendicant misbehavior today is arguably greater than that of most of the brethren's contemporaries outside their orders or the papacy. Rather, it was their ubiquity and high public profile that supplied their critics with ample ammunition.

More than most members of the late-medieval church, the friars were conspicuous. As such, it was incumbent upon them to avoid the wrath of one group or the other in a highly factional environment. But their integration within so many aspects of urban life meant that maintaining neutrality was a nearly impossible feat. Convents tended to attract residents of the local city or its hinterland, a situation that rendered impractical the orders' injunctions against favoring or aiding a particular party.[86] And, when internal urban strife temporarily waned, friars were often accused of collaborating with external enemies: the emperor, the pope, a hostile foreign ruler;[87] or vice versa: an invading power would target them for siding with the local population.[88]

Fame and power, in fine, had their costs above and beyond the tough demands of the mendicant regime, and the threat of the former or the abuse of the latter often led the friars' antagonists to defame them as hypocritical and corrupt. The tension between the mendicant ethos and the direction in which the orders' success took them was evidently a great challenge, not least in terms of the brethren's public relations. As the Franciscan chronicler Salimbene put it: "Wisdom is extremely necessary for men in religious orders, for they have many assailants, detractors, enemies, and persecutors, who gladly put *a blot on the elect* [Eccl. 11:33]."[89] Evidently, it was the kind of wisdom not all friars could boast.

---

[86] *De fundatione*; "Cronaca del convento di Santa Caterina dell'Ordine dei Predicatori in Pisa," *Archivio Storico Italiano*, 1st ser., 6/2 (1845), 397–593. Studies on the friars' provenance include Martin, *Les ordres mendiants en Bretagne*, 127–35; Henderikx, *De oudste bedelordekloosters*, 115–19; Daniel R. Lesnick, *Preaching in Medieval Florence: The Social World of Franciscan and Dominican Spirituality* (Athens, GA: University of Georgia Press, 1989), 47, 72–3, 86–92; Lansing, 137–9; Turck, *Les Dominicaines à Strasbourg*, 159–69; George W. Dameron, *Florence and its Church in the Age of Dante* (Philadelphia: University of Pennsylvania Press, 2005), 104–5; and Piron, "Un couvent sous influence," 331–55. On the orders' unrealistic injunctions against involvement in local politics, see Douais (ed.), *Acta*, i. 32 (Marseille, 1248); and E. Esteban (ed.), "Antiquiores quae extant definitiones capitulorum generalium ordinis," *Analecta Augustiniana*, 4 (1911–12), 235–6 (Milan, 1343).

[87] Josef Wiesehoff, *Die Stellung der Bettelorden in den deutschen freien Reichstädten im Mittelalter* (Leipzig: J. Wiesehoff, 1905); Anne Müller, "Conflicting Loyalties: The Irish Franciscans and the English Crown in the High Middle Ages," *Proceedings of the Royal Irish Academy*, 107 (2007), 87–106; Holly J. Grieco, "Franciscan Inquisition and Mendicant Rivalry in Mid-Thirteenth-Century Marseille," *JMH*, 34 (2008), 275–90.

[88] Lanercost, 254, 260–1, 265, 275, 282; *Chronica*, 22, 24; *Die Chronik Johanns von Winterthur*, ed. Friedrich Bathgen, with C. Brun, MGH SS rer. Germ., NS3 (Berlin: Weidmann, 1924), 197–8, 239–40, 268–9.

[89] Salimbene, 177: "Est autem valde necessaria sapientia viris religiosis, quoniam multos habent mordaces et detractores et inimicos et persecutores, qui libenter ponunt *maculam in electis*."

4
Remembrance: Antifraternalism and Mendicant Identity

We are nowhere and never safe.
        Humbert of Romans, *Letter to the Brethren in Orleans* (1255)[1]

Mendicant authors are often our main if not sole source of information about polemical debates and violent episodes involving the brethren. And it is certainly true, as the previous chapter in particular stressed, that the friars were concerned about—and therefore cared to document—their own misconduct: scandalous behavior that could and at times did precipitate external censure, some of it physically aggressive. Understandably then this study often draws upon medieval mendicants' impressions of their own rejection and abuse by others. Yet so far the friars' agency in shaping a medieval antifraternal tradition remained mostly implicit. To round out the picture, this final chapter focuses on mendicant representations of their own woes, having already established a firm basis for comparison—namely—events described elsewhere by non-mendicants and the broader contours of antifraternal aggression.

As is characteristic of this study generally, here too I interrogate several genres, for mendicants in various capacities shaped the memory of their victimhood, real or imagined, by recording it in local, regional, or universal chronicles, administrative documents, hagiography, martyrology, polemical treatises, liturgy, and figurative art. Through these diverse sources, and as its title hints, the current chapter explores opposition to friars as seen through the eye of an evolving mendicant identity and as driven, among other motivations, by a desire to enhance a particular aspect of this identity—namely, Christological or, more broadly put, eschatological suffering.

To set the stage, the first section introduces the term "mendicant lachrymose history," which I have appropriated from Jewish historiography. While, in the latter field, "lachrymose history" mainly denotes an earlier dominant view of history as a series of misadventures and tragedies afflicting the Jewish people,[2] here I employ

---

[1] *CUP* i. 273 (312): "Non est nobis alicubi securitas ulla ora." The Dominican Master General is writing here about the dangers facing the brethren in the aftermath of the Parisian university quarrels, but before the publication of *De periculis*.
[2] Salo W. Baron, "Ghetto and Emancipation," *Menora*, 14 (1928), 515–26; David Biale, *Power and Powerlessness in Jewish History* (New York: Schocken Books, 1986); David Engel, "Crisis and Lachrymosity: On Salo Baron, Neo-Baronianism, and the Study of Modern European Jewish History," *Jewish History*, 20 (2006), 243–64; Mark R. Cohen, *Under Crescent and Cross: The Jews in*

the term to describe the friars' self-perception as victimized protagonists in an eschatological struggle. Next, we explore three occasions or arenas in which such attitudes were fostered, starting from the Parisian university quarrels of the 1250s, with which this book began. Unlike in Chapter 1, however, where I argued that these events and the polemical literature they generated offer something of a false start to the study of medieval literary, theological, and social antifraternalism, this section identifies them as a seminal moment indeed, albeit only from the perspective of constructing a mendicant lachrymose narrative. A second section illuminates continuities with this tradition in the context of mendicant martyrdom beyond the boundaries of Latin Christendom, with which we have been mainly occupied so far. A third section examines the remembrance of the brethren's rather more ambiguous deaths closer to home, first during the onset of the plague cycle in 1347–8, and then in relation to the brethren's activities as papal inquisitors. It is not the argument of this chapter that suffering was a figment of mendicant propagandists' imagination, but rather that the lachrymose mode of remembrance they fostered regarding their own history became a major, albeit unintentional, vehicle for shaping and transmitting an antifraternal tradition.

A LACHRYMOSE HISTORY

The friars' lives seem to have been beset with all sorts of dangers. According to the fourteenth-century *Annales colmarienses maiores*, for instance, on October 22, 1287 an Alsatian knight named Johannes rode up to the Dominican convent in Colmar and razed its enclosure.[3] The author of the text, probably a Dominican, provides no context for the attack, but his record of the immediately preceding years offers a veritable litany of contemporaries' open and at times violent hostility toward members of the mendicant orders. Among other incidents, he notes that, between 1281 and 1286,

the Penitential Sisters were shamefully thrown out of their cloister;
a friar from the Order of Preachers was lightly injured by a citizen of Strasbourg;
the Friars Preachers received lodgings contrary to the objections of many;
on Easter several citizens of Colmar wounded [certain] slaves and violently forced them into the convent of the Minorites;
the Sisters of St John under the tutelage of the Friars Preachers were forced to give 60 marks to the citizens, against the liberties of the religious;
Lord Heinrich, Bishop of Basel, of the Order of Friars Minor, was made Archbishop of Mainz and was gloriously received by his subjects [albeit] against their [initial] hope;

---

the Middle Ages, rev. edn (Princeton: Princeton University Press, 2008); Ariel Toaff, *Ebraismo virtuale* (Milan: Rizzoli, 2008).

[3] Philipp Jaffé (ed.), *Annales colmarienses maiores*, MGH SS 17 (Hanover, 1861), 214: "Iohannes miles, dictus de Nortgasse, residens in Columbaria, fratribus ordinis Predicatorum in eodem loco residentibus, 8. Idus Octobris, septa domorum per violentiam noscitur destruxisse." This may have been the same or a related assault to that described for Strasbourg in App. II, no. 45.

and so it goes on.[4] The emphasis on harassment, rejection, and violence is typical of numerous mendicant sources in this period. Indeed, texts such as the *Annales colmarienses* and others surveyed in the present chapter suggest that violence and other forms of what is at least implicitly construed as opposition to the friars were a major preoccupation of mendicant authors and an expectation of their intended audiences. Both had to do with the friars' self-perception as belonging to religious orders perched in a precarious state, a world view that the mendicants and their supporters seem rather eager to promote. As the Carmelite John Baconthorpe (d. 1346) put it:

Christian religion was founded by divine inspiration, for no persecution or promulgation of laws was able to dissolve it... And so it is with the Order of the Carmel, for, with God's help, it has persevered since its antiquity, and could be dissolved neither by the persecutions of the Saracens, nor through the laws promulgated against the religious.[5]

Rejection, ranging from physical violence (in this case by Muslims) to legal action (here by fellow Christians), upheld a lachrymose view of mendicant history. As already mentioned, the term "lachrymose history" mainly pertains to Jewish historiography. It is not my intention here to compare the travails of friars and the persecution of Jews in the Middle Ages, except to observe that both groups shared certain psychological, ideological, and eschatological motivations for emphasizing their own victimhood, however great or—as was usually the case with the friars—limited they were.[6]

To recall, the evidence marshaled in Chapter 2 established that the scale of antimendicant aggression across Europe in the thirteenth and fourteenth centuries was modest, especially by comparison to assaults on coeval clergymen. But, however infrequent, in the minds of mendicant apologists such events lent themselves to nourishing their self-perception as members of the church's vanguard, as bold and persecuted evangelists, even martyrs. It is also plausible, to follow an argument propounded by Christopher Haigh in a slightly different context, that

---

[4] Jaffé (ed.), *Annales colmarienses maiores*, 208: "Multi ignobiles facti milites in Argentina. Sorores poenitentes de claustro suo se mutuo turpiter expulerunt"; "Frater ordinis Predicatorum fuit a quibusdam civibus Argentinensibus debiliter vulneratus"; "Item fratres Predicatores domum... pluribus contradicentibus receperunt"; "Item in die pasce quidam ex civibus Columbariensibus servos sculteli vulnaraverunt et eos in claustrum Minorum per violentiam coegerunt"; "Item sorores de Sancto Iohanne-sub-tilia ordinis fratrum Predicatorum contra libertatem religiosorum 60 marcas dare a civibus cogebantur" (p. 212); "Dominus Heinricus, episcopus Basilensis, frater ordinis Minorum, factus est archiepiscopus Maguntinus et receptus est contra spem a suis subditis gloriose" (p. 213). The author, no admirer of the Franciscans, willingly records how one of the Strasbourg brethren drowned and another was struck by lightning (pp. 219, 221, respectively).

[5] John Baconthorpe, *Compendium historiarum et iurium*, MCH 209–10: "Patet christianam religionem divina inspiratione fuisse constitutam, quia nulla persecutione aut legis editione dissolvi poterat... Idem est de ordine Carmeli. Semper enim, Deo disponente, in sua antiquitate insurgente processit, nec per Saracenorum persecutionem, nec per leges editas contra religiosos poterat dissolvi."

[6] See Christopher Ocker, "Contempt for Friars and Contempt for Jews in Late Medieval Germany," in Steven J. McMichael and Susan E. Myers (eds), *Friars and Jews in the Middle Ages and the Renaissance*, The Medieval Franciscans, 2 (Leiden: Brill, 2004), 119–46.

overemphasizing their abuse reflects the brethren's heightened sensitivity to status.[7] Either way, the friars seem to have employed violence to secure the brethren's place within a moral community—that is, a group beyond whose limits suffering would have been difficult to acknowledge.[8]

A tendency to pursue this line has cast a long shadow, from the orders' foundational documents to their recent interpretation, and not least among mendicant historians, still the most committed students of and prolific authors about their orders' formative days. Consider, for instance, the following clause from the earliest extant constitutions of the Franciscan Order, probably written in 1239:

> Should the evident necessity of leaving their dwellings present itself to the brethren of any province, because they cannot be supported even somewhat in that area, let the neighboring ministers [of the order] gather those brethren in their own provinces, so long as letters are sent [on the arriving brethren's behalf] by their own ministers, denoting those brethren in trouble. If, however, the necessity stated above is absent, let no brother be sent to any minister, unless that minister's willingness is first established, namely that he agrees to receive him into his own province. And should anyone be sent otherwise, let him not be received.[9]

For those seeking evidence of the friars' haunted past, the passage begins promisingly, dealing as it does with the contingency of a sudden mass exodus of brethren from their city or town.[10] Its focus, however, appears to lie elsewhere—namely, in curbing the friars' wandering within and especially between their provinces. In other words, a decree seemingly prompted by an external threat quickly assumes the attributes of an inhouse concern with the brethren's *errores*—that is, their un- or misguided movements. True, and as argued earlier in this book, both external threats and the brethren's misbehavior formed distinct threads in a complex antifraternal cloth. Yet the focus on the former at the expense of the latter has prevailed, especially among mendicant interpreters past and present, who often serve as guides to contemporary and later scholars.

Cesare Cenci (1925–2010), the Franciscan friar who edited the present text, was until his recent death among his order's most prominent medievalists. Writing within a mendicant tradition and in his order's most prestigious scholarly

---

[7] Christopher Haigh, "Anticlericalism and Clericalism, 1580–1640," in Nigel Aston and Matthew Cragoe (eds), *Anticlericalism in Britain, c.1500–1914* (Stroud: Sutton, 2000), 37.

[8] David B. Morris, "About Suffering: Voice, Genre, and Moral Community," in Arthur Kleinman, Veena Das, and Margaret Lock (eds), *Social Suffering* (Berkeley and Los Angeles: University of California Press, 1997), 25–45, esp. 39–42.

[9] *Praenarb.*, 86–7 (no. 61; V. 16): "Si contingat fratres alicuius provintie incurrere manifestam necessitatem exeundi a locis suis in tanta multitudine, quod in eadem provincia non possint aliquatenus sustentari, teneantur vicini ministri sic exeuntes in suis provintiis collocare, dummodo ad ipsos per sui ministri litteras transmittantur, facientes de eorumdem fratrum gravamine mentionem. Si autem necessitas huius constitutionis non affuerit, nullus mittatur frater ad aliquem ministrum, nisi prius constiterit sibi de voluntate illius ministri quod velit eum sponte in sua provintia collocare. Et si aliquis aliter missus fuerit, non recipiatur."

[10] Planning for such contingencies was not exclusive to the mendicants. See Anne E. Lester, *Creating Cistercian Nuns: The Women's Religious Movement and its Reform in Thirteenth-Century Champagne* (Ithaca, NY, and London: Cornell University Press, 2011), 1–4.

publication, *Archivum Franciscanum Historicum*, Cenci remarked that the somber passage does not address a hypothetical situation but rather stems from "sad experience" (*Tam grave decretum non nitebatur mera hypothesi sed tristi experientia*). Typically meticulous, he goes on to document this sad experience at length, referring in the first instance to rapid evictions that befell the friars, especially in the Near East, Spain, and, on account of the Mongol invasions, eastern Europe. But there was, avers Cenci, a more pressing reason (*causa proximior*) for the provision than close encounters with intolerant infidels—namely, the brethren's need occasionally to withdraw apace from cities placed under interdict and their sudden ejection from towns subject to the anti-papal emperor Frederick II (1194–1250)—events he subsequently relates for both Franciscans and (charitably?) Dominicans during the period 1237–57.[11] The friars' zeal clearly came at a heavy cost.

On the other hand, the incidents listed in Cenci's note fall almost entirely beyond the passage's estimated composition date of 1239, and mostly between its initial promulgation and that of its redaction around 1260, which Cenci's edition publishes in parallel. The litany of expulsions may thus help explain why the text was barely altered in nearly twenty years, but not what its original *raison d'être* might have been. Further, even if his evidence were entirely pertinent chronologically, at this point in the present book it should be clear that Cenci's version of a *causa proximior* is limited. And for once it cannot be argued that he was oblivious to the variety of grounds for the brethren's evictions or voluntary departures from their host towns, since he himself was among those who documented such grounds for the benefit of modern historians.[12] Rather than in ignorance, then, the tendency to emphasize the friars' victimization across orders and throughout their early history can be understood more fully by recourse to their engrained corporate identity as the church's defenders and, if need be, its new martyrs. For, as we shall see, Cenci's nod at—indeed, his promotion of—a lachrymose narrative of mendicant history follows in the heels of a long tradition, one of whose main points of reference we now move to explore.

THE UNIVERSITY QUARRELS ONCE AGAIN

Violent mostly in a rhetorical sense, the main concerted attempt to abolish religious mendicancy in the Middle Ages dates to the mid-1250s, when, according to the Franciscan chronicler Salimbene (d. 1287), "Master William of St Amour incited the University of Paris against the Order of the Friars Minor and Preachers."[13]

---

[11] *Praenarb.*, 86 n. 39.
[12] Above, Ch. 2, n. 73, and Ch. 3, nn. 19, 37. In 2006 I had the unique privilege of meeting Cesare Cenci, then a lucid and friendly octogenarian living in semi-retirement in Grottaferrata, and discussing my research on mendicant misbehavior with him. He dispelled any apprehensions I may have had by pointing me in several fruitful directions where I could find further evidence.
[13] Salimbene, 436: "cum magister Guillelmus de Sancto Amore provocasset universitatem Parisiensem contra Ordinem fratrum Minorum et Predicatorum." For a recent account of the event and an analysis of its substantial historiography, see *De periculis*, 1–13.

Neither the first nor the last challenge to face the brethren, what came to be known as the university quarrels nonetheless made its mark as a foundational moment, certainly for the mendicants' self-perception as a religious elite prone to being persecuted by its fellow Christians. Indeed, it was in describing the atmosphere in Paris around these very events, in a letter addressed to his brethren in Orleans, that the Dominican Master General, Humbert of Romans (*c.*1200–77), bemoaned the friars' precarious state by insisting that they were "nowhere and never safe."[14]

In the decades and centuries that followed, Dominicans and other mendicant authors echoed Humbert's overblown analysis of his brethren's predicament to a greater or lesser degree, both as an exercise in historical exegesis and as an act of self-preservation. By reinforcing their own order's sense of victimhood during (and implicitly beyond) the original affair, mendicants were enhancing their corporate identity from within by developing a Christological understanding of their orders' tribulations and by building political support from without through becoming, in Bert Roest's phrase, "spokesmen for a strong papal authority."[15]

Though shared among many mendicants, the effort to mythologize the events in Paris, that is to render them into what a recent theorist has called an "ideology in narrative form,"[16] spawned telling discrepancies between the collective memories of different orders, especially those of Dominicans and Franciscans. Writing nearly a century after the event, for instance, the Milanese Dominican Galvano Fiamma (1283–1344) described how William of St Amour

and many other masters in Paris rose against [our] order, wishing to destroy it; and, by deploying arguments made by certain authorities, they tried to prove that an order of [men professing] poverty does not accord with the state of salvation. And a truly mighty book was composed [for this purpose] and sent to the curia.[17]

Fiamma's description is typically Dominican in that it stresses his own order's centrality in the affair and typically mendicant in portraying William's harangues as popular among secular academics. As for the latter and more general claim, Chapter 1 demonstrated that, although St Amour's radicalism was briefly shared by some of the Parisian secular masters, the antimendicant party that formed around it never managed to gather significant and enduring support outside the university. Yet their brief rally became something of a cause célèbre for the volatility of early mendicant life, and as such was often invoked by the orders' apologists and chroniclers as their own counter-rallying cry.

---

[14] See above, n. 1.
[15] Bert Roest, *Reading the Book of History: Intellectual Contexts and Educational Functions of Franciscan Historiography, 1226–c. 1350* (Groningen: Regenboog, 1996), 208; see also pp. 209–14.
[16] Bruce Lincoln, *Theorizing Myth: Narrative, Ideology, and Scholarship* (Chicago: University of Chicago Press, 1999), 147; see also pp. 141–206.
[17] Galvano Fiamma, *Cronica Ordinis Praedicatorum ab anno 1170 usque ad 1333*, ed. Benedictus Maria Reichert, MOFPH 2 (Rome: In Domo Generalita, 1897), 96–7: "Quidam Guillielmus de sancto Amore, canonicus Matisconensis, et multi alii magistri Parisius contra ordinem insurrexerunt, volentes ordinem destruere et probabant racionibus decretalibus de certis auctoritatibus, quod ordo paupertatis non esset in statu salutis, et conscriptus est unus liber magnus valde et portatus ad curiam."

Fiamma's emphasis on the Preachers' central role, on the other hand, is as unsurprising as it is better grounded in the events themselves, notwithstanding the author's wish to portray his brethren as paradigmatic and responsible mendicants. Franciscans and Dominicans responded differently to the secular masters' protest, a disharmony reflecting the groups' diverse agendas and corporate identities that led to different aggrandizing versions of the events of 1254–6. In a nutshell, the masters' prestige was threatened by the friars' growing popularity among students. If the secular masters were to hold onto their jobs, mendicant masters needed to curb their enthusiasm or at least rein in their perceived opportunism. Presented with these claims, the Minorites initially took a more appeasing approach than the Preachers, a line that may have helped forge the notion—warmly adopted by Fiamma and other Dominican chroniclers, and corroborated by well-informed Benedictines[18]—that the Preachers were the sole or at any rate chief targets of the masters' vitriol.

St Amour himself, however, was loath to make any distinctions among religious mendicants, who in his contemporary Paris could be Dominicans, Franciscans, or the very recently arrived Carmelites.[19] This essentialist view justified claims by non-Dominicans (and their later students) of being equal victims of his acrid campaign. As John Fleming put it, William exhibited "an implacable hostility toward the concept of Christian perfection as mendicancy, and to the validity of mendicant ministry." Mediocre in all but his persecuting passion, William's "contribution to the literary history of the Franciscan Order was that which the irritant grain of sand makes to the oyster."[20] The pearls alluded to here by Fleming are mainly theological treatises, notably Bonaventure's *Apologia pauperum*. Yet it seems that, among the orders' run-of-the-mill chroniclers, William's memory conjured up tears.

Salimbene, for instance, no sympathizer of Dominicans and never one to mince his words, was scarcely ready to relinquish persecutorial glory to the Preachers. Of his tendency to play down violence perpetrated against Dominicans, there is some evidence in his treatment of the latter's expulsion from his hometown of Parma in 1279 (discussed in Chapter 2). Unlike in Parma, however, where the Franciscans were absent from the scene, in Paris their role could simply be emphasized at the Dominicans' expense, rather than invented out of whole cloth. Accordingly, Salimbene chose to construe the secular masters' affront as a response to the appearance of the *Liber Introductorius in Evangelium Eternum* (1254), a Joachimite treatise composed without the order's approval by the Paris-based Franciscan

---

[18] See the fifteenth-century anonymous Dominican's continuation of Gerard of Frachet's *Vitae Fratrum*, in *Chronica*, 12. For non-mendicants, see Matthew Paris, *Chronica Majora*, v, ed. Henry Richards Luard, Rolls Series, 57 (London: Longman, 1880), 416; and the Burton annalist in Henry Richards Luard (ed.), *Annales Monastici*, i, Rolls Series, 36 (London: Longman, Green, Longman, Roberts, and Green, 1864), 347.

[19] The Augustinian Hermits arrived in the city several years later. See David Gutiérrez, *The Augustinians in the Middle Ages*, trans. Arthur J. Ennis (Villanova, PA: Augustinian Historical Institute, 1984), 138–9.

[20] John V. Fleming, *An Introduction to the Franciscan Literature of the Middle Ages* (Chicago: Franciscan Herald Press, 1977), 84.

Gerard of Borgo San Donnino.[21] Henceforth, according to Salimbene, the masters' blame and rage afflicted friars of all stripes. The plausible link between the *Introductorius* and St Amour's *De periculis* was particularly useful in carving out a not entirely unwitting role for the Franciscans in the history of the dispute. It also—and perhaps more crucially—opened the door to including other friars among the group indiscriminately targeted by William and his cronies. Not surprisingly, this inclusive approach became quite popular.

Indeed, to follow contemporary and later Franciscan historiography is to trace a familiar path. The mid-fourteenth-century Minorite *Chronicle of Lanercost*, for instance, denies the Dominicans any privileged role in the affair and construes St Amour's struggle as one targeting "the status shared by all religious mendicants," who, "although [in the chronicler's opinion] they evangelize and live according to the gospel, cannot[—according to William—]be saved."[22] Some decades later, the compiler of the *Chronicle of Twenty-Four Generals* initially described the event as a quarrel, initiated by William of St Amour, between the university masters and the mendicant students of theology.[23] Yet what began as a quarrel soon turned into a molestation of all religious mendicants, but especially of the Dominicans and Franciscans, and as a campaign was supported by numerous masters and church prelates, who caused the friars "to endure much suffering and harm *in many countries*." Fortunately, and despite the apparent geographical spread of its message, by 1256 the "pernicious, wicked, malign, and detestable" nature of *De periculis* was made official by the pope, and the treatise was solemnly and publicly burned in Louis IX's court. The tables were turned, and William, now a "miserable man, had to endure all the persecutions that he had levelled against [our] Order," and was presently exiled from Capetian France.[24]

Neither Jordan of Giano nor Thomas of Eccleston discusses these events directly, but subsequent Franciscan historians, while working in different institutional, political, and religious contexts, offered minor variations on a theme. Writing in or around 1508, the German Observant Nicholas Glassberger reported that the secular masters at Paris "began to rise up against the religious mendicants," led by William of St Amour, a fanatic who asserted that neither their begging nor their poverty had any merit. Although William alleged the unorthodoxy of all friars,

---

[21] Salimbene, 341–2; for his anti-Dominican jabs, see pp. 58, 111, 842.

[22] *Lanercost*, 61: "Unus dictus Willelmus de Sancto Amore prius Parisius publice garriens contra statum communiter religiosorum mendicantium, dixit et disputavit, insuper determinavit, quod omnes tales etiam evengelizantes, et de evangelio viventes, salvari non possent." And see A. G. Little, "The Authorship of the Lanercost Chronicle," in *Franciscan Papers, Lists, and Documents*, Publications of the University of Manchester, 284; Publications of the University of Manchester, Historical Series, 81 (Manchester: Manchester University Press, 1943), 42–54.

[23] *XXIV Gen*. 272: "Dissensio inter universitatem clericorum et pauperes Mendicantes Religiosos studentes in theologia, incentore malorum Gulielmo de sancto Amore."

[24] *XXIV Gen*. 280: "Eodem anno [1256...] dictus libellus dicti Gulielmi de sancto Amore tamquam perniciosus, scelestus, exsecrabilis et detestabilis... solemniter est combustus. Dictus vero Gulielmus, libri conditor, de toto regno Franciae est expulsus. Magnam tamen iste miser Ordini persecutionem ingessit. Cum enim callide clerum Parisiensem et prelatos Ecclesiae, quorum se defensorem dicebat, contra Ordinem concitasset, multi fratres oprobria et damna in diversis terris passi sunt. Sed, sicut ostensum est, suae finem malitiae et astutiae confusionem accepit."

Glassberger stresses that the response was issued uniquely by a Franciscan, one Bertrand of Bayonne (whom the chronicler may be confusing here with Thomas of York), who "pleaded so brilliantly on behalf of all mendicants, and rejected William's arguments so thoroughly, that the blaspheming doctor, stupefied, said: 'Either you are an angel, or a devil, or Strabo of Bayonne'."[25] Whether or not such an exchange actually took place, it was unlikely to be limited to one adept Minorite demolishing William's position. Nor did William ever admit defeat.

A decade later, Marianus of Florence (d. 1523) attributed William's assaults to demonic intervention and asserted that his defamatory treatise, while aimed against religious mendicancy *tout court*, prompted a persecution of the Franciscan Order in particular.[26] Happily, by 1255, evangelical poverty had been successfully defended at the papal curia thanks to a collaboration of eminent Franciscan and Dominican scholars, who exposed William's arguments as "frivolous and false" (*frivolas et falsas*), sending his cronies reeling and William himself packing. The matter was finally settled by Louis IX, "a lover of evangelical poverty" (*amator evangelice paupertatis*), who had the book solemnly burned and William promptly expelled from his kingdom.[27] The event is described quite similarly by Marcos of Lisbon (1511–91), later Bishop of Porto, in his immensely popular history of the Franciscan Order. Originally published between 1557 and 1570 in Portuguese, and since then continuously reprinted and translated into German, Spanish, English, French, Polish, and especially Italian, this work tells of a "grande perseguiçao" of the Preachers and Minorites, led by William, who succeeded in establishing himself as "defensor dos clerigos contra os frades mendigantes." His meteoric rise, however, was soon followed by his fall, in large part thanks to able Franciscan polemicists.[28]

At last coming to terms with the strong evidence of the Dominicans' main role in the conflict, Franciscan historians began offering a new twist. The Alsatian Franciscan Malachias Tschamser, an early seventeenth-century historian, rounded off his chronicle's entry for the year 1256 by noting that "William [of St Amour]... wrote a malicious book against the Dominicans, Minorites, and all the religious,

---

[25] *Glassberger*, 72: "Ed eodem anno quidam privati magistri Parisius coeperunt contra Mendicantes Religiosos insurgere, inceptore malorum Gulielmo de sancto Amore, theologiae doctore, qui ad sobrietatem non sapiens, contra dictorum Mendicantium statum libellum diffamatorium promulgavit asserens, eos non esse in statu salvandorum, et eis mendicitatem non esse meritoriam neque paupertatem, cum deberent propriis minibus laborare... Et frater Bertrandus de Baiona de Provincia Aquitaniae pro fratribus Religiosis Mendicantibus splendide peroravit et positiones Gulielmi totaliter improbavit, ita ut ipse doctor blasphemus stupens diceret: 'Vel tu es Angelus, vel diabolus, vel Strabo de Baiona'." Later the author characterizes William's campaign as directed "against the Friars Minor and Preachers" (*contra Fratres Minores et Praedicatores*) (p. 75).

[26] Marianus of Florence, *Compendium chronicarum Fratrum Minorum*, AFH, 2 (1909), 311: "Anno Domini 1251 suscitavit Demon spiritum cuiusdam magistri Guglelmi de Sancta Martha [*sic*], qui contra Religiosorum pauperum statum diffamatorium libellum promulgavit, asserens quod non erant in statu salvandorum, nec eis era⟨n⟩t meritoria eorum mendicitas, cum deberent propriis manibus laborare, et alia plurima. Propter quod magnum Ordinis persecutionem suscitavit."

[27] Marianus of Florence, *Compendium chronicarum Fratrum Minorum*, 313–14.

[28] Marcos de Lisboa, *Croínicas da Ordem dos Frades Menores*, ii (Porto: Faculdade de Letras da Universidade do Porto, 2001), 24, 31.

which was condemned and burned by the pope."[29] The primacy allocated here to the Preachers, however, ultimately came to underscore an irony rather than set the record straight about who suffered more in the event. For, according to Tschamser, all friars endured the secular masters' wrath in equal measure. Thus, as the great Irish Franciscan historian Luke Wadding (1588–1657) put it more pointedly, his brethren fell victim to "evils intended for the Preachers."[30]

It is a measure of Wadding's influence that the "collateral damage" thesis lived on in Franciscan lachrymose memory for many years to come. Less than a century ago, for instance, the French Franciscan Gratien de Paris set the stage for his brethren's ancient ordeal by noting that, "well before 1252, there were already symptomatic scrapings between the secular masters and the religious masters, especially the Friars Preachers." By the time matters came to a head in early 1254, "between the Minorites and the university the case was closed. But since the struggle against the Preachers continued animatedly, bringing the university to detest all friars equally, the Minorites were recast into the conflict."[31] Dominican pride, combined with the ham-fisted approach of the secular masters, spelled more needless suffering for the Franciscans.

Epitomizing this tradition among modern scholars is the Anglican Bishop of Ripon, ecumenist, and accomplished Franciscan historian John Moorman (1905–1989). Echoing many of his predecessors, he too portrayed the Dominicans as implacable in the face of the secular masters' resentment, a line that rendered Franciscan gestures at reconciliation sadly redundant. On the other hand, he acknowledged the inflammatory impact of the *Introductorious* on the already strained relations between seculars and mendicants in that it "gave men like William of Saint-Amour *the opportunity for which they were waiting.*" Thus even here the friars' real fault was their naïveté. Moorman continues:

The friars were now ostracized, and it became dangerous for them to appear in the streets. Scurrilous popular songs began to circulate, and had to be suppressed by authority. But the friars did not remain silent; they employed some of their ablest scholars in writing replies to the charges brought against them.... In these works the defence of the friars' position was so well done that the pope expelled William of Saint-Amour from France.[32]

Moorman was a Franciscan sympathizer, not a mendicant apologist, yet his reading of the evidence here is highly tendentious.[33] On the one hand, he ignores (and thus

---

[29] Malachias Tschamser, *Annales oder Jahrs-Geschichten der Baarfüseren oder Minderen Brüderen*, i (Colmar: Hoffmann, 1864), 145: "Guilielmus ein gewisser Doctor schreibt ein lästerliches Buch wider die P. P. Dominicaner, Baarfüßer und alle Religiosen; wird vom Pabst verdammt und verbrennt den 4 October."

[30] Luke Wadding et al., *Annales Minorum seu trium ordinum a S. Francisco institutorum*, 2nd edn, iv (Rome: Typis Rochi Bernabó, 1732), 21 (1256): "Sub mense Junii jam pertransiit perturbatio ad Minores, et participes facti sunt malorum quae Praedicatoribus evenerant."

[31] Gratien de Paris, *Histoire de la fondation et de l'évolution de l'Ordre des frères mineurs au XIIIe siècle*, with additional bibliography by Mariano D'Alatri and Servus Gieben, Biblioteca Seraphico-Capuccina, 29 (Santa Sabina [Rome]: Institutum Historicum Fratrum Praedicatorum, 1982 [orig. pub. 1928]), 206, 209.

[32] Moorman, *A History of the Franciscan Order*, 128–9 (emphasis added).

[33] Michael Manktelow, *John Moorman: Anglican, Franciscan, Independent* (Norwich: Canterbury Press, 1999), esp. 49–58.

perpetuates) what Maurice Halbwachs famously described as a jelling over time of collective memory;[34] on the other, he downplays the constraints of genre placed upon narrative sources, in this case mostly chronicle entries and polemical notes drafted by mendicant apologists.[35] As we have seen, and as Moorman was surely in a position to recognize, the events at Paris, like other chapters in the order's early history, were mythologized by mendicant authors over the course of many centuries, gradually reaching the dimensions of a clash between Brother David and the University of Goliath. Moreover, notwithstanding St Amour's brazen sermons and Rutebeuf's partisan poetry, the suggestion that any authority had to intervene in order to suppress their works is rather misleading, if only because the friars remained immensely popular both during and after the Parisian affair. The only evidence Moorman marshals of actual threats to the brethren's safety comes from a hysterical letter composed by Humbert of Romans, in which the Dominican Master General refers to some stones being thrown at his underlings and their Parisian convent in a presumably related incident.[36] No other contemporary source, including those composed by pro-mendicant authors, make mention of any physical violence.[37]

Most importantly, and as virtually no mendicant historian was willing to acknowledge, the friars' real challenge at the time was to hold the fort rather than charge at it uphill and unarmed. Their ablest scholars made an eloquent case indeed, but Moorman neglects to mention that their works' immediate audience was a highly sympathetic pope and, crucially, their staunchest secular supporter, Louis IX of France (St Louis), a man venerated by the Dominicans and later championed as a Franciscan Tertiary, albeit not always to his credit.[38] The brethren's triumph and William's exile, in fine, were more likely to have been an outcome of the latter's uncompromising stance, which involved making rather bold allegations of heresy against an antagonistic king and an uncooperative pope, than of any ink spilled by Bonaventure, Thomas of York, or Thomas Aquinas. As the Benedictine chronicler of St Denis, Guillaume de Nangis (d. 1300), remarked, the fate of *De periculis* was sealed "not, as some said, on account of its heretical content, but rather because it was seen to provoke rebellion against the friars and create a scandal."[39]

---

[34] Maurice Halbwachs, *On Collective Memory*, ed. and trans. Lewis A. Coser (Chicago: University of Chicago Press, 1992), 94–5.

[35] James Fentress and Chris Wickham, *Social Memory* (Oxford: Blackwell, 1992), esp. 51–75, 144–99.

[36] *CUP* i. 273 (p. 312): "Et tam in domo quam extra domum, et nocte et die, Israël fili in luto et latere lapidantur. In domum etiam nostram sagitte manu balistarii jaciuntur." The only "insultum cum armis" Humbert refers to (p. 310) is, in my reading, the beating of several secular Parisian students by local guards, an event that originally led to the university strike.

[37] See *CUP* i. 222, 224–5.

[38] A. G. Little, *Franciscan History and Legend in English Mediaeval Art* (Manchester: Manchester University Press, 1937), pp. xvi–xvii. On Louis IX's intimate relations with the mendicant orders, see Ch. 1 and, most recently, William Chester Jordan, "Louis IX: Preaching to Franciscan and Dominican Brothers and Nuns," in Michael F. Cusato and G. Geltner (eds), *Defenders and Critics of Franciscan Life: Essays in Honor of John V. Fleming*, The Medieval Franciscans, 6 (Leiden: Brill, 2009), 219–35.

[39] H. Géraud (ed.), *Chronique Latin de Guillaume de Nangis et de ses continuateurs*, i (Paris: Jules Renouard, 1843), 216–17: "Discordia quae fuerat inter fratres Praedicatores et Minores ac alios religiosos Parisius studentes ex una parte, et magistrum Guillermum de Sancto-Amore ex alia, super

There is little evidence, in short, to suggest that, in the words of the Franciscans' most recent affiliate historian, "the onslaught of the secular masters of the University of Paris in the 1250s was deeply damaging."[40] Rather than being weakened by the events, in Duncan Nimmo's more sober appraisal, the Minorites were "if anything enhanced by the opposition which that success aroused among the secular clergy in general, and at the University of Paris in particular."[41] Which is not to detract from the general significance of the university quarrels: they set the stage for many future debates both within and outside the context of religious mendicancy, including the reformulation of the apostolic life as a precise juridical term, the development of Gallicanism, mendicant reappraisals of papal power and infallibility, and more.[42] In the present context, however, the event served as a major flash of recognition among the friars of their own vulnerability, and—more to the point—as a reminder of how to convert an apparent weakness into strength by retroactively weaving a minor threat into a lachrymose narrative of their orders' history.[43]

In an important sense, then, and beyond the scope of Chapter 1's examination, the Parisian university quarrels of the 1250s do serve as a fulcrum for the history of antifraternalism or else as a focal point for an antifraternal tradition, crafted mostly by contemporary and later mendicant authors in order to perpetuate a social memory of their victimhood. According to this tradition, in cosmopolitan Paris of the mid-thirteenth century, the brethren first recognized the real scale of their opposition, now no longer dismissible as unrelated to local events. We now move to explore two further arenas in which friars developed their identity as sufferers and promoted self-sacrifice in support of their internal goals and in order to secure external backing.

MARTYRDOM AND THE HOME FRONT

While Christians never entirely ceased from dying for their faith following the waning of their persecution in Late Antiquity, the millennium separating early

---

librum quem *De periculis mundi* intitulatum composuerat, recidivavit. Propter quam discordiam sedandam et pacificandam, misit rex Franciae Ludovicus ad curiam Romanam duos clericos, ut per dominum papam [Alexandrum] debitum finem sortiretur. Tandem multis hinc inde propositis, damnatus est et combustus coram Papa, apud Anagniam in ecclesia cathedrali, liber a praedicto magistro Guillermo editus, non propter haeresim, ut quidam dicunt, quam contineret, sed quia contra praefatos religiosos videbatur seditionem et scandalum excitare."

[40] Michael Robson, *The Franciscans in the Middle Ages* (Woodbridge: Boydell, 2006), 4.

[41] Duncan Nimmo, *Reform and Division in the Medieval Franciscan Order (1226–1538)*, Bibliotheca Seraphico-Capuccina, 33 (Rome: Capuchin Historical Institute, 1987), 142.

[42] See Roberto Lambertini, "La scelta francescana e l'Università di Parigi. Il *Bettelordenstreit* fino alla *Exiit qui seminat*," in Francesco Santi (ed.), *Gli studi francescani dal dopoguerra ad oggi* (Spoleto: Centro Italiano di Studi sull'Alto Medioevo, 1993), 143–72.

[43] The strategy was by no means restricted to the Franciscans. See Thomas Ripoll (ed.), *Bullarium ordinis fratrum praedicatorum*, 2 vols (Rome: J. Mainardus, 1729–30), whose index reads like an *improperia* of sorts; for the Parisian affair, see i. 291, 308–9, 311–12, 346–9, 353–4, 372, 375.

martyrs, such as Perpetua and Cyprian,[44] and the neo-martyrs of the thirteenth century saw few such casualties, at least within the boundaries of Western Christendom. The pause is easily explained. On the one hand, Christianity's political triumph by the late fourth century by and large ended its followers' predicament. On the other, few of Jesus's followers, even beyond the former Roman Empire's borders, lived under regimes so intolerant as to openly seek to eradicate their faith.[45] The lingering hiatus in violence did not reduce but rather increased the fame of the early martyrs, whose legends, cults, and relics formed a visible aspect of the literary, spiritual, and material landscape of Christendom, especially in monastic milieus.[46] By practicing self-mortification or else through adopting an ethos of extreme asceticism, medieval monks forged an ancestral link with Christianity's original confessors.[47] Thus the experience of suffering to the point of dying for one's faith maintained a key position in Christian spirituality. In the twelfth century it was expanded and perpetuated through the infusion of the crusading movement with monastic ideals, especially Cistercian,[48] before being appropriated by late-medieval mendicants in their quest to become the church's new vanguard.[49]

In different ways and to varying degrees the friars engaged in defending church doctrine and propagating Christianity, often as cogs in the papal machinery. Pursuing these activities within as well as beyond the shifting borders of Latin Christendom, the brethren encountered both coreligionists and "infidels" who stood in their path. Whether as missionaries to the heathen in Asia, the Balkans, and the Near East, as inquisitors in Languedoc, Lombardy, and elsewhere, or as

---

[44] See Herbert Musurillo (ed. and trans.), *The Acts of the Christian Martyrs* (Oxford: Clarendon Press, 1972).

[45] The notable exception occurred at the meeting point between Latin Christendom and Islam. See Edward P. Colbert, *The Martyrs of Córdoba (850–859): A Study of the Sources* (Washington, D. C.: Catholic University of America Press, 1962); Kenneth Wolf, *Christian Martyrs in Muslim Spain* (Cambridge: Cambridge University Press, 1988); and Jessica A. Coope, *The Martyrs of Córdoba: Community and Family Conflict in an Age of Mass Conversion* (Lincoln, NB: University of Nebraska Press, 1995).

[46] Jacques Dubois, *Les martyrologes du moyen âge latin*, Typologie des sources du moyen âge occidental, 26 (Turnholt: Brepols, 1978); John McCulloh, "Historical Martyrologies in the Benedictine Cultural Tradition," in W. Lourdaux and D. Verhelst (eds), *Benedictine Culture, 750–1050*, Mediaevalia Lovaniensia, 1.11 (Leuven: Leuven University Press, 1983), 114–31; Johan Leemens (ed.), with the collaboration of Jürgen Mettepenningen, *More than a Memory: The Discourse of Martyrdom and the Construction of Christian Identity in the History of Christianity* (Leuven: Peeters, 2005); Candida R. Moss, *The Other Christs: Imitating Jesus in Ancient Christian Ideologies of Martyrdom* (Oxford: Oxford University Press, 2010).

[47] Clare Stancliffe, "Red, White and Blue Martyrdom," in Rosamond McKitterick, David Dumville, and Dorothy Whitlock (eds), *Ireland in Early Mediaeval Europe: Studies in Memory of Kathleen Hughes* (Cambridge: Cambridge University Press, 1983), 21–46. On the friars' "supererogation" or practices of extreme self-mortification, see the Augustinian Jordan of Saxony, *Liber Vitasfratrum*, IV. 10, ed. Rudolf Arbesmann and Winfrid Hümpfner (New York: Cosmopolitan Science & Art Service, 1943), 420–5.

[48] William J. Purkis, *Crusading Spirituality in the Holy Land and Iberia, c.1095–c.1187* (Woodbridge: Boydell, 2008), 86–119.

[49] Nor would they be the last to appropriate that legacy. See Robert Kolb, *For all the Saints: Changing Perceptions of Martyrdom and Sainthood in the Lutheran Reformation* (Macon, GA: Mercer University Press, 1987); Nikki Shepardson, *Burning Zeal: The Rhetoric of Martyrdom and the Protestant Community in Reformation France, 1520–1570* (Bethlehem, PA: Lehigh University Press, 2007); Leemens (ed.), *More than a Memory*, 243–464.

remnants and promoters of a Catholic presence in the Holy Land, mendicants were reared to face serious opposition and consciously to risk their lives in carrying out their ministry.[50] Some locations proved more dangerous than others. While death on doctrinal or even political grounds was uncommon among the brethren within Latin Europe, outside it the risk was significantly higher, notwithstanding what one scholar has identified as the brethren's "remarkable ease of access" to the Muslim-controlled Near East.[51] By the close of the fourteenth century, some forty Franciscans, around thirty Dominicans, and a handful of mendicants from smaller orders lost their lives in faraway lands mainly while proselytizing.[52] At least for some of those donning a mendicant's habit, then, death on the job was being presented as a real possibility, and the brethren as fast en route to becoming the church's new martyrs.

At the same time, there were further motivations for promoting extreme self-sacrifice or at least fostering a martyrological ethos among mendicants. As Maureen Burke has pointed out, the iconographic commemoration of martyrs among Franciscans began in earnest only in the fourteenth century—that is, many decades after the brethren's first achievements in this sphere. Her explanation of the time lag construes the emergence of martyrdom as a pacifying and unifying motif in a religious order until recently embroiled in internal strife, also known as the Spiritual–Conventual conflict.[53] In a yet more recent contribution to this debate, Christopher MacEvitt seems generally amenable to Burke's contextualization, although his analysis of texts describing the brethren's demise in the Near East yields a nuanced set of motivations for both the temporal delay and some of the

---

[50] *The Life of Saint Peter Thomas by Philippe de Mézières*, ed. Joachim Smet, TSHC 2 (Rome: Institutum Carmelitanum, 1954), concerns a single friar engaged in virtually all of these activities.

[51] Andrew Jotischky, "Mendicants as Missionaries and Travellers in the Near East in the Thirteenth and Fourteenth Centuries," in Rosamund Allen (ed.), *Eastward Bound: Travel and Travellers in the Medieval Mediterranean 1050–1500* (Manchester: Manchester University Press, 2004), 90. The Venetian merchant Marco Polo (1254–1323) expressed his surprise at the friars' reluctance to travel to Asia, perhaps as a way to celebrate his own achievement. See *The Travels of Marco Polo*, trans. Robert Latham (London and New York: Penguin Books, 1988), 26. On the other hand, *The Life of Saint Peter Thomas* 36, ed. Smet, 81, construes its protagonist's actions as a wholehearted quest for martyrdom, "velut alter Franciscus" see also 21, 43–4, 74 (pp. 68–9, 88, 114, respectively).

[52] The foremost scholar of Franciscan martyrdom put the figure at forty-two casualties. See Isabelle Heullant-Donat, "Des missionnaires martyrs aux martyrs missionnaires: La Mémoire des martyrs franciscains au sein de leur Ordre aux XIIIe et XIVe siècles," in *Écrire son histoire: Les communautés régulières face à leur passé*, actes du 5e Colloque International du C.E.R.C.O.R., Saint-Étienne (6–8 novembre 2002) (Saint-Étienne: Publications de l'Université de Saint-Étienne–Jean Monnet, 2005), 172 n. 5. See also Isabelle Heullant-Donat, "Les martyrs franciscains de Jérusalem (1391), entre mémoire en manipulation (1391–1970)," in D. Coulon et al. (eds), *Chemins d'Outremer: Études d'Histoire sur la Méditerranée médiévale offertes à Michel Balard*, Byzantina Sorbonensia, 20 (Paris: Publications de la Sorbonne, 2004), 439–59; and her long-awaited *Missions impossibles: Les Franciscains, le martyre et l'islam (XIIIe–XVe siècle)* (Rome: École française de Rome, forthcoming). And see below.

[53] S. Maureen Burke, "The 'Martyrdom of the Franciscans' by Ambrogio Lorenzetti," *Zeitschrift für Kunstgeschichte*, 65 (2002), 465–7. Burke brings no evidence linking the recent upheavals and any decision made by local convents or the order's leadership to begin depicting martyrological activities, however.

common stylistic and ideological features of Franciscan martyrology.[54] In his view, the brethren's portrayals of extreme suffering aimed at underscoring a divide between Christian and Muslim geographies through an affirmation of the latter "as an infidel (that is, Muslim) space in which Christian qualities could find no purchase."[55]

MacEvitt's suggestion of a desired religious dichotomy gestures at two further and interrelated factors converging upon the appropriation of martyrdom as a cherished mendicant value. First and rather obviously, the friars' concept of extreme sacrifice was probably influenced by Near East crusading itself, a movement that not only valorized inflicting as well as suffering death in the name of one's faith, but also received the mendicants' special attention as preachers and promoters of the endeavor.[56] Secondly, born into a reality in which death beyond the borders of Christendom was recognized as a unique act of devotion, mendicants were well positioned to harness such sentiments and events among their brethren in the service of constructing their social memory and identity. As Friederike Pannewick put it in a somewhat broader context, "the shared remembrance [of martyrdom] inscribed in literary texts creates amongst the audience/readers a *community of suffering*."[57]

There are two obvious flaws in trying to bolster the friars' identity as a community of sufferers by recourse to a distilled tradition of Christianity's original martyrs.[58] Judging by the evidence presented in Chapter 2, such a move would require shoehorning a recent and disparate group of events into an ancient and no less complex mould. Further, and as mendicant historians from Bernard Gui to Cesare Cenci have shown, most instances of antifraternal aggression transpired in an intra-Christian rather than inter-religious context and seldom brought into question the legitimacy of religious poverty. To recall, Appendix I (the evidentiary basis for Chapter 2) comprises a roster of chiefly orthodox assailants, including a significant number of priests and monks who resisted the friars on occasions that can hardly be labeled doctrinal disputes, let alone botched conversions. By contrast, pagans, Jews, Muslims, indeed even Christian heretics feature marginally on this

---

[54] Christopher MacEvitt, "Martyrdom and the Muslim World through Franciscan Eyes," *Catholic Historical Review*, 97 (2011), 1–24.
[55] MacEvitt, "Martyrdom and the Muslim World through Franciscan Eyes," 16.
[56] Christoph T. Maier, *Preaching the Crusades: Mendicant Friars and the Cross in the Thirteenth Century* (Cambridge: Cambridge University Press, 1994).
[57] Friederike Pannewick, "Introduction," in Friederike Pannewick (ed.), *Martyrdom in Literature: Visions of Death and Meaningful Suffering in Europe and the Middle East from Antiquity to Modernity* (Wiesbaden: Reichert Verlag, 2004), 9 (emphasis added). On the formation of monastic identity more generally, see Catherine Cubitt, "Monastic Memory and Identity in Early Anglo-Saxon England," in William O. Frazer and Andrew Tyrrell (eds), *Social Identity in Early Medieval Britain* (London and New York: Leicester University Press, 2000), 253–76; Susan Boynton, *Shaping a Monastic Identity: Liturgy and History at the Imperial Abbey of Farfa, 1000–1125* (Ithaca, NY: Cornell University Press, 2006).
[58] Elizabeth A. Castelli, *Martyrdom and Memory: Gender, Theory, and Religion* (New York: Columbia University Press, 2004). For a comparative cross-cultural view, see the essays gathered in Pannewick (ed.), *Martyrdom in Literature*.

118　　　　　　　　　　　　*Deeds and Words*

list, much like clerical reactionaries such as William of St Amour and Richard FitzRalph.[59]

However, the church's vanguard fought internally as well as externally, allowing suffering and self-sacrifice on the home front to fit neatly into the brethren's working assumption that sooner or later they will meet strong opposition. Such expectations ran the gamut from latent eschatology to explicit apocalypticism, and were exemplified through challenges ranging from the quotidian to the truly extraordinary. The Carmelites, for instance, famously traced their origins to Mount Carmel, the site of Elijah's heavenly ascent, thereby drawing a palpable link between their activities and a uniquely eschatological location, from which they claimed they were violently evicted by Muslims in 1187: a firing shot in a cosmic struggle.[60] And among Franciscans, to take another example, the fourteenth-century Irishman John Clyn reported a popular prophecy that associated the millennial era with the brethren's general rejection, this time by their fellow Christians.[61]

Thus, although the clergy as a whole could identify themselves as important agents in the economy of salvation, the friars in particular considered their hardships as uniquely indicative of the end of times. The Dominican Master General Humbert of Romans described William of St Amour and his partisans in 1254 as Satan, Leviathan, and Belial, thus reminding his brethren of the ultimate significance of their struggle.[62] And a Franciscan *Liber exemplorum* composed sometime in the 1270s reports how a certain fra Tomás who, in sermonizing to a group of plague-ridden Irishmen, encouraged his audience to overcome their fear of the Devil by emulating his brethren's example. We Friars Minor, he claimed,

are men who throughout the world do the most against them [i.e., demons] and say many hostile things about them. Here I am, standing and saying all these hostile things about them and preaching. I want to tell them to come to me and do to me what they wish. Let the demons come, I say, if they dare, indeed let them all come! Why do they not come? What are they doing? Where are they? I repeat this abuse for all men to hear.[63]

---

[59] There is no record of Jews assaulting friars in this period, despite major polemical confrontations between the two groups. See Jeremy Cohen, *The Friars and the Jews* (Ithaca, NY: Cornell University Press, 1982); Robert Chazan, *Barcelona and Beyond: The Disputation of 1263 and its Aftermath* (Berkeley and Los Angeles: University of California Press, 1992); and Steven J. McMichael and Susan E. Myers (eds), *Friars and Jews in the Middle Ages and the Renaissance*, The Medieval Franciscans, 2 (Leiden: Brill, 2004).

[60] Jean de Cheminot, *Speculum fratrum ordinis*, MCH 116–23; Jean de Venette, *Speculum status ordinis historiale*, MCH 159–60, both of which explain Elijah's role as a martyr at the end of times.

[61] John Clyn, *Annalium Hiberniae Chronicon ad annum MCCCXLIX*, ed. R. Butler (Dublin: Irish Archaeological Society, 1849), 36. See also the fourteenth-century *Chronicle* by the Franciscan Johannes van Winterthur, which contains a refutation of similar apocalyptic prophecies concerning his brethren, excerpted in Rosmary Horrox (ed. and trans.), *The Black Death* (Manchester: Manchester University Press, 1994), 155. The range of approaches is discussed in Roest, *Reading the Book of History*, 153–92.

[62] *CUP* i. 273 (pp. 309–10).

[63] A. G. Little (ed.), *Liber exemplorum ad usum praedicantium* (Aberdeen: Typis Academicis, 1908), 86: "Nos sumus hominess de mundo qui plus facimus contra eos et plura mala dicimus de eis; et ego sum hic stans et omnia hec mala dicens de eis et predicans; et ego volo et dico eis quod veniant ad me et

Tantalizing demons like a fearless matador (or a Christian gladiator), Tomás purports to bolster the ethos of his order as one situated at the forefront of a perennial struggle for salvation's sake, both personal and collective.

The stance has a long pedigree, from early Christian hermits to later monks, whose function as "those who pray" (*oratores*) was widely accepted and encouraged. However, and to the chagrin of traditional monks, mendicants departed from the accustomed enclosure of monastic life, precisely with the sort of outreach work that the above *exemplum* relates; and, to the chagrin of secular priests, they settled almost exclusively in cities, where they were seen to threaten the stability of existing parish structures. The manifest antagonism created by their unconventional *modus operandi* did little to increase the friars' doubts about their central and potentially hazardous role in the economy of Christian salvation. If anything, and as we shall see, their experiences on the home front did just the opposite.

Black Death

Violent events, from evictions to beatings to murder, offered the mendicants different opportunities to play out, recollect, and reinscribe what they perceived as their unique role in the history and economy of salvation. More than 100 cases lending themselves to such an interpretation were reported in Chapter 2; many of them—not surprisingly—were initially preserved for us by the quills of friars or their sympathizers. Cognizant of these events' value for the orders' identity, mendicants and their advocates were eager to record them in order, on the one hand, to emphasize the brethren's continuous sacrifice and, on the other, to shape "healing narratives" for those who either survived such assaults or were simply able to avoid them.[64] To recall but two such examples, the Minorite Jordan of Giano cast Germany as a land especially fit for those among his brethren seeking martyrdom, albeit on a rather weak basis; and Heinrich von Regensburg, the Dominicans' Protector in Germany, greatly overstated the lethal danger hanging over the Strasbourg brethren's head prior to their eviction in the late 1280s.[65] Despite their generic and circumstantial differences, both texts employ hyperbole as a way to foment their audiences' rage while simultaneously encouraging their recovery.

Yet mendicant authors understood the limited political value of highlighting local and potentially isolated events. Conversely, they recognized the potential of spotlighting their suffering by inserting it into narratives of major calamities that touched upon the lives of numerous others. Among these the most obvious candidate was the Black Death, a plague epidemic that struck down millions

---

faciant michi quicquid possunt. Veniant, inquid, demones si audent, et omnes veniant! Quare non veniunt? Quid faciunt? Ubi sunt? Huiusmodi verba insultatoria replico in auribus totius populi."

[64] On healing narratives, see Patricia Lawrence, "Violence, Suffering, Amman: The Work of Oracles in Sri Lanka's Eastern War Zone," in Veena Das et al. (eds), *Violence and Subjectivity* (Berkeley and Los Angeles: University of California Press, 2000), 171–204.

[65] *Chronica Fratris Jordani*, ed. H. Boehmer (Paris: Librairie Fischbacher, 1908), 5 (pp. 5–6); Wilhelm Wiegand and Aloys Schulte (eds), *Urkunden der Stadt Strassburg*, ii (Strasbourg: Karl J. Trübner, 1886), no. 118.

between 1347 and 1349, in a prelude to several equally disastrous visitations. Friars, monks, and secular clergymen alike perished disproportionately from the disease, a phenomenon requiring clarification if the church was to end common quips about its members' demise as a godly reprisal. "The best of the clergy died, the worst survived," as one modern scholar rationalized.[66] But, whereas medieval parish priests and other secular clergymen generally lacked a united voice to underscore their dedication and altruism, the friars proceeded to construe the Black Death as among their orders' finest hours.

Surprisingly, descriptions of ecclesiastical responses to the plague have yet to be fully studied as examples of "countermemory" or, less subtly put, a form of propaganda war between various entities within the church.[67] Although such an endeavor falls beyond the scope of the present study, it is still worthwhile focusing, however briefly, on mendicants' self-representation during this episode, as we have already dealt with their remembrance of the Parisian university quarrels. This is not to compare the two events, nor to suggest that friars fabricated instances of self-sacrifice during the plague. Yet interrogating mendicant descriptions of suffering in the event illustrates their tendency to employ just such moments in the service of fortifying the orders' social memory and identity, stressing both sacrifice and—by no means less importantly—survival.[68]

In his evocative account of the plague's arrival in Messina, for instance, the Sicilian Franciscan Michele da Piazza (fl. 1349–61) noted how few clergymen, judges, and notaries were willing to help the dying, hear their last confessions, or write down their wills, except the Friars Minor and Preachers, whose extreme selflessness explains why they "died in such large numbers that their priories were *all but deserted.*"[69] Secular clergymen's neglect and the friars' decimation-but-not-annihilation is likewise underscored by the Paris-based Carmelite Jean de Venette (*c.*1300–*c.*1370), who lamented how "in many towns timid priests withdrew, leaving the exercise of their ministry to such of the religious as were more daring." Given that under these circumstances most monks were likely to be religious

---

[66] Philip Ziegler, *The Black Death* (London: Penguin Books, 1982), 270. See also Peter George Mode, *The Influence of the Black Death on the English Monasteries* (Menasha, WI: George Banta, 1916); William J. Dohar, *The Black Death and Pastoral Leadership: The Diocese of Hereford in the Fourteenth Century* (Philadelphia: University of Pennsylvania Press, 1995).

[67] See Natalie Zemon Davis and Randolph Starns (eds), "Collective Memory and Countermemory," *Representations*, 26 (special issue) (1989).

[68] As Michael Vargas, "How a 'Brood of Vipers' Survived the Black Death: Recovery and Dysfunction in the Fourteenth-Century Dominican Order," *Speculum*, 86 (2011), 688–714, has shown, exaggerating the brethren's losses during the plague also played into later narratives of rise, decline, and reform.

[69] Michele da Piazza, *Cronaca*, ed. Antonino Giuffrida, Fonti per la Storia di Sicilia, 3, 3 vols in 1 (Palermo and Sao Paolo: ILA Palma, 1980), i. 27–9 (pp. 82–3): "Et intantum mortalitas ipsa Messanensibus invaluit, quod petebant multi sacerdotibus confiteri sua peccata, et testamenta conficere, et sacredotes, judices, et notarii ad domos eorum accedere recusabant; et si aliqui ipsorum ad eorum hospitia ingrediebantur pro testamentis, et talibus conficiendis, mortem mullatenus repentinam poterant evitare. Fratres vero Ordinis minorum et Predicatorum et aliorum ordinum accedere volentes ad domos infirmorum predictorum, et confitentes eisdem de eorum peccatis, et dantes eis penitentiam juxta velle sermus divinam justitia, adeo letalis mors ipsos infecit, quod *fere in eorum cellulis de eis aliqui remanserunt*" (emphasis added).

mendicants, the text offers a clear vindication of the friars' specifically (and, in the case of the solitude-prone Carmelites, doubly challenging) urban mission. And, just to drive the point home, the author clarifies that "if a healthy man visited the sick he only rarely evaded the risk of death".[70] Other mendicant authors simply took care to record the deaths of their brethren, sometimes to the exclusion of all others', as an effective way of emphasizing their special sacrifice as early responders to the calamity. And, by virtue of doing so, they also implied the healing fact of their survival.[71]

Such descriptions apply a positive gloss to the friars' dying *en masse* and, especially by playing down the suffering of others, imply that their decimation had an important eschatological role to play. Small wonder that a similar emphasis on the brethren's suffering is absent from most secular, let alone monastic and clerical, accounts of the plague, which are uninterested in the specific type of lachrymose narrative the friars were forging. Jean Froissart (*c*.1337–1405), for instance, seems entirely oblivious to the brethren's bravery, as is Matteo Villani (d. 1363) in his more elaborate account of the events in Florence, for which incidentally he relies on at least one mendicant eyewitness.[72] Only the detailed report of Gabriele de' Mussis (d. 1356) concerning the plague's visitation upon his home city of Piacenza recounts the deaths of dozens of friars, albeit alongside those of numerous laypeople and other ecclesiastics: a disaster to be sure, but one in which no unique eschatological role was allocated to the brethren, and no special cause to lament their loss and simultaneously celebrate their survival.[73]

Among some ecclesiastical authors the stakes were evidently even higher. A clerical eyewitness in Narbonne claimed that friars or, as he candidly admitted, men dressed as such, precipitated the plague's onset in the region.[74] The English Benedictine John of Reading (d. 1368/9) describes how, in the immediate aftermath of the plague, local mendicants in particular seized the chance to appropriate

---

[70] H. Géraud (ed.), *Chronique Latin de Guillaume de Nangis et de ses continuateurs*, ii (Paris: Jules Renouard, 1843), 211: "Nam qui sanus aliquem visitabat infirmum, vix aut raro mortis periculum evadebat. Unde in multis vilis parvis et magnis sacerdotes timidi recedebant, religiosis aliquibus magis audacibus ad ministrationem dimittentes."

[71] R. Morçay, "La cronaca del convento di s. Caterina dell'ordine deo Predicatori in Pisa," *Archivio Storico Italiano*, 1st ser., 6/2 (1845), 530 (CLXXXII), records the death of forty friars. Tommaso Kaeppeli, "Cronache domenicane di Giacomo Domenech O.P. in una raccola miscellanea del Card. Niccolò Rosell," *AFP*, 14 (1944), 38–9, mentions that 510 Aragonese Dominicans had perished from the plague. Tschamser, *Annales oder Jahrs-Geschichten*, i. 363–6, likewise records the deaths of friars in numerous houses, juxtaposing their decimation with the lower death rates of the general population. Marianus of Florence, *Compendium Chronicarum Fratrum Minorum*, 301, claims a third of the brethren had perished from the plague, but neglects to mention the parallel rates for non-mendicants, as does *Glassberger*, 184.

[72] Jean Froissart, *Chroniques*, vol. iv, ed. Siméon Luce (Paris: Jules Renouard, 1873), 100–1; Matteo Villani, *Cronica. Con la continuazione di Filippo Villani*, vol. 1, ed. Giuseppe Porta (Parma: U. Guanda, 1995), chs 1–6.

[73] See Horrox (ed. and trans.), *The Black Death*, 21–2, which offers a revised version of the text originally edited by A. W. Henschel, "Document zur Geschichte des schwarzen Todes," in *Archiv für die gesammte Medicin*, 2, ed. Heinrich Haeser (Jena, 1842), 45–7.

[74] Christian Guilleré, "La Pest noire a Gerone (1348)," *Annals de l'Institut d'Estudis Gironins*, 27 (1984), 103–4 and n. 80.

the goods left by the plague's innumerable victims. Suggesting foul play and even fouler outcomes, he wrote that "superfluous wealth flowed their way, through confessions and bequests, in such quantities that they scarcely condescended to accept oblations... Superfluous finery was everywhere: in the chambers, at table, in riding—all unauthorized and prompted by the Devil."[75] And the Regular Canon Henry Knighton (d. 1396) positively relished the demise of 358 Dominicans in Provence, 133 friars in Montpellier, and 153 in Magdalen, and went on to note how

> of 140 Preachers and ten Minorites in Marseille only one remained to bring the news to the rest, which is just fine. Among the Carmelites in Avignon, sixty-six had died before the citizens realized what was happening; they thought that the brothers had been killing one another. Of the English [Augustinian] Hermits not one survived in Avignon, which is of no concern.[76]

As we have seen, mendicant authors were aware of the importance of balancing suffering and survival when depicting the brethren's woes. Conversely, privileging the reporting on the friars' complete destruction over disclosing their continued existence was the obvious path open to Knighton. In this macabre equilibrium, this zero-sum game, the mendicants' loss was at least the clergy's if not Christianity's gain. And it goes almost without saying that Knighton does not portray the friars as having served their communities—that is, other than by dying.

In sum, the half-glass-full view offered by mendicant authors trying to explain their brethren's death during the plague was at times met by an equally tendentious rendering of the events by their clerical antagonists. Securing one's eschatological role was evidently an important factor in shaping mendicant (and clerical) lachrymose narratives, which in turn bolstered their respective audiences' memory and identity. And whatever threatened to compromise an order's understanding of its role in salvation history was squarely met by the friars' resistance. The penitential flagellants' spread in the plague's immediate aftermath is a case in point. According to the German Dominican Heinrich von Herford (d. 1370), two of his brethren were assaulted after accosting a group of flagellants in the outskirts of Meissen in Saxony. One of the friars survived by fleeing, the other was stoned to death.[77] Thus the effect of the plague continued to ripple through the order, creating further

---

[75] James Tait (ed.), *Chronica Johannis de Reading et Anonymi Cantuariensis 1346–1367* (Manchester: Manchester University Press, 1914), 109–10: "superfluae divitiae affluebant ut vix sibi oblate dedignabantur admittere... superfluo ornatu in cameris, mensis, equitaturis ex parte diaboli ceterisque inordinatis, terrene carnalique non coelestia appetebant."

[76] *Chronicon Henrici Knighton, vel Cnitthon, monachi leycestrensis*, ii, ed. Jason Rawson Lumby, Rolls Series, 92 (London: HMSO, 1895), 58–65: "De fratribus praedicatoribus in regione Provinciae in Quadragesima mortui sunt ccclviij. Item apud Monpelers de centum xl. non remanserunt nisi vij. fratres. Apud Magdalen de clx. remanserunt vij. fratres, et tamen satis. Apud Marsiliam de cxl. [praedicatoribus] et x. minoribus non remansit solus unus qui nunciaret caeteris; bene quidem. De Carmelitis mortui sunt Avinionae lxvj. antequam cives casum eventus perciperent. Credebant namque quod alter alterum peremisset. De Heremitis Angliae non remansit unus in Aviniona; nec cura."

[77] *Liber de rebus memorabilioribus sive chronicon Henrici de Hervordia*, ed. August Potthast (Göttingen: Sumptibus Dieterichanis, 1859), 282: "Unde et fratres duos predicatores eis occurentes in campo violentes occidere, cum aglior elpasus aufugisset, alium lapidaverunt, et mortuum lapidibus

victims and simultaneously increasing the friars' conviction in their mission. Continuing a long tradition of Christian spirituality, mendicant authors employed a classic "sweet inversion" of a terrible event into a vindicating one, yet simultaneously compensated for it by creating healing memories that reaffirmed the brethren's survival as a reaffirmation of their virtue.

The Inquisition

Friars' remembrance of home-front violence, with its potential for healing eschatological connotations, could easily draw upon responses to their activities as inquisitors.[78] As we have seen in Chapter 2 and as Appendix I documents, there was no shortage of events at least superficially involving anti-inquisitorial aggression aimed specifically at friars. Yet the brethren's lachrymose historiography is less studded with such incidents than was theoretically feasible, a discrepancy that perhaps has to do, on the one hand, with the Franciscans' only modest effort to recollect this aspect of their mission, and, on the other, with the Dominicans' ambivalence about identifying themselves with their inquisitor-brethren or espousing the institution generally, at least in their early years.[79] This is not to argue that mendicants renounced their involvement in eradicating heresy, but rather that their remembrance of anti-inquisitorial aggression was quite measured, especially when compared with their eagerness to document their suffering in the context of the Parisian affair, martyrdom among non-Christians, or altruism during the Black Death.

To be sure, if dying in the papally organized pursuit of heresy was somewhat elided in the orders' historiography, it was by no means ignored. The vast majority of inquisitors were, after all, friars—a strong and visible overlap that enabled some observers to attribute anti-inquisitorial violence to antifraternal sentiments, while allowing other authors to reduce the latter to the former. Such ambiguity is omnipresent in lists of the orders' saints, a genre whose economy of style leaves much for the imagination regarding the circumstances of each death. An extant copy of a Franciscan list of saints from 1353, for example, includes the names of several brethren who were killed while on duty as inquisitors, such as Gulielmus and Cathelanus, "who were martyred by heretics on account of the inquisition among the faithful" (*qui martyrizati sunt ab haereticis propter inquisitionem fidei*) in

---

obrutum relinquerunt in metis Mysne et Bayoarie, persuassionibus eorum exasperati. Et in plerisque locis similia plura fecerunt."

[78] Contrary to a modern tendency to identify the Dominican Order in particular with the medieval inquisition, the office was in fact largely shared between the two major mendicant orders. Lansing; Holly J. Grieco, "Franciscan Inquisition and Mendicant Rivalry in Mid-Thirteenth-Century Marseille," *JMH*, 34 (2008), 275–90.

[79] Laurent Albaret, "Les Prêcheurs et l'inquisition," in *L'Ordre des Prêcheurs et son histoire en France méridionale*, CdF 36 (Toulouse-Fanjeaux: Privat, 2001), 319–41; Laurent Albaret, "Inquisitio heretice pravitatis: L'Inquisition dominicaine dans le midi de la France aux XIIIe et XIVe siècles ou la première inquisition pontificale," in Wolfram Hoyer (ed.), *Praedicatores, Inquisitores. I. The Dominicans and the Medieval Inquisition* (Rome: Istituto Storico Domenicano, 2004), 421–46. For an opposing view, see Ames.

Valence, and Stephanus, a Benedictine abbot who joined the order and became an inquisitor in Toulouse.[80] These men's ultimate sacrifice is aptly recorded, but not without obfuscating the original circumstances of their demise, which, as I have argued, could be rather diverse.

Unstated assumptions concerning the assailants' original objectives served well the mendicants' changing goals. For instance, a list of Dominican martyrs drafted in the late seventeenth century and preserved today in the order's central archives, makes no qualitative distinction between earlier inquisitors and the Preachers' more recent missionaries to Latin America and Asia, let alone offers concrete contexts for the brethren's deaths other than indicating their geographical locations. Thus the list's record of the thirty-two cases recorded there for the period before 1400 implies that those friars slain in southern France, Lombardy, and Germany faced the same kind of opposition they did synchronically in Bulgaria, Bosnia, and Dalmatia, and diachronically in India, Africa, and Latin America.[81] At the same time, collapsing friars' deaths into a single category reified by a martyrological list offered a convenient way to register such events variously as anti-inquisitorial, anti-Dominican, antifraternal, anticlerical, or anti-colonial violence, or even designate them as acts directed against the papacy by casting the brethren's suffering once again as collateral damage of church policy. This ambiguity and concentricity established the brethren's pursuit of heretics as further evidence of their willingness to sacrifice themselves for salvation's sake by standing at the forefront of a dangerous activity and by appealing only when necessary to their actual involvement as papal inquisitors.

As with the Franciscans' mythologizing of the *De periculis* affair, obscuring the circumstances of the brethren's victimization while exaggerating its scale by using a list form served both internal purposes of corporate remembrance and external quests for secular and church patronage. As Christine Caldwell Ames has shown, Dominican inquisitors routinely leveraged the violence and resistance they faced in order to bolster narratives of suffering and in turn to reinforce the religious value of their mission by casting it—with greater or lesser persuasiveness—as a "further sacralized inquisition."[82] This sweet inversion did not go uncontested, however, as evidenced by the initial reluctance to associate even the order's most famous inquisitorial casualty, Peter of Verona (d. 1252; canonized 1253), with the office under which he died.[83] According to his most recent and rather sympathetic

---

[80] Leonard Lemmens (ed.), *Fragmenta minora: Catalogus sanctorum fratrum minorum* (Rome: Typis Sallustians, 1903), 28, 30.

[81] AGOP XIV, 684, *Lista martyrum OP 1222...1673*. Dozens of Dominicans who died in Hungary in the early thirteenth century, for instance, did so neither at the hands of heretics nor at those of disgruntled orthodox Christians but rather were drowned by the invading Mongols. See John V. A. Fine, *The Bosnian Church: A New Interpretation* (Boulder, CO: East European Quarterly, 1975), 144. A second wave of mendicant missionaries to Bosnia the following century, this time spearheaded by the Franciscan Order, seems to have encountered little resistance. See Fine, *The Bosnian Church*, 180–7.

[82] Ames, 58.

[83] Ames, 89.

biographer, "no early [Dominican] preachers situated Peter's mission in terms of the inquisition."[84]

Such apprehensions seem all the more significant given that the Dominicans failed in promoting the canonization or even local cults of other brethren who died in the inquisitorial line of duty, and despite the fact that the violent circumstances of some of their deaths were virtually uncontested. Petitions in support of these cases fell on deaf ears at the papal curia. Even the case of Guillaume Arnaud, murdered in Avignonet in 1242 alongside several Franciscan inquisitors, failed to get translated into a formal martyr's crown.[85] Nor did the papacy's response change when the Dominicans espoused the inquisitorial office with greater zeal beginning the middle of the fourteenth century.[86]

Peter Martyr is thus not merely a case in point, but the only case in point, of a Dominican who was formally canonized after being clearly, if rather briefly, affiliated with the order's inquisitorial mission during his lifetime. Tellingly, however, Peter's cult was almost immediately made to transcend his unique association with the brethren's sometimes controversial activities. His order awarded him the "triple crown" of a martyr, a theologian, and a virgin, thus embodying major values the Dominicans stood for. Further, the Visconti of Milan chose to promote Peter as the city's patron saint at the expense of the fourth-century archbishop Ambrose, whose cult was deemed too reminiscent of Milan's communal era.[87] Last but not least, from the order's own centralized perspective, the promotion of Peter's cult was directly linked to the events in Paris discussed above. As Ames notes, "the celebration of [...] the order's new saint formed an important part" of a concerted response to the university quarrels, following which "Dominicans aggressively encouraged the dissemination of Peter Martyr's cult."[88]

In other words, efforts to promote the Preachers' first minted martyr were from an early stage rooted in a response to a quite different kind of clash the order faced. Whatever leverage the brethren were able to gain by deploying their recent, if not overwhelmingly popular, saint, they did not shrink from it. Their choice was wise, for it inserted Peter's assassination, which may not have been entirely free from political incentives, into an eschatological narrative shaped in response to the Parisian affair and before an attentive clerical, papal, and royal audience. Tellingly,

---

[84] Donald Prudlo, *The Martyred Inquisitor: The Life and Cult of Peter of Verona (†1252)* (Aldershot: Ashgate, 2008), 100. Prudlo presents Peter's murder purely as a religious event, although it may have had significant political overtones as well. In its immediate aftermath, Leo dai Valvassori, the Franciscan archbishop of Milan, had the podestà run out of the city, allegedly for his incompetence in letting Peter's murderers escape from custody (Prudlo, *The Martyred Inquisitor*, 72–3). Anti-heresy campaigns, however, were politically motivated just as they were politically resisted. See Augustine Thompson, *Revival Preachers and Politics in Thirteenth-Century Italy: The Great Devotion of 1233* (Oxford: Clarendon Press, 1992), 36–7. On Leo dai Valvassori, see Williell R. Thomson, *Friars in the Cathedral: The First Franciscan Bishops, 1226–1261*, Studies and Texts, 33 (Toronto: Pontifical Institute of Medieaval Studies, 1975), 93–101.

[85] App. I, no. 15.
[86] Prudlo, *The Martyred Inquisitor*, 101–2.
[87] Prudlo, *The Martyred Inquisitor*, 138–9.
[88] Ames, 63.

leveraging Peter Martyr's swift canonization was not the Dominicans' only direct response to the events of the 1250s. Equally significant from the perspective of antifraternal opposition was the order's commission of Gerard de Frachet to collect materials for a history of the order, an order that was, in the words of its then leader, "nowhere and never safe."[89] Once again it seems that, however inconsequential politically, *De periculis* exercised a creative influence on mendicant identity as a community of suffering.

Mendicant martyrdom

In their own right, murdered inquisitors never became a staple of mendicant lachrymose narratives. Given that there was no lack of materials available for such purposes, it is plausible that the sometimes controversial contexts of these home-front casualties, alongside mendicant apprehensions about the papal endeavor generally, prevented them from becoming major facets of the orders' social memory. Instead, mendicant martyrdom developed a profile skewed in the direction of early responders to Black Death and especially missionary martyrs operating on the shifting frontiers of Christendom. The trend is exemplified in the case of the Carmelites' most acclaimed martyr, St Angelus of Jerusalem (1185–1220).[90] His first known mention dates to around 1370, some 150 years after he was allegedly stabbed to death in Licata, Sicily, by the incestuous Count Berengar, against whom the Carmelite was prompted to preach in a vision.

The two versions of Angelus' *Life* date to the early fifteenth century, somewhat prior to his first documented incorporation into the Carmelite liturgy, in 1459.[91] Dominican influences are evident in both texts, which borrow handsomely from Gerard de Frachet's *Vitae Fratrum* and Tomasso de Lantini's *Life* of Peter Martyr, especially the close sequence of events leading to and from Peter's assassination.[92] Yet, whoever composed these *vitae* consciously avoided framing the Carmelite's effort as part of a papally organized mission, for Angelus was driven to Licata by a vision—that is, he was sent there by divine inspiration, not an official edict. Further, Berengar's crimes marginalized him as a Christian, one living moreover on an island that for centuries formed a frontier of encounter between Latin Christianity, Greek Orthodoxy, and Islam. If Angelus' *Life* was inspired by Peter's,

---

[89] Andrew Jotischky, *The Carmelites and Antiquity: Mendicants and their Pasts in the Middle Ages* (Oxford: Oxford University Press, 2002), 197–8, 291–2. For Humbert of Romans' quotation, see above, n. 1.

[90] William of Coventry, *De duplici fuga*, MCH 279, refers to several Palestinian brethren martyred in 1187 by the forces of Saladin, but it is a unique mention among numerous early Carmelite texts describing the friars' expulsion from the Holy Land, e.g., *De inceptione ordinis*; Jean de Cheminot, *Speculum fratrum*; Jean de Venette, *Speculum status ordinis historiale*; John Baconthorpe, *Compendium historiarum et iurium*; and William of Coventry's own *Chronica brevis*, all in *MCH* 104–5, 138, 174, 210, 276, respectively. None of these thirteenth- and fourteenth-century works mentions Angelus.

[91] Paschalis Kallenberg, *Fontes liturgiae carmelitanae: Investigatio in decreta, codices et proprium sanctorum*, TSHC 5 (Rome: Institutum Carmelitanum, 1962), 50–1.

[92] Ludovico Saggi, *S. Angelo di Sicilia: Studio sulla vita, devozione, folklore*, TSHC 6 (Rome: Institutum Carmelitanum, 1962), 126–30; Jotischky, *The Carmelites and Antiquity*, 192–201.

the distance between the contexts in which these men attained their martyrs' crowns was nonetheless accentuated, placing Angelus in what appears to be a more digestible tradition of mendicant suffering.

The different emphases in each legend also emerge from the saints' respective iconographies.[93] While both men are portrayed as having been killed similarly (sword or hatchet blow to the head, often followed by a dagger stab), Peter, when he is the focus of the work rather than appearing in a group portrait, is usually depicted alongside his assassin and his *socius*, and is surrounded by references to the urban milieus in which he operated. By contrast, the only trace of humans in Angelus' portrait are the sword and dagger plunged into him. The perpetrator is gone, as are any clues of "civilization" except a book, presumably a preacher's manual or a Bible (an item sometimes clutched by or strewn near Peter as well). The landscape, more importantly, is distinctly rural, comprising some trees and weeds, a bleakness emphasized by the engraving's low horizon. The only other sign of life is a rabbit or hare, a popular symbol of fertility, but also used as an allusion to the Resurrection and the Ascension. Here, however, it is more likely to have been borrowed from a more recent inclination (for example, by Carlo Crivelli [*c*.1435–93] and Giovanni Bellini [1430–1516]), to place rabbits in the desert landscapes surrounding ascetics such as St Jerome and St Francis in order to symbolize solitude.[94] These elements converge to shape precisely the kind of environment idealized by the Carmelites as most amenable to a life of contemplation and the pursuit of Christian perfection. Angelus' superior lifestyle, as compared to Peter's, is driven home by the saints' respective last words: the Preacher commonly dies with the *Credo* upon his lips, while the Carmelite pleads directly with Christ and the angels to accept his martyr's blood, and Jesus reciprocates by noting that Angelus aspires "to celestial glory through martyrdom like another John the Baptist" (see Figure 4.1).

In light of their derivative nature, Angelus' *Life* and iconography illustrate both the challenges of and the motivations for incorporating martyrdom into a

---

[93] One of Angelus' earliest known depictions is reproduced as Figure 4.1. He appears several more times, both individually and among fellow saints, but never earlier than in the late fifteenth or early sixteenth century. For engravings see Arthur M. Hind (ed.), *Early Italian Engraving*, 7 vols (London: M. Knoedler & Co., 1938–48), E.III.67; Walter L. Strauss (gen. ed.), *The Illustrated Bartsch* (New York: Abaris Books, 1978–), 24, commentary, pt 4, 83–4; and 25, 170, and commentary, 307–11. For paintings, see George Kaftal, *Iconography of the Saints in Tuscan Painting* (Florence: Sansoni, 1952), no. 22 (col. 60); George Kaftal, with the collaboration of Fabio Bisogni, *Iconography of the Saints in the Painting of North West Italy* (Florence: Le Lettere, 1985), no. 24 (cols 65–8); George Kaftal, *Iconography of the Saints in Central and South Italian Schools of Painting* (Florence: Le Lettere, 1986), no. 25 (col. 70). Peter Martyr has been depicted numerous times, most famously by his coreligionist Fra Angelico. See Svante Hallberg, Rune Norberg, and Oloph Odenius, "Petrus martyrens död: Ett sfragistiskt bidrag till helgonets äldre ikonografi," *Fornvännen*, 55 (1960), 239–59; Edwin Hall and Horst Uhr, "Aureola Super Auream: Crowns and Related Symbols of Special Distinctions for Saints in Late Gothic and Renaissance Iconography," *Art Bulletin*, 67 (1985), 567–603; William Hood, *Fra Angelico at San Marco* (New Haven: Yale University Press, 1993), 74–5; and in Kaftal's aforementioned works, no. 241 (cols 817–33), no. 184 (551–2), and no. 300 (904–5), respectively.

[94] Mirella Levi d'Ancona, *Lo zoo del Rinascimento: Il significato degli animali nella pittura italiana dal XIV al XVI secolo* (Lucca: Maria Pacini Fazzi Editore, 2001), 109.

Fig. 4.1 Angelus of Jerusalem (Milan, *c*.1470), Staatsbibliothek Bamberg, JH.Inc.typ. IV.317, back cover

By kind permission of the Staatsbibliothek Bamberg.

lachrymose narrative of mendicant history. For the complex appropriations are probably an attempt to fill in the Carmelite roster of saints with a true peer to Francis and Dominic (rather than more obvious parallels such as Anthony of Padua and Peter Martyr), the better to situate the order retroactively as an original fixture of the Christian religious landscape. Several early Carmelite texts make the point explicit that, when Francis and Dominic were only beginning to maneuver for recognition, Elijah's followers were already living under a rule approved by the pope or indeed that they were the Alpha and Omega of religious life.[95]

The Carmelite tendency to punch above their weight emerges most clearly from the episode in Angelus' legend that features a triple summit of mendicant

---

[95] *Universis christifidelibus*, MCH, 85, 88; John Baconthorpe, *Laus religionis carmelitanae*, ch. 2, MCH 235–6.

founders—Francis, Dominic, and Angelus—in Rome, in which trilateral pleasantries are exchanged, the accomplishment of Carmelite life is acknowledged, and the synergy among the three branches is celebrated. Given the relative antiquity of his order and especially in anticipation of his successful bid for martyrdom, Angelus is portrayed in this text as *primum inter pares* not only with Francis and Dominic, but also among mendicant martyrs, a select group to which neither Francis nor Dominic belonged. Indeed, a late fifteenth-century fresco in the Carmelite convent at San Felice del Bencao, near Garda Lake, shows Francis prostrate at the feet of Angelus.[96] Both image and text can be seen as nods, on the one hand, at Francis's mission to al-Malik al-Kâmil in 1219 as an unaccomplished feat,[97] and, on the other, to Peter Martyr's assassination in 1252 as a later emulation. Angelus was less of a founder only because his order was so much more ancient, but he could certainly make a claim to being the original mendicant martyr operating both *extra* and *inter fideles*. There is, of course, no need to take his hagiographers at their word, but their gesture more than confirms that by that point martyrdom had become a sine qua non of mendicant memory.

CONCLUSIONS

Mendicants played an active role in shaping a medieval antifraternal tradition. And they did so, however counterintuitive it may seem at first blush, for their own benefit or at least as one means of self-promotion. While the friars' reputation could be tarnished by their own doings, and was often undermined by their near impossible political situation; and even as aggression toward them was often a response to both, the brethren's own interpretation of these acts and the key in which they were often narrated were instrumental in shaping their social memory and occasionally in raising their value in their own supporters' eyes.

Home and away, lachrymose memory helped consolidate the brethren's identity as a community of sufferers. Some arenas and incidents were more fruitful than others for such purposes, as the friars certainly recognized. Death in the inquisitorial line of duty was on the whole less favored, it seems, while martyrdom on and beyond the borders of Christianity was highly regarded, as were certain sacrifices made on the home front, such as early responses to Black Death. In any case, it is safe to say that by the end of the fourteenth century the shedding of blood and especially of joint tears proved to be a major mendicant activity and a staple of mendicant identity. As such, lachrymosity should be seen as a major, albeit not exclusive, force shaping medieval antifraternalism, no matter how often contemporary and later observers used instances recorded in this key to buttress their resentment of friars.

---

[96] G. M. Fadalti and S. M. Pizzol, *Guida storico-artistica del Santuario del Carmine S. Felice del Benaco (BS)* (Vittorio Veneto: Abitino del Carmine, 1962), 26–8.
[97] On this event's historiography, see, most recently, John Tolan, "The Friar and the Sultan: Francis of Assisi's Mission to Egypt," *European Review*, 16 (2008), 115–26.

General Conclusion
Antifraternalism, Anticlericalism, and Urban Discontent

Polemics, violence, deviance, and remembrance—words and deeds, deeds and words—form distinctive strands of medieval antifraternalism. Each of these revealed certain patterns and consistencies, which partly corroborate and partly challenge the received wisdom about opposition to medieval mendicants, including its origins, scale, and scope. The thrust of much antifraternal polemics, for instance, appears to have substantially departed from what is commonly considered its source, namely William of St Amour's *De periculis novissimorum temporum*, a text rejecting the legitimacy of the new mendicant orders. For by and large theologians and church leaders who aired their views on religious mendicancy (both before and after William's treatise began to circulate) expressed a desire to see the orders curbed, but not—as William would have it—gone. This qualitative difference between William and his alleged followers should inform our view of *medieval* attitudes toward friars and what most contemporaneous authors, be they theologians or poets, found troubling about them.

The choice to include non-abolitionist texts, as argued in Chapter 1, facilitates a broader definition of antifraternalism, one extending beyond opposition to the friars' existence to the challenging of their power. In a short span of time, and thanks to a combination of charismatic leadership and an appealing ideology, mendicants amassed a large following and gained tremendous material and political support. Many among the brethren recognized such success as an obstacle to pursuing a life of Christian perfection. In this sense, what most antifraternal authors did was to echo and inform reformist voices circulating within the orders since their earliest days, rather than chime with the reactionary ecclesiology propounded by St Amour and his short-lived party. This is not to deny the existence of a meaningful difference between internal and external criticisms, but rather to emphasize the overlap in their motivations and their shared views about the positive eschatological role played by mendicants in salvation history. Those few who did not share such a view, or who had a diametrically opposite one, like William and at least some of his original collaborators in Paris, comprised the strong minority voice opposing the new orders—and them alone—on doctrinal principle.

Further, even among those who objected to the friars' presence in their midst, there were numerous cases of pragmatic or circumstantial rather than ideological or categorical opposition. This second distinction is supported by the available evidence for violent responses to the friars' settlement in certain towns and regions.

Here, as always, context proved crucial. The earliest Franciscans to settle in southern France, for instance, were installed among communities already served by an established parish clergy and by local monasteries. No one seems to have challenged the mendicants' orthodoxy or even mission (a situation that would change with their integration into the papal inquisitorial machinery). Rather, the friars simply threatened to undermine existing power relations and presented an added burden on the available material resources. In Ireland, Scotland, and France, to take another group of examples, friars were subjected to violence and expulsion for representing regional interests during armed conflicts. To repeat, this did not mean that local rulers objected to the brethren's conduct or existence in principle. Indeed, indigenous friars in these areas were often replaced by foreign ones (or vice versa) to ensure continuity in their activities, now re-legitimized under a new sovereign. The friars' assailants, using the idiom of physical violence, mostly thought locally and acted locally.

To recap: the first step in revising the traditional account of medieval antifraternalism involved distinguishing between those few authors who objected to the friars' very existence and those who, more commonly, wished to see them return to their founders' ways. The next step required differentiating among the grounds upon which contemporaries took action in response to the brethren's arrival and foreignness, their activities, and their conduct. Jointly these distinctions illustrate how much of the existing scholarship has been limited insofar as it focused on a small number of texts and authors, whose attitude toward religious mendicancy, moreover, has been misrepresented as both abolitionist and typical. Those few scholars who went beyond theological polemics, poetry, and prose fiction, especially by uncovering instances of anti-inquisitorial violence, have illuminated, sometimes inadvertently, further contexts in which friars were opposed. The maximalist approach adopted by the present study has gone farther in illustrating the extent to which the friars' antagonists comprised a highly diverse group, including traditional monks and nuns, clergymen, and orthodox and heterodox lay people, but also—as Chapter 4 recalls—non-Christian individuals and communities, both inside and outside of Latin Christendom.

The latter group in particular, including those who tolerated the friars' presence to a limited degree, underscores the need to make a third distinction—namely, between opposition to the brethren's presence and resentment of their quest for power. To take the most obvious example, the pagan rulers of Lithuania and Poland, as well as a succession of Muslim regimes in the Near East, allowed friars to operate in their territories as pastoral leaders and ecclesiastical administrators among foreign Christian merchants and pilgrims. The persecution of friars in these regions was prompted by or at least couched in terms of the brethren's illicit expansion of their activities—for instance, by advocating conversion or speaking out against the hegemonic religion. As grounds for persecution, the friars' violation of their mandate was construed as an attempt to increase their influence and alter a status quo ante, much like the brethren's perceived threat in encroaching upon the pastoral rights of clergymen in established Christian communities. In both cases, there was no explicit attempt to denounce the orders themselves or their mission, but rather to resist their *modus operandi*, which was often denounced within Europe as hypocritical.

A fourth and final distinction needs to be drawn between those who opposed the friars' power and those who underscored its abuse. Admittedly, it is often difficult to tell the two apart, yet perhaps the most salient instance of violence perpetrated against the brethren in retaliation for their perceived abuse of power, rather than for having a mandate to operate in the first place, occurred in the context of their inquisitorial activities. To recall, when citizens in Parma, Bologna, and elsewhere expelled local friars on occasion or caused them to leave, they cited not the brethren's illicit or threatening presence, nor even their sometimes controversial mission, but rather their botching of an important job. The residents of Strasbourg likewise chased the Dominicans (but not the Franciscans or even the Dominican nuns) out of the city for ignoring the rules within which they were allowed to operate: accumulating numerous urban properties, refusing to pay their taxes, and actively recruiting underage oblates. In a sense, even the Parisian quarrels of the 1250s were ignited and certainly fuelled by the friars' aggressive expansion of their privileges at the expense of reconciliation with the secular masters.

The friars' embrace by the papacy and by numerous secular leaders, their growing wealth and influence, and their popularity in cities was a double-edged sword. The brethren's ascendency meant that they gained the ear of many. But the attention came at a high price, since it was difficult to control, mitigate, or channel at will. Nor did it protect them from envy, hostility, and genuine concern, all of which led to scrutiny of the friars' activities and occasional misconduct. Exacerbating this sometimes-negative attention was the notion that, to a greater degree than secular clergymen or even traditional monks and nuns, most friars belonged to cohesive, well-organized orders. It was thus easy to stereotype them or brand them on the basis of individual and local cases. As Chapter 3 demonstrates, no one was more aware of this challenge than mendicant founders and leaders, whose eagerness to avoid scandal permeates the extant administrative records.

Apart from curbing deviancy, however, the mendicants faced the challenge of having to redirect opposition to them, on whatever grounds, into a productive place. Their chosen strategy had the merit of bolstering their social memory and identity, on the one hand, and enhancing their political status, on the other. Evidence for such practices was explored especially in Chapter 4, which demonstrates that much of the brethren's suffering was recorded by them in an eschatological format and transmitted in such a key and over many centuries to potentially sympathetic audiences. In this way mendicants forged a narrative of Christological suffering, a lachrymose history that accommodated the broad range of their opposition, sometimes consciously ignoring the real diversity of such acts and their original contexts, including their own contribution to them. Throughout the chapters of this book I have tried to point out this complexity, trace the processes and structures by which it has been obfuscated, and restore an element of contingency and diversity that was inherent to the resentment of medieval friars.

These main findings and the distinctions that they call for expand the historical perspective on several related phenomena. The first and most obvious of these is anticlericalism, since assaults on friars lend themselves to studying medieval opposition to figures and institutions of religious authority. Most historical accounts of anticlericalism concern western Europe and within it opposition to the Catholic Church or its members. Insofar as the West is concerned, the perspective is largely justified, at least statistically: Catholicism has had a longer and stronger presence in Europe and later in Latin America than all other forms of Christianity for the better part of two millennia. As such it had gathered allies and foes alike, generating both sympathy and hatred.[1]

To illustrate the latter sentiment in particular, scholars and polemicists have frequently focused on "transitional" events such as the Protestant Reformation, Humanism, the Enlightenment, and of course the French Revolution and various national liberation movements both within and outside of Europe (for example, Spain, Mexico) as examples of or involving anticlerical outbursts, albeit without neglecting similar challenges launched in earlier periods. Indeed, among several historiographies, be they Marxist, Protestant, or secular-nationalist, that sought to extend the pedigree of anticlericalism (itself a nineteenth-century term[2]) back in time, pre-Reformation criticisms (temporarily de-medievalized[3]) were especially prized as early flashes of collective maturity. The theme of anticlericalism as a litmus test for modernity has been so thoroughly engrained in European historiography that, in a recent collection of essays on the topic, one scholar proudly construed it as a bridge between the British Isles and the Continent.[4]

On the face of it, antifraternalism offers further support for such observations concerning the pre-modern period. Much like anti-Jesuit sentiments in the early modern era, opposition to the friars too is often taken as shorthand for anticlericalism or at least anti-papalism, since the brethren were commonly seen as a clear expression of a decadent and power-hungry church, and attacks upon them were easily construed as a cry against broader corruption and abuses. As José Sánchez, the author of a popular monograph on the topic, put it: "anticlericals tend to center their opposition not upon the clergy in general . . . but rather upon specific groups within the clergy. Antipapalism, antiepiscopalism, antimonasticism, and antipastoralism are all specific manifestations of anticlericalism."[5]

---

[1] José Sánchez, *Anticlericalism: A Brief History* (Notre Dame, IN, and London: University of Notre Dame Press, 1972); Peter A. Dykema and Heiko A. Oberman (eds), *Anticlericalism in Late Medieval and Early Modern Europe,* Studies in Medieval and Reformation Thought, 51 (Leiden: Brill, 1993); S. J. Barnell, *Idol Temples and Crafty Priests: The Origins of Enlightenment Anticlericalism* (London: Macmillan, 1999); and Víctor Manuel Arbeloa, *Clericalismo y anticlericalismo en España (1767–1930): Una introducción* (Madrid: Encuentro, 2009). Only recently has the focus shifted outside of Europe. See the *Personal Enemies of God: Anticlericals and Anticlericalism in Revolutionary Mexico, 1915–1940,* special issue of *The Americas*, 65/4 (2009); Vincent Goossaert (ed.), *L'Anticléricalisme en Chine*, Extrême-Orient, Extrême-Occident, 24 (Paris: Presses Universitaires de Vincennes, 2002).
[2] René Rémond, *L'Anticléricalisme en France de 1815 à nos jours* (Paris: Fayard, 1976), 8–9.
[3] Carol Symes, "When We Talk about Modernity," *American Historical Review*, 116 (2011), 715–26.
[4] Keith Robbins, "Foreword," in Nigel Aston and Matthew Cragoe (eds), *Anticlericalism in Britain, c.1500–1914* (Stroud: Sutton, 2000), p. xi—an odd remark given that for centuries anticlericalism has been invoked as a staple of Englishness. See above, Prologue.
[5] Sánchez, *Anticlericalism*, 10–11.

However, to assume that a targeted group is the rule rather than its exception within the church, and moreover that those maligning one order necessarily seek to eradicate (rather than reform) the ecclesiastical establishment, is questionable: Philip IV's violent clampdown on the Templars in the early fourteenth century offers but one famous example to the contrary; Pope John XXII's persecution of the Franciscan Spirituals two decades later provides another, especially given that his actions were in part a response to calls from within the order.

Establishing the critics' identity and goals is paramount. As Sánchez and others have pointed out, anticlerical opinions were often voiced by clerics, the disgruntled Augustinian friar Martin Luther being a famous but not untypical example, one that follows a long line of monastic reformers who challenged church practices without (originally) intending to bring the institution down. Clerics were equally aplenty among the mendicants' opponents, whatever their stripe. As we have seen in Chapter 1, those driven by a conservative ideology that rejected the new orders from the ordained hierarchy of the church were Paris-based theologians, led by William of St Amour. A century later, a similar (but not identical) movement was led by a high-ranking ecclesiastic, Richard FitzRalph, and by yet another theologian, John Wyclif. Most other antifraternal polemicists were reform driven rather than abolitionist, but they too were clerics, as were not a few of those who perpetrated physical assaults on friars and their convents, as we have seen in Chapter 2.

In most of its medieval manifestations, opposition to the friars offers little support for the notion that attacking an organ of the church was tantamount to an attempt at toppling or even substantially revising its structure. Numerous records show the friars' typical opponents in the thirteenth and fourteenth centuries were protesting the brethren's conduct and local presence, not their very existence or even their success. And, although assailants did on occasion generalize about one mendicant order on the basis of local experiences, few thought globally and acted locally—that is, victimized their city's friars as a way to express their broader disaffection with the orders generally, let alone the church at large. To read contemporaries' actions in another key, such as an attempt to promote the priesthood of all the faithful, would involve imposing a much later perspective.

For it was only in the late fifteenth and early sixteenth centuries that ecclesiastical reformers consistently singled out the mendicant orders and their members as the epitome of a degenerate church. And, even then, the charges raised against friars may reflect a more complex situation than is usually recognized. As Geoffrey Dipple and David Loades have argued respectively for Germany and Britain, the reformed (Observant) mendicant orders of that period could and often were seen as a *successful* example of Catholicism and as such posed a greater obstacle for those who wanted to do away with the influence of the papacy.[6] According to

---

[6] Geoffrey Dipple, *Antifraternalism and Anticlericalism in the German Reformation: Johann Eberlin von Günzburg and the Campaign against the Friars* (Aldershot: Scolar Press, 1996); Geoffrey Dipple, "Anti-Franciscanism in the Early Reformation: The Nature and Sources of Criticism," *Franciscan Studies*, 55 (1998), 53–81; David Loades, "Anticlericalism in the Church of England before 1558: An

these and other Reformation scholars, it was the friars' *popularity* in this later period, and not their notoriety, that marked them as the Reformers' obvious targets.[7]

At the same time, antimendicant opposition does tell us something about medieval society's capacity to resist or at least decry corruption in the church, even if it is mostly irrelevant to speak of contemporaries' thinking in terms of a church that was not universal. For students of anticlericalism, the qualitative difference between a world governed by a hegemonic religious establishment and a reality in which people could choose between two or more options (including deism, agnosticism, and atheism) is enormous: John Van Engen was surely right to ask whether "true [i.e., abolitionist or Reformation-style] anticlericalism was even *thinkable* in the middle ages."[8] Historicizing anticlericalism requires adjusting its definition, working as it were with history, not against it. The revised picture of medieval antifraternalism offered by the present study reminds us that there is no need to wait for the Protestant Reformation, Humanism, or the Enlightenment in order to hear voices, read texts, and detect violence aimed against figures of religious authority, and that such opposition did not materialize only during extreme crises or issued by tortured heretics alone. Such instances may be encouraging to those upholding certain values enshrined by modernity, but to see them as veritable precursors falls somewhere between optimistic and tendentious.

Beyond the exigencies of its immediate and numerous contexts, the premise of opposition to the late-medieval church, its spokesmen, and its vanguard was profoundly different before the modern era, when the institution (and later, institutions) had shed much prestige and power. As social observers have long noted, and as shown in Chapter 3, violence can sometimes be employed as a barometer for weakness, rather than power, among its perpetrators. If so, the medieval church and its members sustained a major advantage over lay society. Yet it is also the case that disappointment, however it is expressed, follows great expectations. John Fine, in his work on the medieval Bosnian church, points to a link between people's low hopes from local clergymen and the near absence of opposition to them.[9] Across most of medieval western Europe, however, the situation was varied but markedly different, which explains the intensity of

---

'Eating Canker'?," in Aston and Cragoe (eds), *Anticlericalism in Britain*, 3–4. See also Christopher Haigh, "Anticlericalism in the English Reformation," *History*, 68 (1983), 391–407.

[7] Paul Nyhus, "The Franciscans in South Germany, 1400–1530: Reform and Revolution," *Transactions of the American Philosophical Society*, NS 65 (1975), 1–43; Walter Ziegler, "Reformation und Klosteraulösung: Ein ordensgeschichlicher Vergleich," and Bernhard Neidiger, "Stadtregiment und Klosterreform in Basel," both in Kaspar Elm (ed.), *Reformbemühungen und Observanzbestrebungen im spätmittelaltrichen Ordenswesen*, Berliner historische Studien, 14 (Berlin: Duncker und Humblot, 1989), 585–614, 539–67, respectively.

[8] John Van Engen, "Late Medieval Anticlericalism: The Case of the New Devout," in Dykema and Oberman (eds), *Anticlericalism in Late Medieval and Early Modern Europe*, 20. Lollards, being the partial exception that proves the rule, are analyzed by John Van Engen, "Anticlericalism among the Lollards," in Dykema and Oberman (eds), *Anticlericalism in Late Medieval and Early Modern Europe*, 53–63.

[9] John V. A. Fine, *The Bosnian Church: A New Interpretation* (Boulder, CO: East European Quarterly, 1975), 27–8.

antifraternal and anticlerical criticisms as well as their essentially reformist nature until at least the early sixteenth century, and, some would say, the French Revolution. The scale and scope of pre-modern opposition, whether aimed at friars alone or at the church generally, would be unimaginable in today's secularized society, which, despite no shortage of grounds for resentment against at least the actions of some clergymen, tends to dismiss the latter's access to any substantial form of power.

Further links between medieval antifraternalism and anticlericalism emerge from the present study. It seems, for instance, that the triggers of opposition to the friars were on the whole similar to those of contemporary and later anticlericalism: simony, or spiritual corruption by material considerations; an avid quest for privileges and their abuse; excessive involvement in politics; the accumulation of individual and collective wealth; and sexual misconduct and other forms of specifically clerical deviancy, all commonly tagged as hypocrisy. However, the similarities did not manifest themselves in a temporal and geographical overlap between antifraternalism and anticlericalism. Discrete behaviors could antagonize different groups and social strata for different reasons in different periods and regions. Indeed, it is one of the ironies of mendicant history that the brethren's initial arrival to certain areas actually curbed anticlericalism by furnishing laymen with a living example of evangelical life that they found lacking among the secular clergy and traditional monasticism.[10]

Another suggestive parallel is the unique role of cities in fostering opposition to religious authority. There were obvious reasons for the concentration of antifraternal poetry, sermons, and physical assaults in urban centers, where most friars pursued their ministry. The same cannot be said of the secular clergy in general, however, spread out as they were across a predominantly rural Europe. And yet most of our evidence for anticlerical sentiments comes from Europe's most urbanized regions: central and northern Italy, Languedoc, and the Low Countries. It seems that, even as late as the nineteenth century, rural anticlericalism was still rare, at least in England.[11]

One plausible explanation for the prevalence of urban over rural anticlericalism in the late Middle Ages, and notwithstanding cities' generally superior documentation, is that legal jurisdiction in cities, which often gained their liberties from the church, was more carefully monitored, and its rejection, especially by clerics, was strongly contested. In this sense, sensitivity to the friars' material success, their maintenance of diverse privileges, and their claims of independent jurisdiction fed into a traditional suspicion of clerics among propertied urban elites. And yet, at other times, friars could defy ecclesiastical authorities by siding with their host cities, thereby creating a disjuncture with the secular clergy.[12] If so, it is small

---

[10] *L'Anticléricalisme en France méridionale (milieu XIIe–début XIVe siècle)*, CdF 38 (Toulouse: Privat, 2003), 12.

[11] Frances Knight, "Did Anticlericalism Exist in the English Countryside in the Early Nineteenth Century?" in Aston and Cragoe (ed.), *Anticlericalism in Britain*, 159–78.

[12] Norbert Hecker, *Bettelorden und Bürgertum: Konflikt und Kooperation in deutschen Städten des Spätmittelalters* (Frankfurt: Peter Lang, 1981); Dieter Berg (ed.), *Bettelorden und Stadt: Bettelorden und städlischer Leen im Mittelalter und un der Neuzeit* (Werl: Dietrich Coelde Verlag, 1992).

wonder that the Observance movement among mendicants in the fifteenth and early sixteenth centuries was so strongly supported and even encouraged by secular authorities, including numerous urban regimes.[13]

Last, the concentration of antifraternal and anticlerical action in towns and cities, and especially of physical aggression, demonstrates how violence and its threat were perceived as key elements in maintaining and undermining urban order. True, cities were not necessarily more violent in late medieval Europe than at any other time or place. But it is often the case that social memory is more easily organized around violence, much like individual memory is so often focused on pain.[14] To historians, who are usually much more sensitive to the process of documentary production, this should come as little surprise, given that violence is often an expression of imbalance or rupture and as such, from a narrative perspective, tends to appear as an "event" in our sources more commonly than would indications of stability. This partly explains why medieval urban propaganda, such as *Laudes civitatum*, is typically uneventful in the sense that the pleasant activities this genre describes seem to be perennial, not unlike in Paradise.[15] The threat of change rather than routine, action rather than stillness, drives societies to protest, to fight, and to record. And so it was with opposition to medieval friars, a cluster of often disparate events whose recording and remembrance tell us what contemporaries, be they friars, their critics, or their opponents, valued and feared.

---

[13] Dipple, *Antifraternalism and Anticlericalism*, 24 and n. 16.
[14] Elaine Scarry, *The Body in Pain: The Making and Unmaking of the World* (New York and Oxford: Oxford University Press, 1985).
[15] J. K. Hyde, "Medieval Descriptions of Cities," *Bulletin of The John Rylands Library*, 48 (1966), 308–40; Gina Fasoli, "La coscienza civica nelle 'Laudes civitatum'," in *La coscienza cittadina nei comuni italiani del Duecento* (Todi: Accademia Tedertina, 1972), 9–44.

Epilogue
A New World Twist

Centuries later, and in a land far away, friars continued to upset those whose spiritual welfare they were meant to promote. As missionaries to the natives of Central America, the brethren became subject to abuse not only, as one would expect, by indigenous peoples, but also and perhaps even mainly at the hands of their Old World expats. That the mendicants' proselytizing brought them into conflict with non-Christians should come as no surprise. After all, they were systematically and at times violently altering the world view of their reluctant hosts. However, and to the friars' greater shock, the protection and instruction they sought to provide locals with was perceived as undermining the Spanish Crown's hegemony and, no less importantly, colonizers' efforts at exploiting the land on their own, often ruthless, terms.[1] From a political and material perspective, the brethren's action was seen to block progress.

And so it happened that, as often before, mendicant convents, where Christian values were being taught and fostered, were razed and their residents attacked by fellow Catholics, who also chased away indigenous people attending schools on their premises. "Things were so bad," wrote one contemporary chronicler, "that the friars were forced to go and live among the Indians." But the brethren's woes did not end there. "The Spaniards kept watch on the friars by night, to the scandal of the Indians, and made inquiries into their lives and deprived them of their alms." Moreover, in response to the brethren's support of abolishing personal service in the *audiencia* of Guatemala and of forcing the colonists to marry one spouse rather than live with multiple women, "the Spaniards abominate[d] the friars even more, and they spread defamatory libels against them and ceased going to their Masses."

To be sure, and as the same author clarified, little love was lost between the friars and the Indians themselves, whose numerous "vices" the brethren tried to curb, and who in turn occasionally set fire to local Franciscan monasteries. "But the people on the Spanish side who gave most trouble to the friars, although they did so furtively,

---

[1] See Nancy M. Farriss, *Maya Society under Colonial Rule: The Collective Enterprise of Survival* (Princeton: Princeton University Press, 1984), 90–5, 149–52, 158–64; Inga Clendinnen, *Ambivalent Conquests: Maya and Spaniard in Yucatan, 1517–1570*, 2nd edn (Cambridge: Cambridge University Press, 2003), esp. 57–92; and John F. Chuchiak, "*In Servitio Dei*: Fray Diego de Landa, the Franciscan Order, and the Return of the Extirpation of Idolatry in the Colonial Diocese of Yucatán, 1573–1579," *The Americas*, 61 (2005), 611–46, who also underscores the Maya's success at pitting secular and religious invaders against one another.

were the [Catholic] priests, for they were the people who had lost their offices and the profits to be gained thereby." The friars, unperturbed by their newfound flocks' resistance, their old-countrymen's greed, and the clergymen's hypocrisy, carried on with their mission of spiritual conquest. That, at any rate, is what Diego de Landa (1524–79), a Franciscan missionary in Izamal since 1549, the order's first provincial prior in the Yucatán, and the author of this chronicle, would have us believe.[2]

[2] A. R. Pagden (ed. and trans.), *The Maya: Diego de Landa's Account of the Affairs of Yucatán* (Chicago: J. Philip O'Hara, 1975), 59–61. De Landa's *Relación de las cosas de Yucatán* was composed during the author's temporary repatriation in the 1560s, as he stood trial for the severity of his proceedings against the Indians of Yucatan for idolatry. See Eleanor B. Adams, *A Bio-Bibliography of Franciscan Authors in Colonial Central America* (Washington D.C.: Academy of American Franciscan History, 1953), 40–4.

APPENDIX I

AGGRESSION AGAINST MENDICANT FRIARS AND CONVENTS UNTIL 1400

The following is a chronological list of major cases of violence (including some armed robberies and thefts) perpetrated against friars and mendicant convents in Europe before 1400. Primary sources in or out of print are cited wherever possible, though, where several textual witnesses exist, a secondary source that treats all of them, if one is available, is referred to in the accompanying note. Multiple entries in the same year are organized alphabetically by location.

EARLY THIRTEENTH CENTURY

1. Naples. Sacking of the Dominican convent.[1]

1218–22

2. Prouille (Languedoc). Monks assault a female convent donated to the newly arrived Dominicans.[2]

1224

3. Dover. Local residents reject the newly arrived Franciscans as spies and thieves, citing their appearance and foreignness.[3]

1225

4. Licata (Sicily). Murder of Angelo of Jerusalem, a Carmelite, by a heretical knight he tried to convert.[4]

---

[1] Friedrich von Raumer, *Geschichte der Hohenstaufen und ihrer Zeit*, iii (Leipzig: F. A. Brockhaus, 1841), 470–1.
[2] *De fundatione*, 10–11.
[3] *Lanercost*, 30.
[4] *Acta Sanctorum*, Société des Bollandistes, 68 vols (Brussels and Paris, 1643–1940), 5 May. And see Ludovico Saggi, *S. Angelo di Sicilia: Studio sulla vita, devozione, folklore* (Rome: Institutum Carmelitanum, 1962).

Appendix I

1228

5. Pisa. Local citizens attack the Franciscan convent.[5]

1229

6. Worms. Local citizens assault the Dominicans and Franciscans.[6]

1230-2

7. Orvieto. Locals repeatedly attack the Dominican convent during the city's first inquisition.[7]

1233

8. Piacenza. A mob assaults the Dominican Roland of Cremona, who arrived to preach against heresy, and murders one of his followers.[8]

1234-5

9. Toulouse. Numerous assaults against the local Dominicans, culminating in their expulsion.[9]

1235

10. Narbonne. Heretics assault Dominican inquisitors.[10]

1237

11. Padua. Attempted murder of the Dominican Jordan of Saxony by a nobleman whose son was converted.[11]

---

[5] Mauro Ronzani, "Il francescanesimo a Pisa fino alla metá del Trecento," *Bollettino Storico Pisano*, 54 (1985), 9–10.

[6] Josef Wiesehoff, *Die Stellung der Bettelorden in den deutschen freien Reichstädten im Mittelalter* (Leipzig: Robert Roste, 1905), 16.

[7] Lansing, 57–9.

[8] Augustine Thompson, *Revival Preachers and Politics in Thirteenth-Century Italy: The Great Devotion of 1233* (Oxford: Clarendon Press, 1992), 37.

[9] *De fundatione*, 49–50; Guillaume Pelhisson, *Chronique (1229–1244)*, ed. and trans. Jean Duvernoy (Paris: CNRS Éditions, 1994), 80–6.

[10] Dupré-Thes., 290; Richard W. Emery, *Heresy and Inquisition in Narbonne* (New York: Columbia University Press, 1941), 81.

[11] *Vitae Fratrum*, III. 14 (pp. 110–11). The event could also have taken place in 1229, another year in which Jordan resided in the city. See *Lives of the Brethren of the Order of Preachers, 1206–1259*, trans. Placid Conway, ed. Bede Jarrett (London: Blackfriars Publications, 1955), 103 n. 2.

1239

12. Location unknown. Death of the Franciscan Caesarius of Speyer at the hands of a Franciscan guardian.[12]

1240

13. Orvieto. Locals kill a Dominican inquisitor.[13]
14. Viterbo. Burning of a Dominican convent.[14]

1242

15. Avignonet (Languedoc). Killing of the Dominican inquisitor Guillaume Arnaud and his Franciscan colleague Stephen of Saint Thibéry, along with nine other colleagues.[15]
16. Urgell (Catalonia). Killing of the Dominican inquisitor Pons de Blanes.[16]

1245–6

17. Pamplona. Assaults on the Franciscan convent by clergymen.[17]

1248

18. Milan. Killing of Peter of Arcagnano, a Franciscan inquisitor.[18]

1249

19. Reggio. Expulsion of the Franciscans for supporting the church against the empire.[19]

---

[12] Angelo Clareno, *Historia septem tribulationum Ordinis Minorum*, ed. Orietta Rossini (Rome: Istituto Storico Italiano per il Medio Evo, 1999), 136–7.

[13] Samuel K. Cohn, Jr, *Lust for Liberty: The Politics of Social Revolt in Medieval Europe, 1200–1425* (Cambridge, MA: Harvard University Press, 2006), 101.

[14] Donald Prudlo, *The Martyred Inquisitor: The Life and Cult of Peter of Verona (†1252)* (Aldershot: Ashgate, 2008), 40.

[15] Mark Gregory Pegg, *A Most Holy War: The Albigensian Crusade and the Battle for Christendom* (Oxford: Oxford University Press, 2008), 184–5; Luke Wadding et al., *Annales Minorum seu trium ordinum a S. Francisco institutorum*, 2nd edn, iii (Rome: Typis Rochi Bernabò, 1732), 69; Thomas Ripoll (ed.), *Bullarium Ordinis Fratrum Praedicatorum*, 2 vols (Rome: Ex Typographia Hieronymi Mainardi, 1729), i. 117.

[16] Ames, 65.

[17] *BF* i. 429–30, 431–2.

[18] *BF* i. 720.

[19] Salimbene, 481.

Appendix 1

1252

20. Milan. The Dominican Peter Martyr killed outside the city.[20]

1253–4

21. Paris. The Dominican convent is stoned and the brethren abused.[21]

1257

22. Mantua. Violent resistance against inquisitors.[22]

1258

23. Northern Italy. Followers of Eccelino de Tervis kill numerous Franciscans along with other clergymen.[23]

1259

24. Suffolk. The Franciscans are expelled from Babwell.[24]

1260

25. Urgell (Catalonia). Killing of the Dominican Inquisitor Bernard de Traversa.[25]

1262

26. Treviso. Violent resistance to Franciscan inquisitors.[26]

1264

27. Bergamo. Violent resistance to inquisitors.[27]

---

[20] Prudlo, *Martyred Inquisitor*, 39–65.
[21] *CUP* i. 273 (p. 312).
[22] Dupré-Thes., 290.
[23] O. Holder-Egger (ed.), *Chronica minor auctore minorita erphordiensi*, MGH SS 24 (Hanover, 1879), 201; Giambatista Verci, *Storia degli Eccelini*, iii (Bassano: Stamperia Remodini, 1779), 396–7.
[24] Antonia Gransden (ed.), "A Fourteenth-Century Chronicle from Grey Friars at Lynn," *EHR*, 72 (1957), 270–8.
[25] Ames, 65.
[26] Ilarino da Milano, "Gli antecedenti inediti di un nuovo episodio dell'inquisizione francescana a Treviso (1262–1263)," *Collectanea Franciscana*, 5 (1935), 611–20.
[27] Dupré-Thes., 290.

28. Worms. Sack Friars are rejected by citizens.[28]

1266

29. Apt (Provence). The Franciscans' privileges are ignored by local clergy, and local residents beat the brethren and threaten them at sword point.[29]

1269

30. Mézin (Languedoc). The Carmelite convent is sacked and pillaged by Cluniac monks.[30]

1272

31. Rabastens (Languedoc). Local clergy lead an assault on a new Franciscan foundation and chase the brethren away.[31]

1274

32. Catania. Local residents and clergy damage the Franciscan convent and perpetrate other acts of violence against the brethren.[32]

1276

33. Le Puy. Citizens kill the bishop's *bailli* in the Franciscan church.[33]

1277

34. Urgell (Catalonia). Killing of the Dominican Inquisitor Peter de la Cadireta.[34]
35. Valtellina. Killing of the Dominican Inquisitor Pagano de Lecco.[35]

---

[28] Andrews, 198–9.
[29] *BF* iii. 105–6.
[30] Yves Dossat, "Opposition des anciens ordres à l'installation des mendiants," in *Les mendiants en pays d'Oc au XIIIe siècle*, CdF 8 (Toulouse: Privat, 1973), 287.
[31] Dossat, "Opposition des anciens ordres à l'installation des mendiants," 286.
[32] *BF* iii. 214.
[33] Michel-Jean-Joseph Brial (ed.), *Majus chronicon lemovicense a Petro Coral et aliis conscriptum*, Recueil des Historiens des Gaules et de la France 18 (Paris: Imprimerie Impériale, 1822), 788.
[34] Ames, 65.
[35] Ames, 65.

1278

36. Ferentino. Local residents destroy a new Franciscan convent being built and assault the brethren.[36]

1279

37. Parma. Locals assault the Dominican convent after a contested inquisitorial verdict. One brother is killed, the rest leave the city.[37]

1280

38. Piacenza. Local clergymen dislodge at night the cross from the Franciscan convent and throw it into a gutter.[38]

1281

39. Strasbourg. The Penitential Sisters are expelled.[39]
40. Strasbourg. A Dominican friar is wounded by a local resident.[40]

1285

41. Madrid. Locals forcefully enter the Dominican nuns' convent.[41]

1286

42. Arras. Dominicans harassed and beaten by local canons.[42]

1287

43. Monfalcone. A foiled attempt to attack the Franciscan convent.[43]

---

[36] *BF* iii. 306.
[37] *Salimbene*, 736–7; Giuliano Bonazzi (ed.), *Chronicon parmese ab anno mxxxvii usque ad annum mcccxxxviii*, Rerum Italicarum Scriptores 9 pt. ix (Città di Castello: S. Lapi, 1902), 35–6.
[38] *BF* iii. 432.
[39] Philip Jaffé (ed.), *Annales colmariensis maiores*, MGH SS 17 (Hanover, 1861), 208.
[40] Jaffé (ed.), *Annales colmariensis maiores*, 208.
[41] AGOP, XIV, Lib I I I, fos 16ᵛ–17ʳ.
[42] *Les Olim, ou, Registres des arrêts rendus par la cour du roi*, ii (Paris: Imprimerie Royale, 1842), no. 17 (pp. 258–9).
[43] *Salimbene*, 937.

44. Reggio. Attempted pillaging of the Franciscan convent.[44]
45. Strasbourg. Dominicans are expelled from the city.[45]

1289

46. Bologna. A mob led by a local monk assaults brother Adam, a Franciscan, while leading his brethren in Mass in Santa Maria in Monte.[46]
47. Orense (Spain). Don Pedro Yáñez de Noboa, the local bishop, isolated and violently assaulted the Franciscan convent and its supporters. (See also 1295.)[47]

1291

48. Agen (Languedoc). Laymen led by a Cluniac prior pillage the new Franciscan convent, injuring three friars.[48]
49. Bari (?). Several clerics violently expel Franciscans from the local convent.[49]
50. Cork. Franciscan friars turn on one another during a provincial chapter, leading to the death of sixteen brethren.[50]

1295

51. Orense (Spain). Local bishop (see above, no. 47) sets fire to the Franciscan convent.[51]

1295–96

52. Carcassone. Repeated acts of violence against Dominican inquisitors.[52]

---

[44] Salimbene, 921–2.
[45] "Notae Historicae Argentinenses 1132–1338," in Johannes Friedrich Boehmer (ed.), *Martyrium Arnoldi... und andere Geschichtsquellen Deutschlands* (Stuttgart: J. G. Cotta'scher Verlag, 1853), 117; Heinrich Finke (ed.), *Ungedruckte Dominikanerbriefe des 13. Jahrhunderts* (Paderborn: Ferdinand Schöningh, 1891), nos 97, 108, 112, 120–2, 131 (pp. 120, 128–31, 133–4, 138–42, 147–8); Alfred Hessel (ed.), *Elsässische Urkunden, vornehmlich des 13. Jahrhunderts* (Strasbourg: Karl J. Trübner, 1915), nos XXIV, XXXVI–XXXVIII; Jacob Twinger von Konigsthofen, *Chronicon Universale et Alsaticum*, ed. Johann Schitern (Strasbourg: Josias Städel, 1698), 217d–218b.
[46] ASBo, Curia del podestà, Libri inquisitionum 16, fasc. 8, fos 32^r–43^r (Jan. 20–9, 1289).
[47] *Les Registres de Nicholas IV (1288–91)*, ed. E. Langlois, i (Paris: Ernest Thorin, 1905), no. 1281 (pp. 261–2).
[48] Dossat, "Opposition des anciens orders," 288.
[49] *BF* iv. 308.
[50] Niav Gallagher, "The Franciscans and the Scottish Wars of Independence: An Irish Perspective," *JMH*, 32 (2006), 7–8.
[51] Georges Digard et al. (eds), *Les Registres de Boniface VIII (1294–1303)*, i (Paris: Ernest Thorin, 1884), no. 1108 (p. 395); *BF* iv. 395–6.
[52] *De fundatione*, 102–4.

1296

53. Lanercost (Cumbria). Pillaging of Franciscan convent by Scots.[53]

1297

54. London. Thomas, an English Carmelite, kills his coreligionist Henry of Oxford.[54]

1299

55. Bologna. An aborted mob-assault on Dominican inquisitors.[55]
56. Ludlow. Citizens break into the local Augustinian friary and violently seize John le Berner, a cleric seeking sanctuary there.[56]

EARLY FOURTEENTH CENTURY

57. Germany. Many Dominicans expelled from their convents for siding with John XXII against Louis of Bavaria.[57]

1300

58. Novara. Violent resistance against inquisitors.[58]

1301

59. Exeter. A burial dispute between the Franciscans and the cathedral canons spirals into violence, as the clergy breaks into the friars' convent.[59]
60. Bergamo. Violent resistance against inquisitors.[60]

---

[53] *Lanercost*, 172, 173–5.
[54] The National Archives: PRO JUST1/369/Mem.22-OCarm.
[55] Lorenzo Paolini and Raniero Orioli (eds), *Acta S. Officii Bononie ab anno 1291 usque ad annum 1310*, 3 vols, Fonti per la Storia d'Italia, 106 (Rome: Istituto Storico Italiano per il Medio Evo, 1982–4).
[56] William W. Capes (ed.), *The Register of Richard de Swinfield, Bishop of Hereford, AD 1283–1317*, Cantilupe Society Publications, 3 (Cambridge: Chadwyck-Healey, 1979), 359.
[57] *Chronica*, 22.
[58] Dupré-Thes., 290.
[59] *Calendar of Patent Rolls*, Edward I, iv (London: HMSO, 1898), 79.
[60] Dupré-Thes., 290.

1302–3

61. Albi. Anti-inquisitorial riots, including an assault on the inquisitorial prison, ejecting Dominican preachers from churches, the effacement of Dominican images and texts, and an assault on their convent.[61]

1303

62. Carcassone. The Dominican convent is stoned.[62]
63. Paris. Franciscans are expelled for supporting Boniface VIII.[63]
64. Pavia. Violent resistance against inquisitors.[64]
65. Toulouse. Anti-inquisitorial riot.[65]

1304

66. Florence. Baschiera dela Tosa, leader of the Whites, breaks into the Dominican nunnery and takes two of his nieces by force.[66]

1305–6

67. London. A robbery at the Carmelite convent.[67]

1307

68. Wrocław (Poland). Günter von Biberstein, a papal legate, is assaulted in the local Franciscan church by clergymen and laymen after he rules against Heinrich, the local bishop.[68]
69. Figeac (Languedoc). Local Benedictines attack the Dominican convent over burial rights, causing damage to the cemetery and injuring one friar and one lay brother.[69]

---

[61] *De fundatione*, 201–3; James B. Given, *Inquisition and Medieval Society: Power, Discipline, and Resistance in Languedoc* (Ithaca, NY: Cornell University Press, 1997), 115.

[62] Given, *Inquisition and Medieval Society*, 115.

[63] Michael Robson, *The Franciscans in the Middle Ages* (Woodbridge: Boydell, 2006), 144.

[64] Dupré-Thes., 290.

[65] *Chronique latine de Guillaume de Nangis de 1113 à 1300, avec les continuations de cette chronique de 1300 à 1368*, ed. H. Géraud, i (Paris: Imprimerie de Crapelet, 1843), 338–9.

[66] Dino Compagni, *Cronica*, III.10, ed. Isidoro Del Lungo (Florence: Successori Le Monnier, 1889), 151.

[67] A. H. Thomas (ed.), *Calendar of Early Mayor's Court Rolls . . . 1298–1307* (Cambridge: Cambridge University Press, 1924), 237.

[68] *Monumenta Germaniae Franciscana*, 2.1: Die Kustoden Goldberg und Breslau, 1 Teil: 1240–1517 (Düsseldorf: L. Schwann, 1917), no. 116 (p. 29).

[69] Dossat, "Opposition des anciens ordres," 289.

1309–10

70. Ardfert (Ireland). A local bishop and clergymen abuse the Franciscans and forcibly remove a corpse from their convent.[70]

1315

71. Dundalk (Ireland). The Franciscan convent is sacked and twenty-two friars killed by invading Scots.[71]

1316–17

72. Ireland. Mendicant convents are among the many Irish monasteries destroyed and despoiled that year by Scots.[72]

1321

73. Valence (Languedoc). Killing of two Franciscan inquisitors.[73]

1326

74. Bologna. The family of a young boy admitted into the Franciscan friary lead a violent rescue mission.[74]
75. London. A mob breaks into Dominican convent and steals lead from the turrets.[75]

1333

76. Berwick (and north England generally). Scottish friars are expelled and replaced with English brethren by Edward III.[76]

---

[70] E. B. FitzMaurice and A. G. Little (eds), *Materials for the History of the Franciscan Province of Ireland, AD 1230–1450*, British Society of Franciscan Studies, 9 (Manchester: Manchester University Press, 1920), 91.

[71] FitzMaurice and Little (eds), *Materials for the History of the Franciscan Province of Ireland*, 220.

[72] FitzMaurice and Little (eds), *Materials for the History of the Franciscan Province of Ireland*, 95, 101.

[73] *Glassberger*, 128.

[74] ASBo, Governo, Riformagioni e provvigioni 200, fos 312^v–313^r (Feb. 21, 1326).

[75] A. H. Thomas (ed.), *Calendar of Plea and Memoranda Rolls* (Cambridge: Cambridge University Press, 1926), 46.

[76] Andrews, 103.

1334

77. Bologna. Three men rob Fra Giovanni, a local Franciscan, of a piece of cloth, a tunic, and 40 *soldi*.[77]
78. Prague. The Augustinians excommunicated and expelled by local archdeacon for tax evasion.[78]

1335

79. Dundee. Newcastle seamen burn the Franciscan convent, killing one friar.[79]

1338

80. Location unknown. A Dominican friar is attacked and robbed on his return from the general chapter.[80]

1340

81. Vilnius (Lithuania). Killing of two Franciscans by local authorities for preaching to pagans.[81]

1345

82. London. A mob pursues a Lombard who hides in the Augustinian convent.[82]

1346

83. Cologne. The Dominicans are thrown out of the city; sporadic victimization of the Franciscans.[83]

---

[77] ASBo, Curia del podestà, Libri inquisitionum 137, fasc. 4, fo. 2ʳ (Mar. 30, 1334).
[78] *Glassberger*, 159.
[79] *Lanercost*, 282.
[80] Romanus Fabianus Madura (ed.), *Acta capitulorum provinciae Poloniae Ordinis Praedicatorum*, i. *1225–1600* (Rome: Pontificum Institutum Studiorum Ecclesiasticorum, 1972), 13. The event could also have taken place in 1342.
[81] *XXIV Gen.*, 535–6.
[82] Thomas (ed.), *Calendar of Plea and Memoranda Rolls*, 218.
[83] *Die Chronik Johanns von Winterthur*, ed. Friedrich Bathgen, with C. Brun, MGH SS rer. Germ., new ser. 3 (Berlin: Weidmann, 1924), 268–9.

1347

84. Calais. The Augustinians are expelled as foreigners during the Hundred Years War and are replaced with Englishmen.[84]

1348

85. Meissen (Saxony). Penitential Flagellants assault two Dominicans, killing one of them.[85]

1355

86. Bristol. A former mayor breaks into local Augustinian convent and robs it.[86]

1356

87. Newcastle. Murder of the Franciscan Richard Pestel by the guardian of the house and others.[87]

1359

88. Lucca. The Servite convent is burglarized.[88]

1361

89. Lucca. Armed assault by three men, including a cleric, on two Augustinians.[89]

1362

90. Pisa. A mob forcibly enters the Dominican convent in pursuit of a fleeing enemy.[90]

---

[84] Andrews, 103.
[85] *Liber de rebus memorabilioribus sive chronicon Henrici de Hervordia*, ed. August Potthast (Göttingen: Sumptibus Dieterichanis, 1859), 281–2.
[86] Francis Xavier Roth (ed.), *Sources for a History of the English Austin Friars*, 4 vols in 1 (Heverlee-Leuven: Institutum Historicum Augustinianum Lovanii, 1958–61), no. 420 (pp. 179–80).
[87] *Calendar of Patent Rolls*, Edward III, x (London: HMSO, 1909), 505.
[88] ASDL, Tribunale criminale 14, fo. 42^{r-v} (June 25, 1359).
[89] ASDL, Tribunale criminale 17, fos 102^r–103^v (Aug. 11–Nov. 8, 1361).
[90] AAPi, Atti Straordinari 8, fo. 80^{r-v} (Feb. 14, 1362).

1363

91. Venice. A local thief robs, among others, various items from the Franciscan, Dominican, and Carmelite convents.[91]

1369

92. Vilnius (Lithuania). Five Franciscan friars are executed for preaching to local pagans.[92]

1376

93. Limerick (Ireland). An assault led by Peter, the local bishop, on the Franciscans and their protector, the Franciscan archbishop of Cashel, Philip Torrington.[93]

1379

94. Poggibonzi. Cecco Pieri di Jacopo, a serial violent offender, breaks into the Franciscan convent, destroys property, and threatens to murder one of the brothers.[94]
95. Poggibonzi. Same man robs the local Augustinian convent.[95]

1381

96. Cambridge. Rioting citizens break into Carmelite convent in response to their alleged involvement in the Peasants' Revolt. Some of the friars' books are burnt in the market square.[96]
97. London. William of Appleton, a Franciscan friar and physician associated with John of Gaunt is executed.[97]
98. London. A mob pursues Flemings into the Augustinian convent.[98]
99. York. Rioters assault the Dominican convent, among other ecclesiastical institutions.[99]

---

[91] Stefano Piasentini, *"Alla luce della luna": I furti a Venezia (1270–1403)* (Venice: Il Cardo, 1992), 212–13.
[92] S. C. Rowell, *Lithuania Ascending: A Pagan Empire within East-Central Europe, 1295–1345* (Cambridge: Cambridge University Press, 1994), 275–7.
[93] *BF* vi.576–8.
[94] ASFi, Capitano del popolo 1197, fos 147^v–148^r and 149^r (June 14, 1379).
[95] ASFi, Capitano del popolo 1197, fo. 149r (June 14, 1379).
[96] Andrews, 62–4.
[97] *Westminster*, 6; Jean Froissart, *Chroniques*, x, ed. Gaston Raynaud (Paris: Jules Renouard, 1897), 111.
[98] Jens Röhrkasten, *The Mendicant Houses of Medieval London, 1221–1539* (Münster: Lit, 2004), 290–2.
[99] Christian D. Liddy, "Urban Conflict in Late Fourteenth-Century England: The Case of York in 1380–1," *EHR*, 118 (2003), 29.

Appendix 1

1383

100. Arezzo. The abduction, robbery, and rape of Francesca, a Poor Clare returning to her convent, by Naso, a vagabond from Florence.[100]
101. Villeneuve-sur-Lot (Languedoc). Monks assault the Dominicans and demolish their convent, which was allegedly built against the will of some local abbots.[101]

1384

102. London. A Carmelite friar is tortured to death by antagonists of Richard II for implicating members of the court in treason.[102]

1385

103. London. An English Franciscan is imprisoned at the Tower of London and tortured to death after being caught carrying a letter on behalf of John of Vienne to the king of France.[103]

1391

104. Lucca. Agostino, rector of the church of San Iuso and san Lorenzo de Branchaio in the diocese of Lucca, assaults Benedetto, a local Augustinian friar.[104]

1398

105. Lucca. Ludovico Cittadini of San Miniato assaults Benedetto di Castro Fiorentino, an Augustinian friar.[105]

LATE FOURTEENTH CENTURY

106. London. Lollards attack Augustinians and their convent after they tried to silence former brethren who turned on the order.[106]

---

[100] ASFi, Capitano del popolo 1521, unnumbered folios (May 25, 1383).
[101] Dossat, "Opposition des anciens ordres," 290–1.
[102] *Westminster*, 66–81.
[103] *Westminster*, 136.
[104] ASDL, Tribunale criminale 41, fo. 55^r (May 29, 1391).
[105] ASLu, Sentenze e bandi 94, fo. 15^v (May 5, 1398).
[106] Roth (ed.), *Sources for a History of the English Austin Friars*, no. 584 (pp. 231–2).

APPENDIX II

MAJOR OFFENSES AND PUNISHMENTS AMONG DOMINICAN FRIARS UNTIL 1400

The following is a chronological list of major infractions perpetrated by Dominican friars and mainly reported by the order's own administrative records. Offenses are included (1) when they were explicitly referred to as grave by the sources themselves (e.g., *scandala, excessus, crimen*) and (2) if they resulted in major penalties such as transfer and removal from office/s, incarceration, and expulsion. Cases are grouped by decades and are listed chronologically by modern country in alphabetical order. The number preceding an offense refers to the number of participants involved unless the offense was performed by an individual.

Penalties are denoted as follows:

(t) transfer within the order, often involving the person's being stripped of office and privileges;
(i) imprisonment; and
(e) expulsion.

Twenty-four cases of apostasy among English Dominicans mentioned in Chapter 3 have been omitted from this list since they are reported in great detail in Donald Logan's *Runaway Religious in Medieval England*, 241–2.

1251–60

England: not receiving students (t)[1]
Germany: 2 unknown (t)[2]
Italy: beat prior (e);[3] 3 unknown (e)[4]
Poland: unknown (t)[5]

---

[1] Benedikt Maria Reichert (ed.), *Acta capitulorum generalium Ordinis Praedicatorum*, 9 vols, MOFPH 3, 4, 8–14 (Rome: Typographia Polyglotta S.C. De Propaganda Fide, 1898–1904), i. 110–11.

[2] Reichert (ed.), *Acta*, i. 139–40.

[3] Thomas Kaeppeli and Antonio Dondaine (eds), *Acta capitulorum provincialium provinciae Romanae (1243–1344)*, MOFPH 20 (Santa Sabina [Rome]: Institutum Historicum Fratrum Paedicatorum, 1941), 14.

[4] Kaeppeli and Dondaine (eds), *Acta*, 14.

[5] Reichert (ed.), *Acta*, i. 139–40.

Appendix II 155

1261–70

France: 2 undermining prior;[6] theft (t)[7]
Italy: making a testament[8]

1271–80

France: illicit foundation (t);[9] intercepting letters (t);[10] several gross disobedience[11]
Germany: unknown (i)[12]
Italy: unknown (i);[13] 4 unknown (i);[14] 7 unknown (e)[15]

1281–90

France: 3 speaking against prior;[16] left *studium*[17]
Germany: unknown (i);[18] unknown (i);[19] riot;[20] 2 illicitly entered a convent;[21] allowing illicit visitors;[22] unknown;[23] unknown;[24] unknown (i)/(e);[25] unknown[26]

1291–1300

France: petition against Master General (t)[27]
Italy: 2 unknown (t)[28]

---

[6] Douais (ed.), *Acta capitulorum provincialium Ordinis Fratrum Praedicatoum, première province de Provence, province romaine—province d'Espagne (1239–1302)*, i (Toulouse: Édouard Privat, 1894), 100.
[7] Douais (ed.), *Acta*, i. 147.
[8] Reichert (ed.), *Acta*, i. 155.
[9] Douais (ed.), *Acta*, i. 203.
[10] Douais (ed.), *Acta*, i. 280.
[11] Douais (ed.), *Acta*, i. 290.
[12] Heinrich Finke (ed.), *Ungedruckte Dominikanerbriefe des 13. Jahrhunderts* (Paderborn: Ferdinand Schöningh, 1891), no. 86 (p. 108).
[13] Thomas Kaeppeli (ed.), "Acta capitulorum provinciae Lombardiae (1254–93) et Lombardiae inferioris (1309–1312)," *AFP*, 11 (1941), 156.
[14] Kaeppeli and Dondaine (eds), *Acta*, 39.
[15] Kaeppeli and Dondaine (eds), *Acta*, 39.
[16] Reichert (ed.), *Acta*, i. 241.
[17] Reichert (ed.), *Acta*, i. 246.
[18] Finke (ed.), *Ungedruckte Dominikanerbriefe*, no. 93 (p. 116).
[19] Finke (ed.), *Ungedruckte Dominikanerbriefe*, no. 96 (p. 119).
[20] Finke (ed.), *Ungedruckte Dominikanerbriefe*, no. 109 (pp. 131–2).
[21] Finke (ed.), *Ungedruckte Dominikanerbriefe*, no. 110 (pp. 132–3).
[22] Finke (ed.), *Ungedruckte Dominikanerbriefe*, no. 113 (p. 134).
[23] Finke (ed.), *Ungedruckte Dominikanerbriefe*, no. 114 (p. 135).
[24] Finke (ed.), *Ungedruckte Dominikanerbriefe*, no. 125 (p. 143).
[25] Finke (ed.), *Ungedruckte Dominikanerbriefe*, no. 140 (p. 153).
[26] Finke (ed.), *Ungedruckte Dominikanerbriefe*, no. 141 (pp. 154–5).
[27] Douais (ed.), *Acta*, i. 427.
[28] Kaeppeli and Dondaine (eds), *Acta*, 124.

1301–10

Germany: 20+ unknown (t)[29]
Italy: 5 unknown (e);[30] unknown (t);[31] irreverence (t);[32] wrongful imprisonment;[33] unknown (e);[34] debt[35]

1311–20

Germany: disobedience (t);[36] 2 illicit travel;[37] unknown (t)[38]
Italy: heterodoxy (t);[39] violence (t);[40] *scandala* (t)[41]

1321–30

Germany: 2 assault prior (i);[42] many students conspire against prior (t)[43]
Italy: beating of provincial prior (i)[44]
Spain: 4 gross disobedience (t)[45]

1331–40

France: inept prior (t);[46] forgery (i)[47]

---

[29] Reichert (ed.), *Acta*, i. 307–9.
[30] Kaeppeli and Dondaine (eds), *Acta*, 140–1.
[31] Kaeppeli and Dondaine (eds), *Acta*, 142.
[32] Kaeppeli and Dondaine (eds), *Acta*, 167.
[33] Kaeppeli and Dondaine (eds), *Acta*, 171.
[34] Kaeppeli and Dondaine (eds), *Acta*, 175.
[35] Kaeppeli and Dondaine (eds), *Acta*, 175.
[36] Thomas Kaeppeli (ed.), "Ein Fragment der Akten des in Friesach 1315 gefeierten Kapitels der Provinz Teutonia," *AFP*, 48 (1978), 73.
[37] Kaeppeli (ed.), "Ein Fragment der Akten des in Friesach 1315 gefeierten Kapitels der Provinz Teutonia," 73.
[38] Kaeppeli (ed.), "Ein Fragment der Akten des in Friesach 1315 gefeierten Kapitels der Provinz Teutonia," 73.
[39] Kaeppeli and Dondaine (eds), *Acta*, 197.
[40] Kaeppeli and Dondaine (eds), *Acta*, 200.
[41] Reichert (ed.), *Acta*, i. 66–7.
[42] Reichert (ed.), *Acta*, i. 135.
[43] Reichert (ed.), *Acta*, i. 159–61.
[44] Kaeppeli and Dondaine (eds), *Acta*, 228–9.
[45] "Acta capitulorum provincialium provinciae Aragoniae, 1250–1530," Zaragoza, Biblioteca Universitaria, MS 185 (previously 97), fos 107–8.
[46] Reichert (ed.), *Acta*, i. 281–2.
[47] Reichert (ed.), *Acta*, i. 281–2.

Appendix II 157

[1341–50 NO CASES]

1351–60

France: 7 unknown (t)[48]
Spain: embezzlement and apostasy (t);[49] 2 gross disobedience and apostasy (e);[50] 3 gross disobedience and violence (i);[51] disclosing prior's correspondence (t)[52]

1361–70

Spain: 3 apostasy (i)[53]

1371–80

Germany: debt;[54] blasphemy (t)[55]
Italy: unknown (t)[56]
Spain: 3 rebelliousness (t);[57] apostasy (t)[58]

1381–90

France: theft?[59]
Italy: unknown (i);[60] 2 unknown (i);[61] unknown (i);[62] 2 unknown (i);[63] several theft (i);[64] prison escape;[65] several unknown (e);[66] unknown (i);[67] several disobedience (t);[68] beating;[69] unknown (i)[70]

---

[48] Reichert (ed.), *Acta*, i. 374.
[49] "Acta capitulorum provincialium provinciae Aragoniae, 1250–1530," fo. 233.
[50] "Acta capitulorum provincialium provinciae Aragoniae, 1250–1530," fos 247–8.
[51] "Acta capitulorum provincialium provinciae Aragoniae, 1250–1530," fos 288–9.
[52] "Acta capitulorum provincialium provinciae Aragoniae, 1250–1530," fo. 304.
[53] "Acta capitulorum provincialium provinciae Aragoniae, 1250–1530," fos 376–7.
[54] Heinrich Finke, "Zur Geschichte der deutschen Dominikaner im XIII. und XIV. Jahrhundert," *Römische Quartalschrift für Christliche Altertumskunde und für Kirchengeshichte*, 8 (1894), 383.
[55] Finke, "Zur Geschichte der deutschen Dominikaner im XIII. und XIV. Jahrhundert," 383.
[56] Finke, "Zur Geschichte der deutschen Dominikaner im XIII. und XIV. Jahrhundert," 383.
[57] "Acta capitulorum provincialium provinciae Aragoniae, 1250–1530," fo. 397.
[58] "Acta capitulorum provincialium provinciae Aragoniae, 1250–1530," fo. 448.
[59] *Registrum*, 2.
[60] *Registrum*, 10.
[61] *Registrum*, 10.
[62] *Registrum*, 10.
[63] *Registrum*, 14.
[64] *Registrum*, 16.
[65] *Registrum*, 16.
[66] *Registrum*, 18.
[67] *Registrum*, 18.
[68] *Registrum*, 19.
[69] *Registrum*, 23.
[70] *Registrum*, 26.

158 Appendix II

1391-1400

England: sexual;[71] sexual[72]
Germany: rebellion (e);[73] illicit imprisonment;[74] theft;[75] 10 left convent (e);[76] sexual (e);[77] sexual (i);[78] several desertions;[79] several desertions;[80] several desertions;[81] sexual (i);[82] illicit imprisonment;[83] illicit imprisonment;[84] embezzlement (i);[85] extortion;[86] unknown;[87] unknown;[88] unknown (i);[89] unknown;[90] unknown (t)[91]
Italy: theft;[92] 2 unknown;[93] unknown (i);[94] forgery;[95] illicit imprisonment (i);[96] apostasy (e);[97] unknown;[98] 2 rebellion (e);[99] 5 rebellion (i)[100]
Spain: arson[101]

[71] *Registrum*, 199.
[72] *Registrum*, 199.
[73] *Registrum*, 140.
[74] *Registrum*, 147.
[75] *Registrum*, 150.
[76] *Registrum*, 149–50.
[77] *Registrum*, 152.
[78] *Registrum*, 154.
[79] *Registrum*, 157.
[80] *Registrum*, 158.
[81] *Registrum*, 161.
[82] *Registrum*, 162.
[83] *Registrum*, 163.
[84] *Registrum*, 163.
[85] Fritz Bünger (ed.), "Ein Dominikaner-Provinzialkapitel in Luckau (1400)," *ZfK*, 34 (1913), 85.
[86] Bünger (ed.), "Ein Dominikaner-Provinzialkapitel in Luckau (1400)," 86.
[87] Bünger (ed.), "Ein Dominikaner-Provinzialkapitel in Luckau (1400)," 86.
[88] Benedikt Maria Reichert (ed.), "Akten der Provinzialkapitel der Dominikanerordensprovinz Teutonia, 1398, 1400, 1401, 1402," *Römische Quartalschrift für Christliche Altertumskunde und für Kirchengeshichte* 11 (1897), 300.
[89] Reichert (ed.), "Akten der Provinzialkapitel der Dominikanerordensprovinz Teutonia, 1398, 1400, 1401, 1402," 311.
[90] Reichert (ed.), "Akten der Provinzialkapitel der Dominikanerordensprovinz Teutonia, 1398, 1400, 1401, 1402," 311.
[91] Reichert (ed.), "Akten der Provinzialkapitel der Dominikanerordensprovinz Teutonia, 1398, 1400, 1401, 1402," 311.
[92] *Registrum*, 34.
[93] *Registrum*, 45.
[94] *Registrum*, 46.
[95] *Registrum*, 56.
[96] *Registrum*, 57.
[97] *Registrum*, 84.
[98] *Registrum*, 99.
[99] *Registrum*, 106, 112.
[100] *Registrum*, 122.
[101] "Acta capitulorum provincialium provinciae Aragoniae, 1250–1530," fo. 590.

Bibliography

(Excluding works listed under Abbreviations)

PRIMARY SOURCES

a. Archives
AAPi, Atti straordinari 1, 3, 4, 6–9, 11
AGOP, XIV, Lib. I I I
ASBo, Curia del podestà, Libri inquisitionum 6–31, 115–39, 179–200, 203–4; Governo, Riformagioni e provvigioni 200
ASCMi, Cimeli 146–50, 175
ASDL, Tribunale criminale 1–44
ASFi, Capitano del popolo, 848, 892, 896, 947, 954, 1002bis, 1120, 1197bis, 1198, 1255, 1313, 1371, 1427, 1428, 1496, 1521, 1559
ASLu, Sentenze e bandi 1–9, 19–23, 25, 28, 33, 36, 93–6, 535
ASPa, Conventi, S. Pietro Martire di Parma, Domenicani [= XXXI], B. 3
ASVe, Cancellaria inferiore, Miscellanea testamenti, Notai diversi B. 22; Consiglio di dieci, Deliberazioni (miste) 8
The National Archives: Public Record Office, JUST1/369/M22-OCarm

b. Manuscripts
Barcelona, Biblioteca Universitaria, MS 241
Bologna, Biblioteca dell'Archiginnasio, MS B. 1856 (antica 16*-gg-1-l)
Luzern, Zentralbibliothek, MS BB.129.4°
Milan, Biblioteca Ambrosiana, P25
Zaragoza, Biblioteca Universitaria, MS 185 (previously 97)

c. Edited Sources
Acta Sanctorum, Société des Bollandistes, 68 vols (Brussels and Paris, 1643–1940).
Adam of Usk, *The Chronicle of Adam Usk, 1377–1421*, ed. C. Given-Wilson (Oxford: Clarendon Press, 1997).
Altaner, Berthold (ed.), "Aus den Akten des Rottweiler Provinzialkapitels der Dominikaner vom Jahre 1396," *ZfK*, 48 (1929), 1–15.
Ancelet-Hustace, Jeanne (ed.), "Les 'Vitae Sororum' d'Unterlinden: Édition critique du manuscrit 508 de la Bibliothèque de Colmar," *Archives d'histoire doctrinale et littéraire du moyen age*, 5 (1930), 317–509.
Analecta Sacri Ordinis Fratrum Praedicatorum (Rome: Ex Curia Generalitia ad S. Sabinam, 1893–).
Anonymous, "Cronaca del convento di Santa Caterina dell'Ordine dei Predicatori in Pisa," *Archivio Storico Italiano*, 1st ser., 6/2 (1845), 397–593.
Anonymous, *Universis christifidelibus*, MCH 81–90.
Baconthorpe, John, *Compendium historiarum et iurium*, MCH 199–217.
Baconthorpe, John, *Laus religionis carmelitanae*, MCH 218–53.

Barber, Malcolm, and Keith Bate (eds and trans.), *Letters from the East: Crusaders, Pilgrims and Settlers in the 12th–13th Centuries* (Farnham: Ashgate, 2010).
Bériou, Nicole (gen. ed.), *Les sermons et la visite pastorale de Federico Visconti, archevêque de Pisa (1253–1277)* (Rome: École française de Rome, 2001).
Boccaccio, Giovanni, *Decameron*, ed. Vittore Branca, 8th edn (Milan: Mondadori, 2001).
Boehmer, Johannes Friedrich (ed.), *Martyrium Arnoldi…und andere Geschichtsquellen Deutschlands* (Stuttgart: J. G. Cotta'scher Verlag, 1853).
Bonaventure of Bagnoregio, *Opera omnia*, 10 vols in 9 (Claras Aquas [Quaracchi]: Typographia Collegii S. Bonaventurae, 1882–1902).
Bonazzi, Giuliano (ed.), *Chronicon parmese ab anno mxxxvii usque ad annum mcccxxxviii*, Rerum Italicarum Scriptores, 9, pt ix (Città di Castello: S. Lapi, 1902).
Brial, Michel-Jean-Joseph (ed.), *Majus chronicon lemovicense a Petro Coral et aliis conscriptum*, Recueil des Historiens des Gaules et de la France, 18 (Paris: Imprimerie Impériale, 1822), 761–802.
Bünger, Fritz (ed.), "Ein Dominikaner-Provinzialkapitel in Luckau (1400)," *ZfK*, 34 (1913), 74–88.
Cagnoli, Gerard (ed.), "La leggenda del B. Gerardo Cagnoli, O.Min. (1267–1342) di Frà Bartolomeo Albizi. O.Min. († 1351)," *Miscellanea Francescana*, 57 (1951), 367–446.
Calendar of Patent Rolls, Edward III, 16 vols (London: HMSO, 1891–1916).
Calendar of Patent Rolls, Edward I, 4 vols (London: HMSO, 1893–1901).
Capes, William W. (ed.), *The Register of Richard de Swinfield, Bishop of Hereford, AD 1283–1317*, Cantilupe Society Publications, 3 (Cambridge: Chadwyck-Healey, 1979).
Chaucer, Geoffrey, *The Riverside Chaucer*, gen. ed. Larry D. Benson (Oxford: Oxford University Press, 1988).
Chaucer, Geoffrey, *The Romaunt of the Rose*, ed. Charles Dahlberg (Norman, OK: University of Oklahoma Press, 1999).
Clareno, Angelo, *Historia septem tribulationum Ordinis Minorum*, ed. Orietta Rossini (Rome: Istituto Storico Italiano per il Medio Evo, 1999).
Clyn John, *Annalium Hiberniae Chronicon ad annum MCCCXLIX*, ed. R. Butler (Dublin: Irish Archaeological Society, 1849).
Compagni, Dino, *Cronica*, ed. Isidoro Del Lungo (Florence: Successori Le Monnier, 1889).
Coulon, Auguste, and Suzanne Clemencet (eds), *Lettres secrètes et curiales du pape Jean XXII (1316–1334) relatives à la France*, 4 vols (Paris: Fontemoing, 1965–72).
Dal Pino, Franco Andrea (ed.), *I Frati Servi di S. Maria, dalle origini all'approvazione (1233 ca.–1304)*, 2 vols in 3, Recueil de Travaux d'Histoire et de Philologie, 4th ser., 50 (Louvain: Bureau du Recueil, Bibliotheque de l'Universiteí, 1972).
Di Fonzo, Lorenzo (ed.), "L'Anonimo Perugino tra le fonti francescane nel secolo XIII: Rapporti letterari e testo critico," *Miscellanea Francescana*, 72 (1972), 117–470.
Digard, Georges, et al. (eds), *Les Registres de Boniface VIII (1294–1303)*, 4 vols (Paris: Ernest Thorin [and E. De Bocard], 1884–1939).
Douais, C. (ed.), *Acta capitulorum provincialium Ordinis Fratrum Praedicatoum, première province de Provence, province romaine—province d'Espagne (1239–1302)*, 2 vols (Toulouse: Privat, 1894–95).
Ehrle, Franz (ed.), "Die ältesten Redactionen der Generalconstitutionen des Franziskanerordens," *Archiv für Literatur- und Kirchengeschichte des Mittelalters*, 6 (1892), 1–138.
Esteban, E. (ed.), "Antiquiores quae extant definitiones capitulorum generalium ordinis," *Analecta Augustiniana*, 2–8 (1907–20).

―― (ed.), "Definitiones antiquorum capitulorum provinciae Franciae, O.N.," *Analecta Augustiniana*, 3 (1910), 273–6, 302–6, 321–3; 4 (1911–12), 65–7, 111–15, 162–4, 186–8, 251–3, 476–9.

Haydon, Frank Scott (ed.), *Eulogium historiarum*, 3 vols, Rolls Series, 9 (London: Longman, Brown, Green, Longmans, and Roberts, 1858–63).

Fiamma, Galvano, *Cronica Ordinis Praedicatorum ab anno 1170 usque ad 1333*, ed. Benedikt Maria Reichert, MOFPH 2 (Rome: In Domo Generalitia, 1897).

Finke, Heinrich (ed.), *Ungedruckte Dominikanerbriefe des 13. Jahrhunderts* (Paderborn: Ferdinand Schöningh, 1891).

FitzMaurice, E. B., and A. G. Little (eds), *Materials for the History of the Franciscan Province of Ireland, AD 1230–1450* (Manchester: Manchester University Press, 1920).

FitzRalph, Richard, *Defensio Curatorum*, in Edward Brown (ed.), *Fasciculus rerum expetendarum & fugiendarum*, 2 vols (London, 1690), ii. 466–86.

France, Parlement (Paris), *Les Olim, ou, Registres des arrêts rendus par la cour du roi*, 3 vols in 4 (Paris: Imprimerie Royale, 1839–48).

Froissart, Jean, *Chroniques*, ed. Siméon Luce et al., 11 vols in 12 (Paris: Jules Renouard, 1869–99).

Fuller, Thomas, *The Church History of Britain* (London: John Williams, 1655).

Gerard of Abbevile, "Contra adversarium perfectionis christianae," ed. S. Clasen, *AFH*, 31 (1938), 276–329; 32 (1939), 89–200.

Géraud, H. (ed.), *Chronique Latin de Guillaume de Nangis et de ses continuateurs*, 2 vols (Paris: Jules Renouard, 1843).

Gransden, Antonia (ed.), "A Fourteenth-Century Chronicle from Grey Friars at Lynn," *EHR*, 72 (1957), 270–8.

Gratian, *Concordia discordantium canonum*, in Emil Friedberg (ed.), *Corpus iuris canonici*, 2 vols (Leipzig: B. Tauchnitz, 1879–81).

Gratien de Paris, *Histoire de la fondation et de l'évolution de l'Ordre des frères mineurs au XIIIe siècle*, with additional bibliography by Mariano D'Alatri and Servus Gieben, Biblioteca Seraphico-Capuccina, 29 (Santa Sabina [Rome]: Institutum Historicum Fratrum Praedicatorum, 1982 [orig. pub. 1928]).

Gratius, Ortuin (ed.), *Fasciculus rerum expetendarum & fugiendarum* (Cologne, 1535).

Gregory of Rimini, "Litterae Prioris Generalis Ordinis Fr. Gregorii Ariminensis," in *Analecta Augustiniana*, 4 (1911–12), 372–6, 423–6, 443–7, 465–71; 5 (1913–14), 5–11, 26–30, 122–6, 152–6.

Heinrich von Herford, *Liber de rebus memorabilioribus sive chronicon Henrici de Hervordia*, ed. August Potthast (Göttingen: Dieterich, 1859).

Henschel, W., "Document zur Geschichte des schwarzen Todes," in *Archiv für die gesammte Medicin*, 2, ed. Heinrich Haeser (Jena, 1842), 26–59.

Hessel, Alfred (ed.), *Elsässische Urkunden, vornehmlich des 13. Jahrhunderts* (Strasbourg: Karl J. Trübner, 1915).

Heyworth, P. L. (ed.), *Jack Upland, Friar Daw's Reply, and Upland's Rejoinder* (Oxford: Oxford University Press, 1968).

Hind, Arthur M. (ed.), *Early Italian Engraving*, 7 vols (London: M. Knoedler & Co., 1938–48).

Holder-Egger, O. (ed.), *Chronica minor auctore minorita erphordiensi*, MGH SS 24 (Hanover, 1879), 172–204.

Horrox, Rosmary (ed. and trans.), *The Black Death* (Manchester: Manchester University Press, 1994).

Humbert of Romans, *Opera de vita regulari*, ed. Joachim Joseph Berthier, 2 vols (Rome: Typis A. Befani, 1888–9).

Ilarino da Milano, "Gli antecedenti inediti di un nuovo episodio dell'inquisizione francescana a Treviso (1262–1263)," *Collectanea Franciscana*, 5 (1935), 611–20.

Jaffé, Philipp (ed.), *Annales colmarienses maiores*, MGH SS 17 (Hanover, 1861), 202–32.

Jean de Cheminot, *Speculum fratrum ordinis, MCH* 115–46.

Johanns von Winterthur, *Die Chronik Johanns von Winterthur*, ed. Friedrich Bathgen, with C. Brun, MGH SS rer. Germ., NS3 (Berlin: Weidmann, 1924).

Jordan of Giano, *Chronica Fratris Jordani*, ed. H. Boehmer (Paris: Librairie Fischbacher, 1908).

Jordan of Saxony, *Love among the Saints: The Letters of Blessed Jordan of Saxony to Blessed Diana of Andalò*, ed. and trans. Kathleen Pond (London: Bloomsbury, 1958).

Jordan of Saxony [=de Quedlinburg], *Liber Vitasfratrum*, ed. Rudolf Arbesmann and Winfrid Hümpfner (New York: Cosmopolitan Science & Art Service, 1943).

Kaeppeli, Thomas, "Cronache domenicane di Giacomo Domenech O.P. in una raccola miscellanea del Card. Niccolò Rosell," *AFP*, 14 (1944), 5–42.

Kaeppeli, Thomas (ed.), "Acta capitulorum provinciae Lombardiae (1254–93) et Lombardiae inferioris (1309–1312)," *AFP*, 11 (1941), 140–67.

—— (ed.), "Ein Fragment der Akten des in Friesach 1315 gefeierten Kapitels der Provinz Teutonia," *AFP*, 48 (1978), 71–5.

Kaeppeli, Thomas, and Antoine Dondaine (eds), *Acta capitulorum provincialium provinciae Romanae (1243–1344)*, MOFPH 20 (Santa Sabina [Rome]: Institutum Historicum Fratrum Praedicatorum, 1941).

Knighton, Henry, *Chronicon Henrici Knighton, vel Cnitthon, monachi leycestrensis*, ed. Jason Rawson Lumby, 2 vols, Rolls Series, 92 (London: HMSO, 1889–95).

Langlois, E. (ed.), *Les Registres de Nicholas IV (1288–91)*, 2 vols (Paris: Ernest Thorin, 1905).

Le Baker, Geoffrey, *Chronicon Galfridi le Baker de Swynebroke*, ed. Edward Maude Thompson (Oxford: Clarendon Press, 1889).

Lemmens, Leonard (ed.), *Fragmenta minora: Catalogus sanctorum fratrum minorum* (Rome: Typis Sallustians, 1903).

Little, A. G. (ed.), "Decrees of the General Chapters of the Franciscan Order, 1260–1282," *EHR*, 13 (1898), 703–8.

—— (ed.), *Liber exemplorum ad usum praedicantium* (Aberdeen: Typis Academicis, 1908).

Lorris, Guillaume de, and Jean de Meun, *Le Roman de la Rose*, ed. Ernest Langlois, 5 vols (Paris: Librairie Ancienne Honoré Champion, 1914–24).

Luard, Henry Richards (ed.), *Annales monastici*, 5 vols, Rolls Series, 36 (London: Longman, Green, Longman, Roberts, and Green, 1864–9).

Madura, Romanus Fabianus (ed.), *Acta capitulorum provinciae Poloniae Ordinis Praedicatorum*, i. *1225–1600* (Rome: Pontificum Institutum Studiorum Ecclesiasticorum, 1972).

Maiarelli, Andrea (ed.), *La cronaca di S. Domenico di Perugia*, Quaderni del Centro per il Collegamento degli Studi Medievali e Umanistici nell'Umbria, 36 (Spoleto: Centro Italiano di Studi sull'Alto Medioevo, 1995).

Marcos de Lisboa, *Crónicas da Ordem dos Frades Menores*, 3 vols (Porto: Faculdade de Letras da Universidade do Porto, 2001).

Marianus of Florence, *Compendium chronicarum Fratrum Minorum, AFH*, 1 (1908), 98–107; 2 (1909), 92–107, 305–18, 457–72, 626–41; 3 (1910), 294–309, 700–15.

Masetti, Thomas (ed.), *Monumenta et antiquitates veteris disciplinae Ordinis Praedicatorum ab anno 1216 ad 1348*, 2 vols (Rome: Camera Apostolica, 1864).

Matthew of Janov, *Matthiae de Janov Regulae Veteris et Novi Testamenti*, ed. V. Kybal, 6 vols (Innsbruck: Wagner University, 1908–11).
Mézières, Philippe de, *The Life of Saint Peter Thomas by Philippe de Mézières*, ed. Joachim Smet, TSHC 2 (Rome: Institutum Carmelitanum, 1954).
Milioli, Albertus, *Liber de temporibus et etatibus*, ed. Oswald Holder-Egger, MGH SS 31 (Hanover, 1903), 336–668.
Monumenta Germaniae Franciscana, 2.1: *Die Kustoden Goldberg und Breslau*, 1 Teil: *1240–1517* (Düsseldorf: L. Schwann, 1917).
Musurillo, Herbert (ed. and trans.), *The Acts of the Christian Martyrs* (Oxford: Clarendon Press, 1972).
Nicolas of Lisieux, "Liber de Antichristi," in Edmond Martène and Ursin Durand (eds), *Veterum scriptorum et monumentorum historicorum...*, ix (Paris: Montalant, 1724–33), cols 1271–1446.
Pagden, A. R. (ed. and trans.), *The Maya: Diego de Landa's Account of the Affairs of Yucatán* (Chicago: J. Philip O'Hara, 1975).
Paolini, Lorenzo, and Raniero Orioli (eds), *Acta S. Officii Bononie ab anno 1291 usque ad annum 1310*, 3 vols, Fonti per la Storia d'Italia, 106 (Rome: Istituto Storico Italiano per il Medio Evo, 1982–4).
Paris, Matthew, *Chronica Majora*, ed. Henry Richards Luard, 7 vols, Rolls Series, 57 (London: Longman, 1872–83).
Pelhisson, Guillaume, *Chronique (1229–1244)*, ed. and trans. Jean Duvernoy (Paris: CNRS Éditions, 1994).
Piazza, Michele da, *Cronaca*, ed. Antonino Giuffrida, Fonti per la Storia di Sicilia, 3, 3 vols in 1 (Palermo and Sao Paolo: ILA Palma, 1980).
Polo, Marco, *The Travels of Marco Polo*, trans. Robert Latham (London and New York: Penguin Books, 1988).
Reichert, Benedikt Maria (ed.), "Akten der Provinzialkapitel der Dominikanerordensprovinz Teutonia, 1398, 1400, 1401, 1402," *Römische Quartalschrift für christliche Altertumskunde und für Kirchengeschichte*, 11 (1897), 287–331.
——, *Acta capitulorum generalium Ordinis Praedicatorum*, 9 vols, MOFPH 3, 4, and 8–14 (Rome: Typographia Polyglotta S.C. De Propaganda Fide, 1898–1904).
Ripoll, Thomas (ed.), *Bullarium Ordinis Fratrum Praedicatorum*, 2 vols (Rome: J. Mainardus, 1729–30).
Robles Sierra, Adolfo, and Vito T. Gómez García (eds), "Actas de los Capitulos Provinciales de la Provincia de Aragon de la Orden de Predicadores," *Escritos del Vedat*, 20–7 (1990–7); 31–5 (2001–5).
Roth, Francis Xavier (ed.), *Sources for a History of the English Austin Friars*, 4 vols in 1 (Heverlee-Leuven: Institutum Historicum Augustinianum Lovanii, 1958–61).
Rowlands, John K., Fedja Anzelewsky, and Robert Zijlma (eds), *Hollstein's German Engravings, Etchings and Woodcuts*, xi. *Urs Graf* (Amsterdam: Van Gendt & Co., 1977).
Rummel, Erika (ed. and trans.), *Scheming Papists and Lutheran Fools: Five Reformation Satires* (New York: Fordham University Press, 1993).
Rutebeuf, *Œuvres complètes*, ed. Edmond Faral and Julia Bastin, 2 vols (Paris: A. et J. Picard, 1959–60).
Sabatini, Andrea (ed.), *Atti dei capitoli provinciali di Toscana dei carmelitani, 1375–1491*, Archivum Historicum Carmelitanum, 4 (Rome: Institutum Carmelitanum, 1975).
St Amour, William of, "Les 'Responsiones' de Guillaume de Saint-Amour," ed. E. Faral, *Archives d'histoire doctrinale et littéraire du moyen age*, 18 (1950–1), 337–94.

St Amour, William of, *Guillielmi de S. Amore Opera Omnia*... (Constance [Paris]: Alitophilos, 1632; repr. Hildesheim and New York: G. Olms, 1997).
——, *The Opuscula of William of Saint-Amour: The Minor Works of 1255–1256*, ed. Andrew G. Traver (Münster: Aschendorff, 2003).
Salgado, James, *The Fryer, or An Historical Treatise*, 2 vols in 1 (London, 1680).
SS. Ecclesiae Doctorum Thomae Aquinatis et Bonaventurae Opuscula adversus Guillelmum a S. Amore, 2 vols (Rome: G. Salomon, 1773).
Scolaro, Luigina Carratori, et al. (eds), *Carte dell'Archivio Arcivescovile di Pisa, Fondo Luoghi Vari*, 3 vols (Pisa: Pacini, 1988–99).
Somerset, Fiona (ed.), *Four Wycliffite Dialogues*, Early English Text Society, OS 333 (Oxford: Oxford University Press, 2009).
Speght, Thomas, *The Works of our Antient and Learned English Poet Geffrey Chaucer* (London, 1598).
Stephens, G. (ed.), "Brottstycken av en Dominikaner-Ordens eller Predikare-Brödernas Statut- eller Capitel-Bok infrån XIII. Århundradet, och gällande för 'Provincia Dacia' eller de Nordiska Riken," *Kirkehistoriske Samlinger*, 1 (1849–52), 545–642; 2 (1853–6), 128–9.
Strauss, Walter L. (gen. ed.), *The Illustrated Bartsch* (New York: Abaris Books, 1978–).
Tait, James (ed.), *Chronica Johannis de Reading et Anonymi Cantuariensis 1346–1367* (Manchester: Manchester University Press, 1914).
Thomas, A. H. (ed.), *Calendar of Early Mayor's Court Rolls... 1298–1307* (Cambridge: Cambridge University Press, 1924).
——, *Calendar of Plea and Memoranda Rolls* (Cambridge: Cambridge University Press, 1926).
——, *Calendar of Select Pleas and Memoranda of the City of London*, 6 vols (Cambridge: Cambridge University Press, 1926–61).
Tirelli, Vito, and Matilde Tirelli Carli (eds), *Le pergamene del convento di S. Francesco in Lucca (secc. XII–XIX)* (Rome: Ministero per I Beni Culturali e Ambientali, 1993).
Tschamser, Malachias, *Annales oder Jahrs-Geschichten der Baarfüseren oder Minderen Brüderen*, 2 vols (Colmar: Hoffmann, 1864).
Twinger von Konigsthofen, Jacob, *Chronicon Universale et Alsaticum*, ed. Johann Schitern (Strasbourg: Josias Städel, 1698).
Venette, Jean de, *Speculum status ordinis historiale*, MCH 152–75.
Villani, Matteo, *Cronica. Con la continuazione di Filippo Villani*, 2 vols, ed. Giuseppe Porta (Parma: U. Guanda, 1995).
Voragine, Jacobus de, *The Golden Legend; Readings on the Saints*, trans. William Granger Ryan, 2 vols (Princeton: Princeton University Press, 1993).
Wadding, Luke, et al., *Annales Minorum seu trium ordinum a S. Francisco institutorum*, 2nd edn, 25 vols (Rome: Typis Rochi Bernabo, 1731–1886).
Wessels, Gabriel (ed.), *Acta capitulorum generalium Ordinis B. V. Mariae de Monte Carmelo*, i (Rome: Apud Curiam Generalitiam, 1912).
Wiegand, Wilhelm, and Aloys Schulte (eds), *Urkunden der Stadt Strassburg*, 4 vols (Strasbourg: Karl J. Trübner, 1879–98).
William of Cremona, "Litterae Prioris Generalis Fr. Guillelmi de Cremona," *Analecta Augustiniana*, 4 (1911–12), 29–32; 57–65.
William of Coventry, *Chronica brevis*, MCH 272–7.
William of Coventry, *De duplici fuga*, MCH 278–81.

Wright, Thomas (ed.), *Political Poems and Songs Relating to English History, Composed during the Period from the Accession of Edw. III to that of Ric. III*, 2 vols (London: Longman, 1859–61).

Wyclif, John, *Two Short Treatises, against the Orders of the Begging Friars* (Oxford: Iospeh Barnes, 1608).

Wyclif, John, *Select English Works of John Wyclif*, ed. Thomas Arnold, 3 vols (Oxford: Clarendon Press, 1869–71).

MODERN STUDIES

Adams, Eleanor B., *A Bio-Bibliography of Franciscan Authors in Colonial Central America* (Washington, D.C.: Academy of American Franciscan History, 1953).

Albaret, Laurent, "Les Prêcheurs et l'inquisition," in *L'Ordre des Prêcheurs et son histoire en France méridionale*, CdF 36 (Toulouse: Privat, 2001), 319–41.

Albaret, Laurent, "Inquisitio heretice pravitatis: L'Inquisition dominicaine dans le midi de la France aux XIIIe et XIVe siècles ou la première inquisition pontificale," in Wolfram Hoyer (ed.), *Praedicatores, Inquisitores I. The Dominicans and the Medieval Inquisition* (Rome: Istituto Storico Domenicano, 2004), 421–46.

Althoff, Gerd, *Family, Friends and Followers: Political and Social Bonds in Medieval Europe*, trans. Christopher Carroll (Cambridge and New York: Cambridge University Press, 2004).

Andreas, James, "'New Science' from 'Olde Bokes': A Bakhtinian Approach to the *Summoner's Tale*," *Chaucer Review*, 25 (1990), 138–51.

Anscombe, G. E. M., "On Brute Facts," *Analysis*, 18 (1958), 69–72.

Arbeloa, Víctor Manuel, *Clericalismo y anticlericalismo en España (1767–1930): Una introducción* (Madrid: Encuentro, 2009).

Arden, Heather M., *The Roman de la Rose: An Annotated Bibliography* (New York: Garland, 1993).

Arendt, Hannah, *On Violence* (Orlando, FA: Harcourt, 1970).

Aston, Nigel, and Matthew Cragoe (eds), *Anticlericalism in Britain, c.1500–1914* (Stroud: Sutton, 2000).

Badel, Pierre-Yves, *Le Roman de la Rose au XIVe siècle* (Geneva: Librairie Droz, 1980).

Bakhtin, Mikhail, *Rabelais and his World*, trans. Hélène Iswolsky (Cambridge: Cambridge University Press, 1968).

Barret, Sébastien, and Gert Melville (eds), *Oboedientia: Zu Formen und Grenzen von Macht und Unterordnung im mittelalterlichen Religiosentum*, Vita Regularis, 27 (Münster: Lit, 2005).

Barnell, S. J., *Idol Temples and Crafty Priests: The Origins of Enlightenment Anticlericalism* (London: Macmillan, 1999).

Baron, Salo W., "Ghetto and Emancipation," *Menora*, 14 (1928), 515–26.

Barron, Caroline, "The Deposition of Richard II," in John Taylor and Wendy Childs (eds), *Politics and Crisis in Fourteenth-Century England* (Gloucester: Alan Sutton, 1990), 132–49.

Bataillon, Louis Jacques, "Les crises de l'université de Paris d'après les sermons universitaires," in Albert Zimmermann (ed.), *Die Auseinandersetzungen an der Pariser Universität im XIII. Jahrhundert*, Miscellanea Medievalia, 10 (Berlin: Walter de Gruyter, 1976), 155–69.

Batamy, Jean, "L'Image des franciscaines dans les 'revues d'États' du XIIIe au XVIe siècle," in André Vauchez (ed.), *Mouvements franciscains et société française, XIIe–XXe siècles*, Beauchesne Religions, 14 (Paris: Beauchesne, 1984), 61–74.

Bayon, Balbino Velasco, *Historia del carmeli español*, 2 vols, TSHC 17–18 (Rome: Institutum Carmelitanum, 1990–92).

Beltran de Heredia, V., "El convento de s. Esteban en sus relaciones con la iglesia y la universita," *La Ciencia Tomista*, 84 (1926), 95–116.
Bennett, R. F., *The Early Dominicans: Studies in Thirteenth-Century Dominican History* (Cambridge: Cambridge University Press, 1937).
Benz, E., "Die Excerptsätze der Pariser Professoren aus dem Evangelium aeternum," *ZfK*, 51 (1932), 415–55.
Berg, Dieter (ed.), *Bettelorden und Stadt: Bettelorden und städlischer Leen im Mittelalter und un der Neuzeit* (Werl: Dietrich Coelde Verlag, 1992).
Biale, David, *Power and Powerlessness in Jewish History* (New York: Schocken Books, 1986).
Bierbaum, Max, *Bettelorden und Weltgeistlichkeit an der Universität Paris: Texte und Unterschungen zum literarischen Armuts- und Exemtionsstreit des 13. Jahrhunderts (1255–1272)*, Franzikanische Studien 2. Beiheft (Münster: Aschendorff, 1920).
Bloomfield, Morton W., "Joachim of Flora: A Critical Survey of his Canon, Teaching, Sources, Bibliography, and Influence," *Traditio*, 13 (1957), 249–311.
Bloomfield, Morton W., "Recent Scholarship on Joachim of Fiore and his Influence," in Ann Williams (ed.), *Prophecy and Millenarianism: Essays in Honour of Marjorie Reeves* (Harlow: Longman, 1980), 21–52.
Boreczky, Elemér, *John Wyclif's Discourse on Dominion in Community*, Studies in the History of Christian Traditions, 139 (Leiden and Boston: Brill, 2008).
Bornstein, Daniel, "Women and Religion in Late Medieval Italy: History and Historiography," in Daniel Bornstein and Roberto Rusconi (eds), *Women and Religion in Medieval and Renaissance Italy*, trans. Margery J. Schneider (Chicago and London: University of Chicago Press, 1996), 1–27.
Bougerol, Jacques Guy, *Les manuscrits franciscains de la Bibliothèque de Troyes*, Spicilegium Bonaventurianum, 23 (Grottaferrata: Collegii S. Bonaventurae ad Claras Aquas, 1982).
Boyd, David Lorenzo, and Ruth Mazo Karras, "'Ut cum muliere': A Male Transvestite Prostitute in Fourteenth Century London," in Louise Fradenburg and Carl Freccero (eds), *Premodern Sexualities* (London: Routledge, 1996), 99–116.
Boynton, Susan, *Shaping a Monastic Identity: Liturgy and History at the Imperial Abbey of Farfa, 1000–1125* (Ithaca, NY: Cornell University Press, 2006).
Brackett, John K., "The Language of Violence in the Late Italian Renaissance: The Example of the Tuscan Romagna," in Donald J. Kagay and L. J. Andrew Villalon (eds), *The Final Argument: The Imprint of Violence on Society in Medieval and Early Modern Europe* (London: Boydell, 1998), 97–105.
Bryan, Lindsay, "'Scandle is heaued sunne,'" *Florilegium*, 14 (1995–6), 71–86.
Bryan, Lindsay, "*Periculum animarum:* Bishops, Gender, and Scandal," *Florilegium*, 19 (2002), 49–73.
Burke, S. Maureen, "The 'Martyrdom of the Franciscans' by Ambrogio Lorenzetti," *Zeitschrift für Kunstgeschichte*, 65 (2002), 460–92.
Burr, David, *The Spiritual Franciscans: From Protest to Persecution in the Century after Saint Francis* (University Park, PA: Pennsylvania State University Press, 2001).
Cal Pardo, E., "Pleito promovido por los freiles de Santo Domingo y San Francisco de Viveiro contra los curas de las parroquias de Santa María y Santiago de dicha villa... Santiago. Rupeforte, 10.V.1334," *Estudios Mindonienses*, 7 (1991), 124–31.
Campbell, J. K., *Honour, Family and Patronage: A Study of Institutions and Moral Values in a Greek Mountain Community* (Oxford: Oxford University Press, 1964).
Cassi, Paolo, "Per una revisione: Fra' Gherardo da Borgo S. Donnino," *Aurea Parma*, 19 (1935), 5–13.

Castelli, Elizabeth A., *Martyrdom and Memory: Gender, Theory, and Religion* (New York: Columbia University Press, 2004).

Cattini, Marco, and Marzio A. Romani (eds), *Il potere di giudicare: Giustizia, pena, e controllo sociale negli stati d'Antico regime*, Cheiron, 1 (Brescia: Grafo, 1983).

Chazan, Robert, *Barcelona and Beyond: The Disputation of 1263 and its Aftermath* (Berkeley and Los Angeles: University of California Press, 1992).

Chuchiak, John F., "*In Servitio Dei*: Fray Diego de Landa, the Franciscan Order, and the Return of the Extirpation of Idolatry in the Colonial Diocese of Yucatán, 1573–1579," *The Americas*, 61 (2005), 611–46.

Cicconetti, Carlo, *La Regola del Carmelo: Origine, Natura, Significato*, TSHC 12 (Rome: Institutum Carmelitanum, 1973).

Clasen, Sophronius, *Der hl. Bonaventura und das Mendikantentum: Ein Beitdrag zur Ideengeschichte der Pariser Mandikantenstreites (1252–1272)*, Franziskanische Forschungen, Heft 7 (Werl in Wesfalen: Verlag Franziskus-Drukerei, 1940).

Clendinnen, Inga, *Ambivalent Conquests: Maya and Spaniard in Yucatan, 1517–1570*, 2nd edn (Cambridge: Cambridge University Press, 2003).

Clopper, Lawrence M., *"Songs of Rechlesnesse": Langland and the Franciscans* (Ann Arbor, MI: University of Michigan Press, 1997).

Cohen, Esther, "'To Die a Criminal for the Public Good': The Execution Ritual in Late Medieval Paris," in D. Nicholas and B. Bachrach (eds), *Law, Custom, and the Social Fabric in Medieval Europe: Essays in Honor of Bryce Lyon* (Kalamazoo, MI: Medieval Institute Publications, 1990), 285–304.

Cohen, Jeremy, *The Friars and the Jews* (Ithaca, NY: Cornell University Press, 1982).

Cohen, Mark R., *Under Crescent and Cross: The Jews in the Middle Ages*, rev. edn (Princeton: Princeton University Press, 2008).

Cohn, Samuel K., Jr, *Women in the Streets: Essays on Sex and Power in Renaissance Italy* (Baltimore: Johns Hopkins University Press, 1996).

Cohn, Samuel K., Jr, *Lust for Liberty: The Politics of Social Revolt in Medieval Europe, 1200–1425* (Cambridge, MA: Harvard University Press, 2006).

Colbert, Edward P., *The Martyrs of Córdoba (850–859): A Study of the Sources* (Washington, D.C.: Catholic University of America Press, 1962).

Constable, Giles, "The Ceremonies and Symbolism of Entering Religious Life and Taking the Monastic Habit, from the Fourth to the Twelfth Century," *Segni e riti nella chiesa altomedievale occidentale* (Spoleto: Centro Italiano di Studi sull'Alto Medioevo, 1987), 822–31.

Coope, Jessica A., *The Martyrs of Córdoba: Community and Family Conflict in an Age of Mass Conversion* (Lincoln, NB: University of Nebraska Press, 1995).

Cooper, Helen, *The Canterbury Tales*, 2nd edn (Oxford: Oxford University Press, 1996).

Copeland, Jean L., "The Relations between the Secular Clergy and the Mendicant Friars in England during the Century after the Issue of the Bull *Super Cathedram* (1300)," MA thesis, University of London, 1937.

Cowan, Ian B., and David E. Easson, *Medieval Religious Houses: Scotland*, 2nd edn (London: Longman, 1976).

Crouzet-Pavan, Elisabeth, "Violence, société et pouvoir à Venise (XIVe–XVIe siècles): Forme et evolution de rituels urbains," *Mélanges de l'École française de Rome: Moyen âge*, 96 (1984), 903–36.

Crow, Martin M., and Clair C. Olson (eds), *Chaucer Life-Records* (Oxford: Oxford University Press, 1966).

Cubitt, Catherine, "Monastic Memory and Identity in Early Anglo-Saxon England," in William O. Frazer and Andrew Tyrrell (eds), *Social Identity in Early Medieval Britain* (London and New York: Leicester University Press, 2000), 253–76.

Cusato, Michael F., and G. Geltner (eds), *Defenders and Critics of Franciscan Life: Essays in Honor of John V. Fleming*, The Medieval Franciscans, 6 (Leiden: Brill, 2009).

Dameron, George W., *Florence and its Church in the Age of Dante* (Philadelphia: University of Pennsylvania Press, 2005).

Daniel, E. Randolph, *The Franciscan Concept of Mission in the High Middle Ages* (Lexington, KY: University of Kentucky Press, 1975).

Das, Veena, et al. (eds), *Violence and Subjectivity* (Berkeley and Los Angeles: University of California Press, 2000).

Davis, Natalie Zemon, and Randolph Starns (eds), "Collective Memory and Countermemory," *Representations*, 26 (special issue) (1989).

Dawson, James Doyne, "William of Saint-Amour and the Apostolic Tradition," *Mediaeval Studies*, 40 (1978), 223–38.

De La Salle, Xavier, *Le service des âmes à la cour: Confesseurs et aumôniers des rois de France du XIIIe au XVe siècle*, Mémoires et Documents de l'École des Chartes, 43 (Paris: École des Chartes, 1995).

Dean, Trevor, *Crime in Medieval Europe, 1200–1550* (London: Longman, 2001).

Dean, Trevor, *Crime and Justice in Late Medieval Italy* (Cambridge: Cambridge University Press, 2007).

Dean, Trevor, "Theft and Gender in Late Medieval Bologna," *Gender & History*, 20 (2008), 399–415.

Delcorno, Carlo, "La 'predica' di Tedaldo," *Studi sul Boccaccio*, 27 (1999), 55–80.

Dickens, A. G., "The Shape of Anticlericalism and the English Reformation," in *Late Monasticism and the Reformation* (London and Rio Grande: Hambledon Press, 1994), 151–76.

Dimier, A., "Violence, rixes et homicides chez les Cisterciens," *Revue des Sciences Religieuses*, 46 (1972), 38–57.

Dipple, Geoffrey, *Antifraternalism and Anticlericalism in the German Reformation: Johann Eberlin von Günzburg and the Campaign against the Friars* (Aldershot: Scolar Press, 1996).

Dipple, Geoffrey, "Anti-Franciscanism in the Early Reformation: The Nature and Sources of Criticism," *Franciscan Studies*, 55 (1998), 53–81.

Dipple, Geoffrey, "'Si sind all glichsner': Antifraternalism in Medieval and Renaissance German Literature," in Cusato and Geltner (eds), *Defenders and Critics of Franciscan Life*, 177–92.

Dohar, William J., *The Black Death and Pastoral Leadership: The Diocese of Hereford in the Fourteenth Century* (Philadelphia: University of Pennsylvania Press, 1995).

Dolan, T. P., "Richard FitzRalph's 'Defensio Curatorum' in Transmission," in Howard B. Clarke and J. R. S. Phillips (eds), *Ireland, England and the Continent in the Middle Ages and Beyond: Essays in Memory of a Turbulent Friar, F. X. Martin, OSA* (Dublin: University College Dublin Press, 2006), 177–94.

Dossat, Yves, "Opposition des anciens ordres à l'installation des mendiants," in *Les mendiants en pays d'Oc au XIIIe siècle*, CdF 8 (Toulouse: Privat, 1973), 263–306.

Douglas, Mary, *Purity and Danger: An Analysis of Concepts of Pollution and Taboo* (Abingdon: Routledge, 2007 [orig. pub. 1966]).

Downes, David, and Paul Rock, *Understanding Deviance: A Guide to the Sociology of Crime and Rule-Breaking*, 5th edn (Oxford: Oxford University Press, 2007).

Doyle, Brian, *English and Englishness* (London and New York: Routledge, 1989).

Dubois, Jacques, *Les martyrologes du moyen âge latin*, Typologie des sources du moyen âge occidental, 26 (Turnholt: Brepols, 1978).

Dufeil, M.-M., *Guillaume de Saint-Amour et la polémique universitaire parisienne, 1250–1259* (Paris: Picard, 1972).

Dufeil, M.-M., "Guilelmus de Sancto Amore, Opera Omnia (1252–1270)," in Albert Zimmermann (ed.), *Die Auseinandersetzungen an der Pariser Universität im XIII. Jahrhundert*, Miscellanea Medievalis, 10 (Berlin: Walter de Gruyter, 1976), 215–19.

Duffy, Eamon, *The Stripping of the Altars: Traditional Religion in England, c.1400–c.1580*, 2nd edn (New Haven and London: Yale University Press, 2005).

Durkheim, Émile, *The Rules of Sociological Method*, trans. Sarah A. Solovay and John H. Mueller, 8th edn (New York: Free Press, 1962).

Dykema, Peter A., and Heiko A. Oberman (eds), *Anticlericalism in Late Medieval and Early Modern Europe*, Studies in Medieval and Reformation Thought, 51 (Leiden: Brill, 1993).

Elm, Kaspar, "Ausbreitung, Wiksamgeit und Ende der Provençalischen Sackbrüder (Fratres de Poenitentia Jesu Christi) in Deutschland und den Niederlanden," *Francia*, 1 (1973), 257–324.

Elm, Kaspar (ed.), *Reformbemühungen und Observanzbestrebungen im spätmittelaltrichen Ordenswesen*, Berliner historische Studien, 14 (Berlin: Duncker und Humblot, 1989).

Emery, Richard W., *Heresy and Inquisition in Narbonne* (New York: Columbia University Press, 1941).

Emery, Richard W., *The Friars in Medieval France: A Catalogue of French Mendicant Convents, 1200–1550* (New York and London: Columbia University Press, 1962).

Engel, David, "Crisis and Lachrymosity: On Salo Baron, Neo-Baronianism, and the Study of Modern European Jewish History," *Jewish History*, 20 (2006), 243–64.

Fadalti, G. M., and S. M. Pizzol, *Guida storico-artistica del Santuario del Carmine S. Felice del Benaco (BS)* (Vittorio Veneto: Abitino del Carmine, 1962).

Farriss, Nancy M., *Maya Society under Colonial Rule: The Collective Enterprise of Survival* (Princeton: Princeton University Press, 1984).

Fasoli, Gina, "La coscienza civica nelle 'Laudes civitatum,'" in *La coscienza cittadina nei comuni italiani del Duecento* (Todi: Accademia Tedertina, 1972), 9–44.

Fentress, James, and Chris Wickham, *Social Memory* (Oxford: Blackwell, 1992).

Ferrari, Rino, *Fra Gherardo da Fidenza (il Martin Lutero del 1200)* (Parma: STEP, 1950).

Fine, John V. A., *The Bosnian Church: A New Interpretation* (Boulder, CO: East European Quarterly, 1975).

Finke, Heinrich, "Zur Geschichte der deutschen Dominikaner im XIII. und XIV. Jahrhundert," *Römische Quartalschrift für Christliche Altertumskunde und für Kirchengeshichte*, 8 (1894), 367–92.

Fleming, John V., "The *Collationes* of William of Saint-Amour against St. Thomas," *Recherches de théologie ancienne et médiévale*, 32 (1965), 132–8.

Fleming, John V., "The Antifraternalism of the *Summoner's Tale*," *Journal of English and Germanic Philology*, 65 (1966), 688–700.

Fleming, John V., *The Romance of the Rose: A Study in Allegory and Iconography* (Princeton: Princeton University Press, 1969).

Fleming, John V., *An Introduction to the Franciscan Literature of the Middle Ages* (Chicago: Franciscan Herald Press, 1977).

Fleming, John V., "The Friars and Medieval English Literature," in David Wallace (ed.), *The Cambridge History of Medieval English Literature* (Cambridge: Cambridge University Press, 1999), 349–75.

Foucault, Michel, *Surveiller et punir: Naissance de la prison* (Paris: Gallimard, 1975).

Freed, John B., *The Friars and German Society in the Thirteenth Century* (Cambridge, MA: Medieval Academy of America, 1977).

Freeman Sandler, Lucy, *Omne Bonum: A Fourteenth-Century Encyclopedia of Universal Knowledge*, 2 vols (London: Harvey Miller Publishers, 1996).

Füser, Thomas, *Mönche im Konflikt: Zum Spannungsfeld von Norm, Devianz und Sanktion bei den Cisterziensern und Cluniazensern (12. bis frühes 14. Jahrhundert)*, Vita Regularis, 9 (Münster: Lit, 2000).

Galbraith, G. R., *The Constitution of the Dominican Order, 1216 to 1360*, Publications of the University of Manchester, Historical Series, 44 (Manchester: Manchester University Press, 1925).

Galiano, Franco, *Interpretazione esoterica della storia in Gioacchino da Fiore, frate calabrese*, 2nd edn (Cosenza: Brenner, 2000).

Gallagher, Niav, "The Franciscans and the Scottish Wars of Independence: An Irish Perspective," *JMH*, 32 (2006), 3–17.

García-Serrano, Francisco, *Preachers of the City: The Expansion of the Dominican Order in Castile (1217–1348)* (New Orleans: University Press of the South, 1997).

Gauvard, Claude, *Violence et ordre public au Moyen Âge*, Les Médiévistes Français, 5 (Paris: Picard, 2005).

Geertz, Clifford, "Thick Description: Toward an Interpretive Theory of Culture," in *The Interpretation of Cultures* (New York: Basic Books, 1973), 3–30.

Geltner, G., "Faux Semblants: Antifraternalism Reconsidered in Jean de Meun and Chaucer," *Studies in Philology*, 101 (2004), 357–80.

Geltner, G., *The Medieval Prison: A Social History* (Princeton: Princeton University Press, 2008).

Geltner, G., "A False Start to Medieval Antifraternalism? William of St. Amour's *De periculis novissimorum temporum*," in Cusato and Geltner (eds), *Defenders and Critics of Franciscan Life*, 127–43.

Geltner, G., "Brethren Behaving Badly: A Deviant Approach to Medieval Antifraternalism," *Speculum*, 85 (2010), 47–64.

Geltner, G., "Friars as Victims: Scale, Scope, and the Idiom of Violence," *JMH*, 36 (2010), 126–41.

Geltner, G., "I registri criminali dell'Archivio Arcivescovile di Lucca: Prospettive di ricerca per la storia sociale del medioevo," in Sergio Pagano and Pierantonio Piatti (eds), *Il patrimonio documentario della Chiesa di Lucca: Prospettive di ricerca* (Florence: Edizioni SISMEL, 2010), 331–40.

Gill, Katherine, "*Scandala*: Controversies Concerning *Clausura* and Women's Religious Communities in Late Medieval Italy," in Scott L. Waugh and Peter D. Diehl (eds), *Christendom and its Discontents: Exclusion, Persecution, and Rebellion, 1000–1500* (Cambridge: Cambridge University Press, 1996), 177–203.

Given, James B., *Inquisition and Medieval Society: Power, Discipline, and Resistance in Languedoc* (Ithaca, NY: Cornell University Press, 1997).

Glorieux, Palémon, "Prélats français contre religieux mendiants: Autour de la bulle 'Ad fructus uberes' (1281–1290)," *Revue de l'histoire de l'eglise de France*, 11 (1925), 309–31, 471–95.

Glorieux, Palémon, "Une offensive de Nicolas de Lisieux contre saint Thomas d'Aquin," *Bulletin de Littérature Ecclésiastique*, 39 (1938), 121–9.

Goffman, Erving, *Asylums: Essays on the Social Situation of Mental Patients and Other Inmates* (Garden City, NY: Anchor Books, 1961).

Goldstein, Daniel M., *The Spectacular City: Violence and Performance in Urban Bolivia* (Durham, NC, and London: Duke University Press, 2004).
Gonthier, Nicole, *La châtiment du crime au moyen âge, XIIe–XVIe siècles* (Rennes: Presses universitaires de Rennes, 1998).
Goodich, Michael E., *Violence and Miracle in the Fourteenth Century* (Chicago and London: University of Chicago Press, 1995).
Goossaert, Vincent (ed.), *L'Anticléricalisme en Chine*, Extrême-Orient, Extrême-Occident, 24 (Paris: Presses Universitaires de Vincennes, 2002).
Graña Cid, María del Mar, "La Iglesia Orensana durante la crisis de la segunda mitad del siglo XIII," *Hispania sacra*, 42/86 (1990), 689–720.
Grieco, Holly J., "A Dilemma of Obedience and Authority: The Franciscan Inquisition and Franciscan Inquisitors in Provence, 1235–1340," Ph.D. dissertation, Princeton University, 2004.
Grieco, Holly J., "Franciscan Inquisition and Mendicant Rivalry in Mid-Thirteenth-Century Marseille," *JMH*, 34 (2008), 275–90.
Gross, John (ed.), *New Oxford Book of Literary Anecdotes* (Oxford: Oxford University Press, 2006).
Guattari, Félix, *Soft Subversions: Texts and Interviews 1977–1985*, ed. Sylvère Lotringer, trans. Chet Wiener and Emily Wittman (Los Angeles: Semiotex(e), 2009).
Guilleré, Christian, "La Pest noire a Gerone (1348)," *Annals de l'Institut d'Estudis Gironins*, 27 (1984), 87–161.
Gunn, Alan M. F., *The Mirror of Love* (Lubbock, TX: Texas Tech Press, 1952).
Gutiérrez, David, *The Augustinians in the Middle Ages*, trans. Arthur J. Ennis (Villanova, PA: Augustinian Historical Institute, 1984).
Gwynn, Aubrey, *The English Austin Friars in the Time of Wyclif* (Oxford: Oxford University Press, 1940).
Gwynn, Aubrey, and R. Neville Hadcock, *Medieval Religious Houses: Ireland* (London: Longman, 1970).
Habermas, Jürgen, *The Structural Transformation of the Public Sphere: An Inquiry into a Category of Bourgeois Society*, trans. Thomas Burger with Frederick Lawrence (Cambridge, MA: MIT Press, 1989).
Haigh, Christopher, "Anticlericalism in the English Reformation," *History*, 68 (1983), 391–407.
Haigh, Christopher, "Anticlericalism and Clericalism, 1580–1640," in Aston and Cragoe (eds), *Anticlericalism in Britain*, 18–41.
Halbwachs, Maurice, *On Collective Memory*, ed. and trans. Lewis A. Coser (Chicago: University of Chicago Press, 1992).
Hale, J. R., "Violence in the Late Middle Ages: A Background," in Lauro Martines (ed.), *Violence and Civil Disorder in Italian Cities, 1200–1500* (Berkeley and Los Angeles: University of California Press, 1972), 19–37.
Hall, Edwin, and Horst Uhr, "Aureola Super Auream: Crowns and Related Symbols of Special Distinctions for Saints in Late Gothic and Renaissance Iconography," *Art Bulletin*, 67 (1985), 567–603.
Hallberg, Svante, Rune Norberg, and Oloph Odenius, "Petrus martyrens död: Ett sfragistiskt bidrag till helgonets äldre ikonografi," *Fornvännen*, 55 (1960), 239–59.
Ham, Edward Billings, *Rutebeuf and Louis IX*, University of North Carolina Studies in the Romance Languages and Literatures, 42 (Chapel Hill, NC: University of North Carolina Press, 1962).

Hammerich, L. L., *The Beginning of the Strife between Richard FitzRalph and the Mendicants with an Edition of his Autobiographical Prayer and his Proposition "Unusquisque"* (Copenhagen: Levin & Munksgaand, 1938).

Hanawalt, Barbara, "The Female Felon in Fourteenth-Century England," *Viator*, 5 (1974), 253–68.

Haren, Michael, "Diocesan Dimensions of a Die-Hard Dispute: Richard FitzRalph and the Friars in Evolving Perspective," in Howard B. Clarke and J. R. S. Phillips (eds), *Ireland, England and the Continent in the Middle Ages and Beyond: Essays in Memory of a Turbulent Friar, F. X. Martin, OSA* (Dublin: University College Dublin Press, 2006), 164–76.

Harriss, Gerald, *Shaping the Nation: England 1360–1461* (Oxford: Clarendon Press, 2005).

Havely, Nicholas, "Chaucer's Friar and Merchant," *Chaucer Review*, 13 (1978–89), 337–45.

Havely, Nicholas, "Chaucer, Boccaccio, and the Friars," in P. Boitani (ed.), *Chaucer and the Italian Trecento* (Cambridge: Cambridge University Press, 1983), 249–68.

Hecker, Norbert, *Bettelorden und Bürgertum: Konflikt und Kooperation in deutschen Städten des Spätmittelalters* (Frankfurt: Peter Lang, 1981).

Heers, Jacques, *Family Clans in the Middle Ages: A Study of Political and Social Structures in Urban Areas*, trans. Barry Herbert (Amsterdam and New York: North-Holland, 1977).

Henderikx, P. A., *De oudste bedelordekloosters in het graafschap Holland en Zeeland*, Hollandse Studiën, 10 (Dordrecht: Historische Vereniging Holland, 1977).

Henriet, Patrick, "*In injuriam ordinis clericalis*: Traces d'anticléricalisme en Castille et León (XIIe–XIIIe s.)," in *L'Anticléricalisme en France méridionale*, 289–325.

Heullant-Donat, Isabelle, "Les martyrs franciscains de Jérusalem (1391), entre mémoire en manipulation (1391–1970)," in D. Coulon et al. (eds), *Chemins d'Outremer: Études d'Histoire sur la Méditerranée médiévale offertes à Michel Balard*, Byzantina Sorbonensia, 20 (Paris: Publications de la Sorbonne, 2004), 439–59.

Heullant-Donat, Isabelle, "Des missionnaires martyrs aux martyrs missionnaires: La Mémoire des martyrs franciscains au sein de leur Ordre aux XIIIe et XIVe siècles," in *Écrire son histoire: Les communautés régulières face à leur passé*, actes du 5e Colloque International du C.E.R.C.O.R., Saint-Étienne (6–8 novembre 2002) (Saint-Étienne: Publications de l'Université de Saint-Étienne–Jean Monnet, 2005), 171–84.

Heullant-Donat, Isabelle, *Missions impossibles: Les Franciscains, le martyre et l'islam (XIIIe–XVe siècle)* (Rome: École française de Rome, forthcoming).

Hinnebusch, William A., *The History of the Dominican Order*, 2 vols (New York: Alba House, 1966–73).

Hissette, Roland, "Nicolas de Lisieux," *Catholicisme*, 9 (1982), 1254–5.

Historical Research on Crime and Criminal Justice, Collected Studies in Criminological Research, 22 (Strasbourg: European Committee on Crime Problems, 1985).

Hood, William, *Fra Angelico at San Marco* (New Haven: Yale University Press, 1993).

Hudson, Anne, *Lollards and their Books* (London: Hambledon Press, 1985).

Huot, Sylvia, *The Romance of the Rose and its Medieval Readers: Interpretation, Reception, Manuscript Transmission* (Cambridge: Cambridge University Press, 1993).

Hyde, J. K., "Medieval Descriptions of Cities," *Bulletin of The John Rylands Library*, 48 (1966), 308–40.

Israel, Uwe, *Fremde aus dem Norden: Transalpine Zuwanderer im spätmittelalterlichen Italien* (Tübingen: Max Niemeyer, 2005).

Jones, Karen, *Gender and Petty Crime in Late Medieval England: The Local Courts in Kent, 1460–1560*, Gender in the Middle Ages, 2 (London: Boydell, 2006).

Jordan, William Chester, *Louis IX and the Challenge of the Crusade: A Study in Rulership* (Princeton: Princeton University Press, 1979).
Jordan, William Chester, "The Case of Saint Louis," *Viator*, 19 (1988), 209–17.
Jordan, William Chester, "Louis IX: Preaching to Franciscan and Dominican Brothers and Nuns," in Cusato and Geltner (eds), *Defenders and Critics of Franciscan Life*, 219–35.
Jotischky, Andrew, *The Carmelites and Antiquity: Mendicants and their Pasts in the Middle Ages* (Oxford: Oxford University Press, 2002).
Jotischky, Andrew, "Mendicants as Missionaries and Travellers in the Near East in the Thirteenth and Fourteenth Centuries," in Rosamund Allen (ed.), *Eastward Bound: Travel and Travellers in the Medieval Mediterranean 1050–1500* (Manchester: Manchester University Press, 2004), 88–106.
Kaftal, George, *Iconography of the Saints in Tuscan Painting* (Florence: Sansoni, 1952).
Kaftal, George, with the collaboration of Fabio Bisogni, *Iconography of the Saints in the Painting of North West Italy* (Florence: Le Lettere, 1985).
Kaftal, George, *Iconography of the Saints in Central and South Italian Schools of Painting* (Florence: Le Lettere, 1986).
Kahneman, Daniel, Jack L. Knetsch, and Richard H. Thaler, "Anomalies: The Endowment Effect, Loss Aversion, and Status Quo Bias," *Journal of Economic Perspectives*, 5 (1991), 193–206.
Kallenberg, Paschalis, *Fontes liturgiae carmelitanae. Investigatio in decreta, codices et proprium sanctorum*, TSHC 5 (Rome: Institutum Carmelitanum, 1962).
Karras, Ruth Mazo, *Common Women: Prostitution and Sexuality in Medieval England* (New York: Oxford University Press, 1996).
Keene, Derek, *Survey of Medieval Winchester* (Oxford: Clarendon Press, 1985).
Kennard, Joseph Spencer, *The Friar in Fiction: Sincerity in Art and Other Essays* (New York: Brentano's, 1923).
Kerby-Fulton, Kathryn, "Hildegard of Bingen and Anti-Mendicant Propaganda," *Traditio*, 43 (1987), 386–99.
Kerby-Fulton, Kathryn, *Books under Suspicion: Censorship and Tolerance of Revelatory Writing in Late Medieval England* (Notre Dame, IN: University of Notre Dame Press, 2006).
Kerby-Fulton, Kathryn, Magda Hayton, and Kenna Olsen, "Pseudo-Hildegardian Prophecy and Antimendicant Propaganda in Late Medieval England: An Edition of the Most Popular Insular Text of 'Insurgent gentes,'" in Nigel Morgan (ed.), *The Millennium, Social Disorder and the Day of Doom: Prophecy, Revolution, Apocalypse and Judgement in Medieval England and France*, Proceedings from the Harlaxton Symposium XVII, July 2000 (Stamford: Paul Watkins, 2004), 160–94.
Knight, Frances, "Did Anticlericalism Exist in the English Countryside in the Early Nineteenth Century?" in Aston and Cragoe (ed.), *Anticlericalism in Britain*, 159–78.
Knowles, David, *The Religious Orders in England*, 3 vols (Cambridge: Cambridge University Press, 1961–2).
Knowles, David, and R. Neville Hadcock, *Medieval Religious Houses: England and Wales* (London: Longman, 1971).
Koegler, Hans (ed.), *Beschreibendes Verzeichnis der Basler Handzeichnungen des Urs Graf* (Basel: Banno Schwabe & Co., 1926).
Kolb, Robert, *For all the Saints: Changing Perceptions of Martyrdom and Sainthood in the Lutheran Reformation* (Macon, GA: Mercer University Press, 1987).
Kuehn, Thomas, "Reading Microhistory: The Example of Giovanni and Lusanna," *Journal of Modern History*, 61 (1989), 512–34.

Lacassagne, Alexandre, "Les transformations du droit pénal et les progrès de la médecine légale, de 1810 à 1912," *Archives d'anthropologie criminelle*, 28 (1913), 321–64.

Lahey, Stephen E., *Philosophy and Politics in the Thought of John Wyclif* (Cambridge: Cambridge University Press, 2003).

Lambertini, Roberto, "La scelta francescana e l'Università di Parigi : Il *Bettelordenstreit* fino alla *Exiit qui seminat*," in Francesco Santi (ed.), *Gli studi francescani dal dopoguerra ad oggi* (Spoleto: Centro Italiano di Studi sull'Alto Medioevo, 1993), 143–72.

Langlois, Ernst, *Les manuscrits du Roman de la Rose: Description et classement* (Lille and Paris: Champion, 1910).

L'Anticléricalisme en France méridionale (milieu XIIe–début XIVe siècle), CdF 38 (Toulouse: Privat, 2003).

Lawrence, C. H., *The Friars: The Impact of the Early Mendicant Movement on Western Society* (Harlow: Longman, 1994).

Lawrence, Patricia, "Violence, Suffering, Amman: The Work of Oracles in Sri Lanka's Eastern War Zone," in Das et al. (eds), *Violence and Subjectivity*, 171–204.

Le Goff, Jacques, et al., "Ordres mendiants et urbanisation dans la France médiévale," *Annales: Économies, Sociétés, Civilisations*, 25 (1970), 924–87.

Lea, Henry Charles, *A History of the Inquisition in the Middle Ages*, 3 vols (New York: Macmillan, 1906).

Leemens, Johan (ed.), with the collaboration of Jürgen Mettepenningen, *More than a Memory: The Discourse of Martyrdom and the Construction of Christian Identity in the History of Christianity* (Leuven: Peeters, 2005).

Leff, Gordon, *Paris and Oxford Universities in the Thirteenth and Fourteenth Centuries: An Institutional and Intellectual History* (New York: John Wiley and Sons, 1968).

Les ordres mendiants et la ville en Italie centrale, extrait de *Mélanges de l'École Française de Rome. Moyen Age, Temps Modernes*, 89.2 (1977).

Lesnick, Daniel R., *Preaching in Medieval Florence: The Social World of Franciscan and Dominican Spirituality* (Athens, GA: University of Georgia Press, 1989).

Lester, Anne E., *Creating Cistercian Nuns: The Women's Religious Movement and its Reform in Thirteenth-Century Champagne* (Ithaca, NY, and London: Cornell University Press, 2011).

Levi d'Ancona, Mirella, *Lo zoo del Rinascimento: Il significato degli animali nella pittura italiana dal XIV al XVI secolo* (Lucca: Maria Pacini Fazzi Editore, 2001).

Lickteig, Franz-Bernard, *The German Carmelites at the Medieval Universities*, TSHC 13 (Rome: Institututm Carmelitanum, 1981).

Liddy, Christian D., "Urban Conflict in Late Fourteenth-Century England: The Case of York in 1380–1," *EHR*, 118 (2003), 1–32.

Lincoln, Bruce, *Theorizing Myth: Narrative, Ideology, and Scholarship* (Chicago: University of Chicago Press, 1999).

Linehan, Peter, "A Tale of Two Cities: Capitular Burgos and Mendicant Burgos in the Thirteenth Century," in David Abulafia et al. (eds), *Church and City, 1000–1500: Essays in Honour of Christopher Brooke* (Cambridge: Cambridge University Press, 1992), 81–110.

Linehan, Peter, *The Ladies of Zamora* (Manchester: Manchester University Press, 1997).

Lippini, Pietro, *La vita quotidiana di un convento medievale: Gli ambienti, le regole, l'orario e le mansioni dei frati domenicani del trecesimo secolo*, Collana Attendite ad Petram, 5 (Bologna: Studio Domenicano, 1990).

Little, A. G., *Studies in English Franciscan History*, The Ford Lectures in 1916 (Manchester: Manchester University Press, 1917).

Little, A. G., "The Friars v. the University of Cambridge," *EHR*, 50 (1935), 686–96.
Little, A. G., *Franciscan History and Legend in English Mediaeval Art* (Manchester: Manchester University Press, 1937).
Little, A. G., *Franciscan Papers, Lists, and Documents*, Publications of the University of Manchester, 284; Publications of the University of Manchester, Historical Series, 81 (Manchester: Manchester University Press, 1943).
Little, Lester K., "Saint Louis' Involvement with the Friars," *Church History*, 2 (1964), 125–43.
Little, Lester K., *Religious Poverty and the Profit Economy in Medieval Europe* (Ithaca, NY: Cornell University Press, 1978).
Loades, David, "Anticlericalism in the Church of England before 1558: An 'Eating Canker'?," in Aston and Cragoe (eds), *Anticlericalism in Britain*, 1–17.
Logan, F. Donald, *Runaway Religious in Medieval England, c.1240–1540*, Cambridge Studies in Medieval Life and Thought, 4th ser., 32 (Cambridge: Cambridge University Press, 1996).
Luria, Maxwell, *A Reader's Guide to the Roman de la Rose* (Hamden, CN: Archon Books, 1982).
Lutz, Catherine, *Homefront: A Military City and the American 20th Century* (Boston: Beacon Press, 2001).
McCord, Joan (ed.), *Violence and Childhood in the Inner City* (Cambridge: Cambridge University Press, 1997).
McCulloh, John, "Historical Martyrologies in the Benedictine Cultural Tradition," in W. Lourdaux and D. Verhelst (eds), *Benedictine Culture, 750–1050*, Mediaevalia Lovaniensia, 1.11 (Leuven: Leuven University Press, 1983), 114–31.
MacEvitt, Christopher, "Martyrdom and the Muslim World through Franciscan Eyes," *Catholic Historical Review*, 97 (2011), 1–24.
McGinn, Bernard, *Apocalyptic Spirituality* (New York: Paulist Press, 1979).
McGinn, Bernard, *The Calabrian Abbott: Joachim of Fiore in the History of Western Thought* (New York and London: Macmillan, 1985).
McGinn, Bernard, "Apocalypticism and Church Reform, 1100–1500," in Bernard McGinn (ed.), *Encyclopedia of Apocalypticism*, ii (New York: Continuum, 1999), 74–109.
McKeon, Peter R., "The Status of the University of Paris as *Parens Scientiarum*: An Episode in the Development of its Autonomy," *Speculum*, 39 (1964), 651–75.
McMichael, Steven J., and Susan E. Myers (eds), *Friars and Jews in the Middle Ages and the Renaissance*, The Medieval Franciscans, 2 (Leiden: Brill, 2004).
Maier, Christoph T., *Preaching the Crusades: Mendicant Friars and the Cross in the Thirteenth Century* (Cambridge: Cambridge University Press, 1994).
Major, Emil, and Erwin Gradmann, *Urs Graf* (Basel: Holbein Verlag, 1942).
Malinowski, Bronislaw, *Crime and Custom in Savage Society* (London: Kegan Paul, 1926).
Manktelow, Michael, *John Moorman: Anglican, Franciscan, Independent* (Norwich: Canterbury Press, 1999).
Mann, Jill, *Chaucer and Medieval Estates Satire* (Cambridge: Cambridge University Press, 1973).
Marin, Olivier, *L'Archevêque, le maître et le dévot: Genèses du mouvement réformateur pragois (1360–1419)* (Paris: Honoré Champion, 2005).
Martin, Herve, *Les ordres mendiants en Bretagne (vers 1230–vers 1530)* (Paris: Klincksieck, 1975).
Mathis, Burkhard, *Die Privilegien des Franziskanerordens bis zum Konzil von Vienne (1311)* (Paderborn: Schöningh, 1928).
Mode, Peter George, *The Influence of the Black Death on the English Monasteries* (Menasha, WI: George Banta, 1916).

Montagnes, Bernard, "Les Inquisiteurs martyrs de la France méridionale," in Wolfram Hoyer (ed.), *Praedicatores, Inquisitores I. The Dominicans and the Medieval Inquisition* (Rome: Istituto Storico Domenicano, 2004), 513–38.

Moorman, John R. H., *A History of the Franciscan Order from its Origins to the Year 1517* (Oxford: Clarendon Press, 1968).

Moorman, John R. H., *Medieval Franciscan Houses* (St Bonaventure, NY: Franciscan Institute, 1983).

Morçay, R., "La cronaca del convento di s. Caterina dell'ordine deo Predicatori in Pisa," *Archivio Storico Italiano*, 1st ser., 6/2 (1845).

Morris, David B., "About Suffering: Voice, Genre, and Moral Community," in Arthur Kleinman, Veena Das, and Margaret Lock (eds), *Social Suffering* (Berkeley and Los Angeles: University of California Press, 1997), 25–45.

Moss, Candida R., *The Other Christs: Imitating Jesus in Ancient Christian Ideologies of Martyrdom* (Oxford: Oxford University Press, 2010).

Muir, Edward, "The Idea of Community in Renaissance Italy," *Renaissance Quarterly*, 55 (2002), 1–18.

Mulchahey, M. Michèle, *"First the Bow is Bent in Study...": Dominican Education before 1350* (Toronto: Pontifical Institute of Mediaeval Studies, 1998).

Müller, Anne, "Conflicting Loyalties: The Irish Franciscans and the English Crown in the High Middle Ages," *Proceedings of the Royal Irish Academy*, 107 (2007), 87–106.

Müller, Christian, *Urs Graf: Die Zeichnungen im Kupferstichkabinett Basel*, Beschreibender Katalog der Zeichnungen, Band III. Die Zeichnungen des 15. und 16. Jahrhunderts, Teil 2B (Basel: Schwabe, 2001).

Murray, Alexander, "Archbishop and Mendicants in Thirteenth-Century Pisa," in Kaspar Elm (ed.), *Bettelorden und Wirksamkeit der Bettelorden in den städtischen Geselschaft* (Berlin: Duncker & Humblot, 1981), 19–75.

Muscatine, Charles, *Chaucer and the French Tradition: A Study in Style and Meaning* (Berkeley and Los Angeles: University of California Press, 1960).

Musson, Anthony (ed.), *Boundaries of the Law: Geography, Gender and Jurisdiction in Medieval and Early Modern Europe* (Aldershot: Ashgate, 2005).

Neidiger, Bernhard, "Stadtregiment und Klosterreform in Basel," in Elm (ed.), *Reformbemühungen und Observanzbestrebungen*, 539–67.

Nimmo, Duncan, *Reform and Division in the Medieval Franciscan Order (1226–1538)*, Biblioteca Seraphico-Capuccina, 33 (Rome: Capuchin Historical Institute, 1987).

Nirenberg, David, *Communities of Violence: Persecution of Minorities in the Middle Ages* (Princeton: Princeton University Press, 1996).

Nyhus, Paul, "The Franciscans in South Germany, 1400–1530: Reform and Revolution," *Transactions of the American Philosophical Society*, NS 65 (1975), 1–43.

Ocker, Christopher, "Contempt for Friars and Contempt for Jews in Late Medieval Germany," in Steven J. McMichael and Susan E. Myers (eds), *Friars and Jews in the Middle Ages and the Renaissance*, The Medieval Franciscans, 2 (Leiden: Brill, 2004), 119–46.

Ocker, Christopher, "*Lacrima ecclesie:* Konrad of Megenberg, the Friars, and the Beguines," in Claudia Märtle, Gisela Drossbach, and Martin Kintzinger (eds), *Konrad von Megenberg (1309–1374) und sein Werk Das Wissen der Zeit* (Munich: C. H. Beck, 2006), 169–200.

Odber de Baubeta, Patricia Anne, *Anticlerical Satire in Medieval Portuguese Literature* (Lewiston, NY: Edwin Mellen Press, 1992).

Oliger, Livarius, "De pueris oblatis in Ordinis Minorum (cum textu hucusque ineditum Fr. Iohannis Pecham)," *AFH*, 8 (1915), 389–447.

——, "De pueris oblatis in Ordinis Minorum: Additamentum," *AFH*, 10 (1917), 271–88.
Ott, Karl August, *Der Rosenroman* (Darmstadt: Wissenschaftliche Buchgesellschaft, 1980).
Pannewick, Friederike (ed.), *Martyrdom in Literature: Visions of Death and Meaningful Suffering in Europe and the Middle East from Antiquity to Modernity* (Wiesbaden: Reichert Verlag, 2004).
Pegg, Mark Gregory, *A Most Holy War: The Albigensian Crusade and the Battle for Christendom* (Oxford: Oxford University Press, 2008).
Pellegrini, Luigi, "L'ordine francescano e la società cittadina in epoca bonaventuriana: Un'analisi del 'Determinationes quaestionum super Regulam Fratrum Minorum,'" *Laurentianum*, 15 (1974), 154–200.
——, "Mendicanti e parroci: Coesistenza e conflitti di due strutture organizzative della '*cura animarum*,'" in *Francescanesimo e vita religiosa dei laici nel '200. Atti dell'VIII Convegno Internazionale (Assisi, 16–18 ottobre 1980)* (Assisi: Universitá degli Studi di Perugia, 1981), 129–67.
Pelster, F., "Der Traktat 'Manus que contra Omnipotentem tenditur' und sein Verfasser," *AFH*, 15 (1923), 3–22.
Personal Enemies of God: Anticlericals and Anticlericalism in Revolutionary Mexico, 1915–1940, The Americas, 65/4 (special issue) (2009).
Peuchmaurd, M., "Mission canonique et predication," *Recherches de Théologie Ancienne et Médiévale*, 29 (1962), 52–76, 30 (1963), 122–44, 251–76.
Phythian-Adams, Charles V., "Rituals of Personal Confrontation in Late Medieval England," *Bulletin of the John Rylands Library*, 73 (1991), 65–90.
Piasentini, Stefano, *"Alla luce della luna": I furti a Venezia (1270–1403)* (Venice: Il Cardo, 1992).
Piron, Sylvain, "Un couvent sous influence: Santa Croce autour de 1300," in Nicole Bériou and Jacques Chiffoleau (eds), *Économie et religion: L'Expérience des ordres mendiants (XIIIe–XVe siècle)* (Lyons: Presses universitaires de Lyon, 2009), 331–55.
Pollmann, Judith, "Off the Record: Problems in the Quantification of Calvinist Church Discipline," *Sixteenth Century Journal*, 33 (2002), 423–38.
Prudlo, Donald, *The Martyred Inquisitor: The Life and Cult of Peter of Verona (†1252)* (Aldershot: Ashgate, 2008).
Purkis, William J., *Crusading Spirituality in the Holy Land and Iberia, c.1095–c.1187* (Woodbridge: Boydell, 2008).
Rashdall, H., *The Universities of Europe in the Middle Ages*, ed. F. M. Powicke and A. B. Emden, 3 vols (Oxford: Clarendon Press, 1936).
von Raumer, Friedrich, *Geschichte der Hohenstaufen und ihrer Zeit*, 6 vols (Leipzig: F. A. Brockhaus, 1840–2).
Rémond, René, *L'Anticléricalisme en France de 1815 à nos jours* (Paris: Fayard, 1976).
Riedl, Matthias, *Joachim von Fiore: Denker der vollendeten Menschheit* (Würzburg: Königshausen & Neumann, 2004).
Ríos, Rita, "The Role of the Mendicant Orders in the Political Life of Castile and León in the Later 13th Century," in Ausana Cimdiņa (ed.), *Religion and Political Change in Europe: Past and Present* (Pisa: Edizioni Plus, 2003), 21–32.
Robertson, D. W., Jr., *A Preface to Chaucer* (Princeton: Princeton University Press, 1962).
Robson, Michael, *The Franciscans in the Middle Ages* (Woodbridge: Boydell, 2006).
——, "The Greyfriars at Lincoln *c*.1230–1330: The Establishment of the Friary and the Friars' Ministry and Life in the City and its Environs," in Robson and Röhrkasten (eds), *Franciscan Organisation*, 113–37.

——, and Jens Röhrkasten (eds), *Franciscan Organisation in the Mendicant Context: Formal and Informal Structures of the Friars' Lives and Ministry in the Middle Ages*, Vita Regularis, 44 (Berlin: Lit, 2010).

Roest, Bert, *Reading the Book of History: Intellectual Contexts and Educational Functions of Franciscan Historiography, 1226*–ca. *1350* (Groningen: Regenboog, 1996).

——, *A History of Franciscan Education (c.1210–1517)* (Leiden: Brill, 2000).

Röhrkasten, Jens, *The Mendicant Houses of Medieval London: 1221–1539*, Vita Regularis, 21 (Münster: Lit, 2004).

Ronzani, Mauro, "Il francescanesimo a Pisa fino alla metá del Trecento," *Bollettino Storico Pisano*, 54 (1985), 1–55.

Rotolo, Filippo, "San Bonaventura e fra Gerardo da Borgo S. Donnino: Riflessi del Gioachimismo in Sicilia," *O Theologos: Cultura Cristiana di Sicilia*, 2 (1975), 263–97.

Rowell, S. C., *Lithuania Ascending: A Pagan Empire within East-Central Europe, 1295–1345* (Cambridge: Cambridge University Press, 1994).

Rüther, Andreas, *Bettelorden in Stadt und Land: Die Straßburger Mendikantenkonvente und das Elsaß im Spätmittelalter*, Berliner historische Studien, 26; Ordensstudien, 11 (Berlin: Duncker & Humblot, 1997).

Saggi, Ludovico, *S. Angelo di Sicilia: Studio sulla vita, devozione, folklore*, TSHC 6 (Rome: Institutum Carmelitanum, 1962).

Sánchez, José, *Anticlericalism: A Brief History* (Notre Dame, IN, and London: University of Notre Dame Press, 1972).

Scanlon, Larry, *Narrative, Authority and Power: The Medieval* Exemplum *and the Chaucerian Tradition* (Cambridge: Cambridge University Press, 1994).

Scarry, Elaine, *The Body in Pain: The Making and Unmaking of the World* (New York and Oxford: Oxford University Press, 1985).

Scase, Wendy, *"Piers Plowman" and the New Anticlericalism* (Cambridge: Cambridge University Press, 1989).

Schmidt, Hans-Joachim, "Povertá e politica: I frati degli ordini mendicanti alla corte imperiale nel XIV secolo," in Giorgio Chittolini and Kaspar Elm (eds), *Ordini religiosi e societá politica in Italia e Germania nei secoli XIV e XV* (Bologna: Il Mulino, 2001), 373–417.

——, "Establishing an Alternative Territorial Pattern: The Provinces of the Mendicant Orders," in Robson and Röhrkasten (eds), *Franciscan Organisation*, 1–18.

Schmitt, Clément, "Documents sur la province franciscaine de Strasbourg aux XIV–XVe siècles d'après un formulaire de Lucerne," *AFH*, 59 (1966), 209–300.

Schnapper, Bernard, *Les peines arbitraires du XIIIe au XVIIIe siècle: Doctrines savantes et usages français* (Paris: R. Pichon et R. Durand-Auzias, 1974).

Scott, James C., *Weapons of the Weak: Everyday Forms of Peasant Resistance* (New Haven and London: Yale University Press, 1985).

Şenocak, Neslihan, *The Rise of Learning in the Franciscan Order* (Ithaca, NY: Cornell University Press, 2012).

Shepardson, Nikki, *Burning Zeal: The Rhetoric of Martyrdom and the Protestant Community in Reformation France, 1520–1570* (Bethlehem, PA: Lehigh University Press, 2007).

Sickert, Ramona, "*Extra obedientiam evagari* . . . : Zur zeitgenössischen Deutung der Mobilität von Franziskanern und Dominikanern im 13. Jahrhundert," in Barret and Melville (eds), *Oboedientia*, 159–80.

——, *Wenn Klosterbrüder zu Jahrmarktsbrüdern werden: Studien zur Wahrnehmung der Franziskaner und Dominikaner im 13. Jahrhundert*, Vita Regularis, 28 (Berlin: Lit, 2006).

Smail, Daniel Lord, *The Consumption of Justice: Emotions, Publicity, and Legal Culture in Marseille, 1264–1423* (Ithaca, NY, and London: Cornell University Press, 2003).

Smail, Daniel Lord, "Aspects of Procedural Documentation in Marseille (14th–15th Centuries)," in Susanne Lepsius and Thomas Wetzstein (eds), *Als die Welt in die Akten kam: Prozeßschriftgut im europäischen Mittelalter* (Frankfurt: Vittorio Klostermann, 2008), 139–69.

Smith, Julie A., "Prouille, Madrid, Rome: The Evolution of the Earliest Dominican Instituta for Nuns," *JMH*, 35 (2009), 340–52.

Snyder, Susan Taylor, "Orthodox Fears: Anti-Inquisitorial Violence and Defining Heresy," in Anne Scott and Cynthia Kosso (eds), *Fear and its Representations in the Middle Ages and Renaissance* (Turnholt: Brepols, 2002), 92–106.

Sofsky, Wolfgang, *Saggio sulla violenza*, trans. Barbara Trapani and Luca Lamberti (Turin: Einaudi, 1998).

Somerset, Fiona, *Clerical Discourse and Lay Audience in Late Medieval England*, Cambridge Studies in Medieval Literature, 37 (Cambridge: Cambridge University Press, 1998).

Soria, Myriam, "Les violences anti-épiscopales dans la province de Narbonee (fin XIIe– début XIIIe sècle): Des manifestations anticléricales?," in *L'Anticléricalisme en France méridionale*, 161–79.

Stakel, Susan, *False Roses: Structures of Duality and Deceit in Jean de Meun's Roman de la Rose* (Stanford: ANMA Libri, 1991).

Stancliffe, Clare, "Red, White and Blue Martyrdom," in Rosamond McKitterick, David Dumville, and Dorothy Whitlock (eds), *Ireland in Early Mediaeval Europe: Studies in Memory of Kathleen Hughes* (Cambridge: Cambridge University Press, 1983), 21–46.

Starcke-Neuman, Susanne, *Johannes von Anneux: Ein Fürstenmahner und Mendikantengegner in der ersten Hälfte des 14. Jahrhunderts* (Mammendorf: Septem Artes, 1996).

Storch, Robert D., "The Study of Urban Crime," *Social History*, 4 (1979), 117–22.

Stouff, Louis, "Le couvent des prêcheurs d'Arles, XIIIe–XVe siècle," in *L'Ordre des Prêcheurs et son histoire en France méridionale*, CdF 36 (Toulouse: Privat, 2001), 61–80.

Symes, Carol, *A Common Stage: Theater and Public Life in Medieval Arras* (Ithaca, NY: Cornell University Press, 2007).

——, "Out in the Open, in Arras: Sightlines, Soundscapes, and the Shaping of a Medieval Public Sphere," in Caroline Goodson, Anne E. Lester, and Carol Symes (eds), *Medieval Cities, Texts and Social Networks, 400–1500: Experiences and Perceptions of Medieval Urban Space* (Aldershot: Ashgate, 2010), 279–302.

——, "When We Talk about Modernity," *American Historical Review*, 116 (2011), 715–26.

Szittya, Penn R., *The Antifraternal Tradition in Medieval Literature* (Princeton: Princeton University Press, 1986).

——, "Kicking the Habit: The Campaign against the Friars in a Fourteenth-Century Encyclopedia," in Cusato and Geltner (eds), *Defenders and Critics of Franciscan Life*, 159–75.

Taitt, Peter S., *Incubus and Ideal: Ecclesiastical Figures in Chaucer and Langland*, Salzburg Studies in English Literature, 44 (Salzburg: Institut für Englische Sprache und Literatur, 1975).

Toaff, Ariel, *Ebraismo virtuale* (Milan: Rizzoli, 2008).

Tolan, John, "The Friar and the Sultan: Francis of Assisi's Mission to Egypt," *European Review*, 16 (2008), 115–26.

Thompson, Augustine, *Revival Preachers and Politics in Thirteenth-Century Italy: The Great Devotion of 1233* (Oxford: Clarendon Press, 1992).

Thompson, Augustine, "Lay versus Clerical Perceptions of Heresy: Protests against the Inquisition in Bologna, 1299," in Wolfram Hoyer (ed.), *Praedicatores, Inquisitores I. The Dominicans and the Medieval Inquisition* (Rome: Istituto Storico Domenicano, 2004), 701–30.

——, *Cities of God: The Religion of the Italian Communes, 1125–1325* (University Park, PA: Pennsylvania State University Press, 2005).

Thomson, Williell R., *Friars in the Cathedral: The First Franciscan Bishops, 1226–1261*, Studies and Texts, 33 (Toronto: Pontifical Institute of Medieaval Studies, 1975).

Tönsing, Michael, *Johannes Malkaw aus Preussen (ca.1360–1416): Ein Kleriker im Spannungsfeld von Kanzel, Ketzerprozess und Kirchenspaltung*, Studien zu den Luxemburgern und ihrer Zeit, 10 (Warendorf: Fahlbusch, 2004).

Toureille, Valérie, *Vol et brigandage au moyen âge* (Paris: Presses universitaires de France, 2006).

Traver, Andrew G., "Rewriting History? The Parisian Secular Masters' *Apologia* of 1254," *History of Universities*, 15 (1997–9), 9–45.

——, "Thomas of York's Role in the Conflict between Mendicants and Seculars at Paris," *Franciscan Studies*, 57 (1999), 1–24.

——, "The Liber de Antichristo and the Failure of Joachite Expectations," *Florensia*, 14 (2001), 1–12.

Tugwell, Simon, "The Evolution of Dominican Structures of Government, II: The First Dominican Provinces," *AFP*, 70 (2000), 5–109.

Tugwell, Simon, "The Evolution of Dominican Structures of Government, III: The Early Development of the Second Distinction of the Constitutions," *AFP*, 71 (2001), 1–182.

Tugwell, Simon, "For whom was Prouille Founded," *AFP*, 74 (2004), 5–125.

Turck, Sandrine, *Les Dominicaines à Strasbourg entre prêche, prière et mendicité (1224–1429)*, Publications de la Société savante d'Alsace et des regions de l'Est, Collection Recherches et Documents, 68 (Strasbourg: Société Savante d'Alsace, 2002).

Tyerman, Christopher, *God's War: A New History of The Crusades* (London: Penguin Books, 2007).

Van Engen, John, "Late Medieval Anticlericalism: The Case of the New Devout," in Dykema and Oberman (eds), *Anticlericalism in Late Medieval and Early Modern Europe*, 19–52.

Vargas, Michael, "How a 'Brood of Vipers' Survived the Black Death: Recovery and Dysfunction in the Fourteenth-Century Dominican Order," *Speculum*, 86 (2011), 688–714.

Vargas, Michael, "Weak Obedience, Undisciplined Friars, and Failed Reforms in the Medieval Order of Preachers," *Viator*, 42 (2011), 283–307.

Vauchez, André, "Les stigmates de saint François et leurs détracteurs dans les derniers siècles du moyen âge," *Mélanges d'archéologie et d'histoire*, 80 (1968), 595–625.

Verci, Giambatista, *Storia degli Eccelini*, 3 vols (Bassano: Stamperia Remodini, 1779).

Verga, Ettore, "Le sentenze criminali dei podestà milanesi 1385–1429," *Archivio Storico Lombardo*, 16 (1901), 96–142.

Villani, Matteo, *Cronica. Con la continuazione di Filippo Villani*, vol. 1, ed. Giuseppe Porta (Parma: U. Guanda, 1995).

Vialler, Ludovic, "Le Role du gardien dans les couvents franciscains," in Robson and Röhrkasten (eds), *Franciscan Organisation*, 225–51.

Wallace, Samuel E. (ed.), *Total Institutions* (Chicago: Transaction Books, 1971).

Walsh, Katherine, *A Fourteenth-Century Scholar and Primate: Richard FitzRalph in Oxford, Avignon and Armagh* (Oxford: Clarendon Press, 1981).

Wattenbach, W., "Über erfundene Briefe in Handschriften des Mittelalters, besonders Teufelsbriefe," *Sitzungsberichte der königlich preussischen Akademie der Wissenschaften zu Berlin*, 1 (1892), 92–123.
Weiss, Alexander, *Chaucer's Native Heritage* (New York and Berne: Peter Lang, 1985).
Wessley, Stephen E., *Joachim of Fiore and Monastic Reform* (New York: Peter Lang, 1990).
West, Delno C., and Sandra Zimders-Swartz, *Joachim of Fiore: A Study in Spiritual Perception and History* (Bloomington, IN: Indiana University Press, 1983).
Wiesehoff, Josef, *Die Stellung der Bettelorden in den deutschen freien Reichstädten im Mittelalter* (Leipzig: J. Wiesehoff, 1905).
Williams, Arnold, "Chaucer and the Friars," *Speculum*, 28 (1953), 499–513.
Wolf, Kenneth, *Christian Martyrs in Muslim Spain* (Cambridge: Cambridge University Press, 1988).
Wrong, Dennis H., *The Problem of Order: What Unites and Divides Society* (New York: Free Press, 1994).
Yuval, Israel Jacob, *Two Nations in your Womb: Perceptions of Jews and Christians in Late Antiquity and the Middle Ages*, trans. Barbara Harshav and Jonathan Chipman (Berkeley and Los Angeles: University of California Press, 2006).
Zerfaß, Rolf, *Der Streit um die Laienpredigt: Eine pastoralgeschichliche Undersuchung zum Verstandnis des Predigtamtes und zu zeinder Entwicklung im 12. und 13. Jahrhundert* (Freiburg: Herder, 1974).
Ziegler, Philip, *The Black Death* (London: Penguin Books, 1982).
Ziegler, Walter, "Reformation und Klosteraulösung: Ein ordensgeschichlicher Vergleich," in Elm (ed.), *Reformbemühungen und Observanzbestrebungen*, 585–614.
Žižek, Slavoj, *Violence* (London: Profile, 2008).

Index of Names and Subjects

Alexander IV, pope 22
al–Kâmil, al–Malik, Sultan 129
Ames, Christine Caldwell 124
Andreas, James 15, 41
Angelus of Jerusalem, OCarm 126–9
Anthony of Padua, OFM 128
anticlericalism 1, 2, 5, 8–9, 27, 75, 132–7
Antichrist 19, 20, 21, 22, 23, 42
Antifraternalism 1–3, 4–9, 130–7
   abolitionist 4, 16, 27, 41, 43, 130, 131, 134, 135; *see also* antifraternalism, contrarian; St Amour, William of
   contrarian 16, 23, 24–5, 26, 29, 37, 74
   doctrinal 23–7, 116, 117, 130
   legal 8, 17, 22, 25, 105
   literary and poetic 7, 28–43
   reformist 4, 6, 16, 25, 37, 42, 43, 81–102
   violent 7, 8, 14, 45–75, 81, 104–19, 123–9, 140–53
apocalypticism 18–23, 42, 118; *see also* eschatology
Aquinas, Thomas, OP 24, 56, 113
Arendt, Hannah 56
Arnaud, Guillaume, OP 125, 142
Augustinian Order vii, 5, 18, 22, 52, 63, 64, 71, 86, 94, 97, 100, 122, 147, 150, 151, 152, 153

Baconthorpe, John, OCarm 105
Batamy, Jean 15, 41
Bennett, R. F. 101
Bertrand of Bayonne, OFM 111
Blackadder, Edmund, 28
Black Death 51, 101, 119–23, 126, 129
Boccaccio, Giovanni 7, 28, 79, 82
   Decameron 41
Bonaventure of Bagnoregio, OFM 24, 43, 81, 97, 109, 113
Boniface VIII, pope 65, 148
Burke, S. Maureen 116

Caesarius of Speyer, OFM 70, 142
Campbell, John 72
Catherine of Siena 53
Chaucer, Geoffrey 1–3, 7, 16, 28, 79, 82
   Canterbury Tales 40, 41, 42
      Friar John 37–40
Carmelite Order vii, 5, 17, 22, 52, 58, 63, 64, 70, 71, 86, 97, 109, 118, 121, 122, 126–9, 140, 144, 147, 148, 152, 153
Cenci, Cesare, OFM 106–7, 117
Charles VI of France 64

children, friars' recruitment of 53, 57, 59, 60, 81, 100, 132
Clare of Assisi 56
Clopper, Lawrence 41
Clyn, John, OFM 118
Cooper, Helen 40
Cotter, Francis 99
Coulton, G. G. 28
criminal court records 7, 8, 48–9, 54, 70, 81, 83, 94
criminality; *see* deviancy
crusades, friars' role in 63

da Piazza, Michele, OFM 120
da Vicenza, Guido, OP 68
Dean, Trevor 49
de Adam, Salimbene, OFM 4, 57, 67–8, 70, 102, 107, 109–10
de Ferrara, Jacopo, OP 66
de Frachet, Gerard, OP 126
de Landa, Diego, OFM 138–9
de Lantini, Tomasso, OP 126
de Meun, Jean 7, 28, 37, 39, 40, 79
   Roman de la Rose 16, 29
      False Seeming (Faus Semblant) 29–37
de' Mussis, Gabriele 121
de Nangis, Guillaume 113
de Venette, Jean, OCarm 120
de Vitry, Jacques 61
deviancy, among friars: 8, 79, 81–102, 130, 132, 154–8
deviancy, modern study of 49, 85
Diana d'Andalò 56
Dipple, Geoffrey 27, 134
Dionysius the Pseudo–Areopagite 21
discipline 6, 70, 83, 85, 90
   see also deviancy
Dominican Order vii, 5, 6, 8, 17, 22, 24, 49, 52, 56, 57, 60, 63–71, 73, 85–93, 94–8, 101, 104–5, 107–13, 116, 122, 124–6, 132, 140–8, 150–3, 154–8
Dominican nuns 53, 58, 90, 98, 132, 145, 148
Dominic of Guzman 43
Dossat, Yves 58
Duffy, Eamon 65
Durkheim, Émile 95

education, among mendicants 17–8, 53, 58
Edward III of England 63, 149
Englishness 1
Enlightenment 9, 27, 133, 135
Erasmus, Desiderius 28
eschatology 19, 118; *see also* apocalypticism

184 Index of Names and Subjects

Fernando III of Castile 70
Fiamma, Galvano, OFM 108–9
FitzRalph, Richard 16, 25–7, 45, 54, 118, 134
Fleming, John V. 109
Franciscan Order vii, 1–2, 4–6, 17, 19–21, 22, 24–6, 41, 47, 52, 55–66, 70–1, 73, 86, 90, 93–4, 99, 101, 106–14, 116–8, 123, 125, 131–2, 134, 138–9, 140–53
   Poor Clares 50, 53, 71, 153
   Francis of Assisi 43, 127, 129
   Spirituals 13, 43
Frederick II, emperor 65, 107
French Revolution 9, 133, 136
Froissart, Jean 121
Fuller, Thomas 2

Gallicus, Nicholas, OCarm 43
Gerard of Abbeville 23
Gerard of Borgo San Donnino, OFM 20, 110
   Introductorius in evangeliumeternum 19–22, 109–10
Glassberger, Nicholas, OFM 110–1
Gower, John 28
Gratian 21, 22
Grosseteste, Robert 61
Guattari, Félix 56
Gui, Bernard, OP 58, 59, 117

Haigh, Christopher 105
Halbwachs, Maurice 113
Hale, J. R. 47
Harriss, Gerald 49, 82
Havely, Nicholas 15, 41
Heinrich von Herford, OP 122
Heinrich von Regensburg 60, 119
Henry IV of England 65
Henry VIII of England 3
Henry of Ghent, OSA 24
Henry of Oxford, OCarm 70, 147
Heresy 6, 13, 19, 24, 25, 36, 47, 51, 55, 56, 65, 66–7, 68, 69, 73, 91, 99, 113, 117, 123, 124, 135, 140, 141, 142, 143
   see also inquisition
Hermann von Minden, OP 89–90
Hildegard of Bingen 42
Hugh of Lincoln [=Little St. Hugh] 73
Humanism 9, 133, 135
Humbert of Romans, OP 43, 103, 108, 113, 118

Innocent IV, pope 65
inquisition, papal 6, 8, 13, 47, 50, 51, 52, 53, 55, 58–9, 82, 101, 104, 115, 123–6, 129, 131, 132
   violent responses to: 65–70, 141–9; *see also* violence
Islam 105, 116–7, 118, 126, 131

Jews 55, 73, 103, 105, 117
Jack Upland 42
James le Palmer 42
   Omne Bonum 42
Jan Milíč of Kroměříž 27
Jean d'Anneux 16, 24
Joachim of Fiore 20
Johann Eberlin von Günzburg 27
John XXII, pope 13, 24, 26, 65, 134, 147
John of Gaunt 63, 152
John of Pouilly 24
John of Reading 121
Jordan of Giano, OFM 56, 110, 119
Jordan of Saxony, OP 57, 141
Jordan of Saxony [=De Quedlinburg], OSA 96

Karras, Ruth Mazo 99
Kennard, Joseph Spencer 82
Kerby–Fulton, Kathryn 41–2
Knighton, Henry 122
Knowles, David 82
Konrad of Megenberg 24
Konrad of Waldhäusen 27
Kybal, Vlastimil 27

Lacassagne, Alexandre 95
Langland, William 7, 28, 41, 82
   Piers Plowman 41
Lansing, Carol 6
Little, A. G. 86
Liturgy 48, 90, 103, 126
Loades, David 134
Logan, F. Donald 91, 99, 154
Lollards 65, 82, 153
Louis IV of Bavaria 65, 147
Louis IX (St Louis) of France 22, 110, 111, 113
Luther, Martin 134

Machiavelli, Niccolò 28
MacEvitt, Christopher 116–7
McMunn, Meradith 33
Mann, Jill 15, 41
Marcos of Lisbon, OFM 111
Margaret of Città di Castello 53
Marianus of Florence, OFM 111
Marlowe, Christopher 28
Martin IV, pope 34
martyrdom 8
   ancient 114–5
   medieval 115
   mendicant 47, 48, 56, 103–4, 105, 107, 115–9, 123–9; *see also* Peter Martyr, OP
Masetti, Thomas, OP 84
Matthew of Janov 27
memory 3
   lachrymose 4, 8, 59, 79, 103–29
   social 8, 103, 112–3, 117, 120, 122, 126, 129, 132, 137

Index of Names and Subjects

missionary activities of mendicants 6, 17, 56, 101, 124
   among Muslims 126, 129
   among Native Americans 124, 138–9
   among pagans 115
monasticism 6, 20, 63, 133, 134, 136
   ascetic practices of 81, 85, 96, 115
   antagonism toward friars 73, 119, 121
Moorman, John, R. H. 112–3
moral community 106

narrative healing 119, 121, 123
Nicholas IV, pope 57
Nicolas of Lisieux 16, 23

Ocker, Christopher 24, 27

Pannewick, Friederike 117
Paris, Gratien de, OFM 112
Paris, Matthew 73
Peasants' Revolt 62, 63, 153
Peter of Verona [=Peter Martyr], OP 50, 55, 124–9, 143
Philip IV of France 65, 134
prostitutes, friars' involvement with 45–6, 99–100
Protestant Reformation 1–3, 27, 133–5
punishment, deviant friars receiving 73, 85, 88–94, 154–8

Rabelais, François 28, 54
Raymond of Capua, OP 86–9, 93
Richard II of England 64, 153
Robertson, D. W. 39
Roest, Bert 108
Rutebeuf 28, 32, 54, 113

St Amour, William of 3, 6, 7, 13, 14, 22–3, 54, 58, 59, 74, 81, 107–13, 118, 130, 134
   De periculis
      context for 15–18
      reception of 23–44
      themes and ecclesiology 18–22
Sacchetti, Franco 28
Salgado, James 82–4
Sánchez, José 133–4

Scase, Wendy 16, 41
Scott, James C. 74
scandal 79, 86–9, 95–8, 103, 113, 132, 138, 154, 156
Servite Order 52, 71, 86, 99, 151
Smail, Daniel Lord 49
Speght, Thomas 2
Szittya, Penn R. 15

Thomas of Eccleston, OFM 57, 110
Thomas of York, OFM 111, 113
Thomson, Williell R. 101
Tschamser, Malachias, OFM 111–2

Ugo of Ravenna, OP 87
urban environment 5, 8–9, 18, 43, 46–8, 50–1, 53, 59, 71, 72–5, 98–9, 102, 121, 127, 132, 136–7

Van Engen, John 135
Vauchez, André 47
Villani, Matteo 121
violence against friars
   as communicative act 9, 72–4
   distribution among mendicant orders 52
   diversity of grounds for 54–72
   regional distribution of 50
   rural lack of 136
   scale of 48
   urban focus of: *see* urban environment
violence perpetrated by friars 63, 70, 86–98, 146, 156–8
   see also deviancy
violence, modern study of 9, 47, 56, 72, 74–5, 64, 124, 136–7
Visconti, Federigo 61

Wadding, Luke, OFM 112
William of Appleton, OFM 63, 152
women
   as friars' opponents 5, 45–6, 53
   as victims of friars' abuses 19
Wyclif, John 2, 3, 25–6, 82, 134

Žižek, Slavoj 56

Index of Places

Note: Placenames are listed alphabetically by modern country.

Belgium:
  Bruges 87
Bosnia: 124, 135
Bulgaria: 124

Czech Republic:
  Prague 27, 150

England: 1–3, 25, 50, 62, 91, 92, 93, 136, 149, 154, 158
  Berwick 63, 149
  Bristol 71, 151
  Cambridge 2, 27, 58, 63, 152
  Dover 55, 140
  Exeter 147
  Lanercost 147
  Lincoln 73,
  London 1, 25, 57, 62, 64, 71, 73, 147, 148, 149, 150, 152, 153
  Ludlow 64, 147
  Newcastle 62–3, 70, 150, 151
  Oxford 2, 25, 27, 58
  Suffolk 143
  York 64, 152
  Winchester 99, 100

France: 50, 51, 55, 58, 92, 112, 124, 131, 155–7
  Agen 58, 146
  Albi 148
  Apt 144
  Arles 98
  Arras 145
  Avignon 25, 122
  Avignonet 125, 142
  Calais 63, 151
  Carcassonne 146, 148
  Colmar 90, 104
  Figeac 148
  Le Puy 144
  Magdalen 122
  Marseille 122
  Mézin 58, 144
  Montpellier 122
  Narbonne 100, 121, 141
  Nice 64
  Paris 17–8, 20–1, 27, 32, 36, 42, 58, 60, 65, 73, 97, 107–10, 113–4, 120, 143, 148
  Prouille 58, 140
  Rabastens 58, 144
  Rouen 89
  Strasbourg 50, 57, 60, 67, 89, 90, 98, 104, 119, 132, 145, 146
  Toulouse 124, 141, 148
  Valence 124, 149
  Villeneuve-sur-Lot 153

Germany: 50, 56, 60, 62, 65, 70, 92, 93, 119, 124, 134, 147, 154–8
  Cologne 50, 87, 150
  Goldberg 90
  Greifswald 89, 98
  Mainz 104
  Meissen 122, 151
  Sechdorf 87
  Stralsund 89
  Worms 50, 59, 141, 144

Ireland: 50, 62, 63, 101, 131, 149
  Ardfert 149
  Cork 63, 70, 93, 146
  Dundalk 149
  Limerick 152
Italy: 48, 49, 50, 51, 52, 54, 55, 56, 62, 66, 92, 93, 136, 143, 154–8
  Ancona 87
  Arezzo 50, 71, 153
  Bari 146
  Bergamo 143, 147
  Bologna 48, 57, 68–9, 70, 97, 132, 146, 147, 149, 150
  Camerino 86, 98
  Catania 144
  Cremona 65
  Faenza 87
  Ferentino 145
  Fermo 87
  Florence 48, 67, 121, 148
  Licata 126, 140
  Lucca 48, 54, 71, 94, 99, 151, 153
  Mantua 143
  Milan 48, 50, 125, 142, 143
  Modena 65
  Monfalcone 70, 145
  Naples 70, 140
  Padua 141
  Parma 66–8, 109, 132, 145
  Pavia 148
  Pesaro 87
  Piacenza 121, 141, 145
  Pisa 49, 61, 64, 70, 94, 98, 151

Italy: (*cont.*)
  Poggibonzi 71, 152
  Novara 147
  Orvieto 69, 141, 142
  Recanati 87
  Reggio 65, 67, 70, 142, 146
  Rimini 87
  Rome 36, 129
  Siena 99
  Treviso 143
  Urbino 86
  Valtellina 144
  Venice 71, 94, 152
  Viterbo 87, 97, 142

Lithuania: 131
  Vilnius 150, 152

Netherlands: 27, 54
  Holland 55
  Zeeland 55

Poland: 131, 154
  Wrocław 68

Scotland: 50, 62, 131
  Dundee 62, 150
Spain: 50, 92, 93, 107, 133, 138, 156-8
  Madrid 70, 145
  Orense 59, 146
  Pamplona 55, 142
  Salamanca 58
  Urgell 142, 143, 144
Switzerland: 27
  Basel 104